The Genealogy of Jesus Christ

The genealogy of Jesus Christ is essentially an abstract of the Old Testament, continuing the line of David up to the New Testament times. It is divided into three periods: from Abraham to David, from David to the Babylonian Exile, from the Exile to Christ. In sum, there are 42 generations from Abraham to Christ, a number which corresponds with the 42 stations in the wilderness through which the children of Israel wandered before entering the promised land.

The genealogy of Christ in Matthew begins with Abraham and presents Christ as King, descendant of Abraham, the father of the called race, and not Adam, the father of the created race. The Gospel of Luke, on the other hand, goes all the way back to Adam, in order to show that Jesus was a man. The Gospels of Mark and John do not give genealogies, because they present Christ in two aspects for which a genealogy is unnecessary: in Mark Christ is presented as the Servant of God, and a servant does not require any detailed recording of genealogy; John shows Christ as the Son of God and thus not requiring any human genealogy since as the "Word" he was in the beginning, "and the word was God" (John 1:1).

In the genealogy of Jesus given in Luke (Luke 3:23–38), the title "Christ" is not mentioned since Luke's gospel shows Jesus as the proper man to be the Savior of mankind. However, Matthew's genealogy emphasizes the title "Christ" repeatedly (Matthew 1:16–17) in line with the aspect of Christ as King, the anointed one of God.

Luke gives the genealogy of David's son Nathan, who was Mary's forefather. In Matthew, Solomon is given as the forefather of Joseph. Thus both Mary and Joseph were descendants of David, and Christ may be counted as the descendant of David through both Solomon and Nathan. Actually, Solomon was not a direct forefather of Christ, and his relation to Christ is indirect through Joseph's marriage to Mary.

There are several omissions in the genealogy of Jesus Christ. Three generations, the descendants of Joram, given in the Old Testament, are left out from the genealogy of Christ, most likely due to Joram's marriage to the daughter of Ahab and Jezebel, which corrupted Joram's descendants (II Chronicles 21:5–6; 22:1–4). Such an omission of three generations is in line with Exodus 20:5. Another generation – Jehoiakim – is also omitted from the genealogy of Christ, probably because Jehoiakim was made king by Pharaoh and collected taxes for him (II Kings 23:34–35).

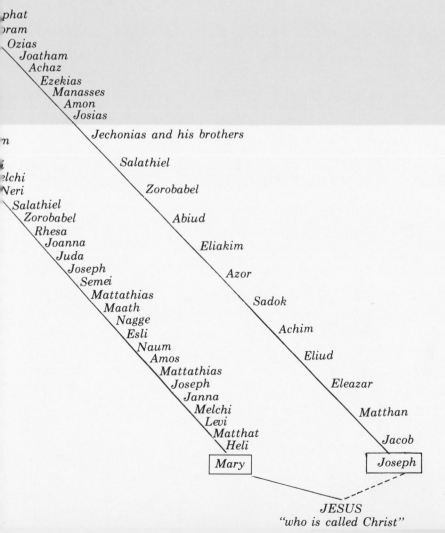

…ba) wife of Urias

…phat
…ram
…Ozias
…Joatham
…Achaz
…Ezekias
…Manasses
…Amon
…Josias
…Jechonias and his brothers
…Salathiel
…Zorobabel
…Abiud
…Eliakim
…Azor
…Sadok
…Achim
…Eliud
…Eleazar
…Matthan
…Jacob

…elchi
…Neri
…Salathiel
…Zorobabel
…Rhesa
…Joanna
…Juda
…Joseph
…Semei
…Mattathias
…Maath
…Nagge
…Esli
…Naum
…Amos
…Mattathias
…Joseph
…Janna
…Melchi
…Levi
…Matthat
…Heli

Mary   Joseph

JESUS
"who is called Christ"

VILLARD BOOKS / NEW YORK / 1984

THE GLORY OF THE
NEW TESTAMENT

Concept and design: SHLOMO S. (YOSH) GAFNI

General Editor: GEORGETTE CORCOS

Editor for the Epistles: GALEN MARQUIS

Managing editor: RACHEL GILON

Language editor: YAEL LOTAN

Assistant designer: CONSTANTIN PRESMAN

Main Photographers: ERICH LESSING
A. VAN DER HEYDEN
DAVID HARRIS
ZEV RADOVAN

The Publishers wish to express their sincere gratitude to the following persons for their help:
Mrs Irène Lewitt; Mr Mietek Orbach; Mr Uri Palit; Mrs Margalit Bassan; Mr Yoel Zimmerman;
Mrs Judith Meissner-Joseph; Miss Susan Fogg; Miss Hilary Cemel; Mr Yehuda Reshef;
Miss Hanna Dahan.

Title page:
The Sea of Galilee seen from
the Golan Heights.

Library of Congress Cataloging in Publication Data
Main entry under title:

The Glory of the New Testament

Includes index.
1. Palestine – Description and travel – Views
2. Bible N.T. – Illustrations
DS108.5.G55   1984   225.9'1   83-840322
ISBN 0-394-53659-2

The scripture quotations in this publication are from the Authorized Version of the King James' Bible.

Phototypesetting: S.T.I. Scientific Translations International Ltd., Jerusalem

Manufactured in Hong Kong by Mandarin Offset (International) Ltd.

9   8   7   6   5   4   3   2
First Edition

CONTENTS

INTRODUCTION

The New Testament, with its account of the life and works of Jesus and the founding of the Christian Church, has been the most influential book of the Western World. For close on 2,000 years, it has been a source of faith, guidance and inspiration for Christians of every denomination, who have found in its pages the roots of their theology and ethics. Non-Christians too have turned to it as a supreme literary creation, as a major historical document and as a pillar of human civilization. Its central story, told in the Gospels, with their tender portrayal of Jesus, has captured man's imagination at all times and in all places, appealing equally to Byzantine emperors, medieval peasants and remote African tribes. For untold millions of individuals through the ages, the New Testament has been a beacon illuminating their lives.

In size, the New Testament is less than a third of the Old Testament, and whereas the Old Testament covers a period of over a thousand years and was written by a variety of authors over many centuries, the events described in the New Testament take place within a few decades, and it was written by a closely connected fraternity of men within less than a century. It was committed to writing to assist the early Christians to formulate their belief and worship and to shape their daily life.

Although its authorship was more homogeneous than that of the Old Testament, its early audience was more diverse. They were of many nations, spread throughout the Roman Empire – in Palestine and Syria, in Egypt, Turkey and Greece, in Rome herself and in remote outposts. The setting of the New Testament is also more spacious than that of the Old Testament. The latter occasionally extends briefly to neighboring lands, such as Egypt, Syria and even Babylonia, but it is firmly centered in the Land of Israel. The life of Jesus, as related in the Gospels, also takes place entirely within the Holy Land, but the Epistles take us farther afield. St Paul comes from Tarsus in Turkey and spends the crucial part of his life bringing the Gospel of Christianity to Asia Minor, Greece and even to Rome. The understanding of the New Testament, therefore, emerges from the three great cities of Jerusalem, Athens and Rome, and requires us to take a leap across time and space to gain an insight into two very different worlds. The first is the world of Judaism and the Jewish world, which was the milieu in which Jesus lived – Jewish everyday customs and festivals, its Law and its rabbinic interpretations, the Temple, the Sadducees and the Pharisees, the ascetic sect of the Essenes, the belief in and constant longing for the Messiah. The second is the Greco-Roman world, dominated by Hellenistic culture and aesthetics, and ruled by Roman law and power.

Despite the overwhelming influence of the New Testament on the history and culture of the world, its intensive study down the ages, it is only in the past century that its real face has been uncovered. Previously the reader, scholar and believer lacked the context in which to set it, and tended to recreate it in familiar images. Today a variety of disciplines has brought to us the world of Jesus and Paul in the reality of its place and time. In particular, the modern science of biblical archaeology has brought to light material remains and provided perspectives which enable us to penetrate, comprehend and visualize the background to the Gospels and the Epistles. The development of social sciences, such as anthropology, economics and psychology, and a profounder appreciation of ancient history, linguistics, etc., have all provided fresh and vivid insights.

One greatly significant discovery was the Dead Sea Scrolls and the place where they were written — an Essene monastery on the shore of the Dead Sea. Its location near the mouth of the Jordan river, and the practices and teachings described in its literature, bring us very close to the world of John the Baptist. Excavations in Galilee and Jerusalem also shed light on the environment in which Jesus grew up, lived and died. We can see the Herodian masonry of the Temple which he visited and the very cobbled street along which he walked on his last journey. In Corinth we can traverse the Lechaeum Road, which St. Paul must have trodden, and on which the synagogue from which he was ejected was probably situated. By studying the features of the present-day inhabitants of Middle Eastern countries we gain a better idea of the real appearance of the personalities of the New Testament than the familiar but imaginary creations of Western art. We know now much more about the houses in which they lived, the clothes they wore, the food they ate, the languages they spoke. We can see the sheep and goats, the vineyards and mustard seeds, the new wine and the old bottles, the tares and the fig trees, all of which illuminated Jesus' parables. Thanks to photography, we can see the actual sites and experience the selfsame colors that so profoundly affected Jesus: the hills of Galilee, the roads along which he went — the Sea of Galilee, the Mount of Olives, the Garden of Gethsemane, Jerusalem and Nazareth, Caesarea where Peter preached, Corinth and its judgement seat, which Paul had to face, and the great ancient city of Antioch, home of the first and largest community of Gentile Christians.

For many centuries, pilgrims sought evidence of early Christianity in Palestine. Their devotions were directed to shrines built from the fourth century onwards. These sites were hallowed by tradition and faith but the buildings, their interiors and the forms of worship, reflected periods and mentalities much later than the events they commemorated. It is only the new knowledge that has given authenticity to our perception of the period and a view of the historic Jesus, whose life becomes more real and immediate when seen in its actual setting.

This volume shows the world of the New Testament as we now know it was. It adds a new and vivid dimension, enhancing our appreciation of the text as a document of its time and all times, as superb literature and as religious inspiration.

Geoffrey Wigoder

The book of the generation of Jesus Christ, the son of David, the son of Abraham.

Abraham begat Isaac; and Isaac begat Jacob; and Jacob begat Judas and his brethren;

And Judas begat Phares and Zara of Thamar; and Phares begat Esrom; and Esrom begat Aram . . .   (1:1–3)

And Salmon begat Booz of Rachab; and Booz begat Obed of Ruth; and Obed begat Jesse;

And Jesse begat David the king; and David the king begat Solomon of her that had been the wife of Urias;

And Solomon begat Roboam; and Roboam begat Abia; and Abia begat Asa;

And Asa begat Josaphat; and Josaphat begat Joram; and Joram begat Ozias;

And Ozias begat Joatham; and Joatham begat Achaz; and Achaz begat Ezekias;

And Ezekias begat Manasses; and Manasses begat Amon; and Amon begat Josias;

And Josias begat Jechonias and his brethren, about the time they were carried away to Babylon.

(1:5–11)

1. The Patriarchs, depicted in a stone sculpture at the 13th-century cathedral of Chartres, France.

The Patriarchs are buried in the Cave of Machpelah, in Hebron. The Old Testament tells us that Abraham bought the Cave as a burial place for his wife Sarah (Genesis 23). Subsequently, Abraham, Isaac, Rebecca, Jacob and Leah were also interred there.

The first page of the New Testament opens with a genealogy – the genealogy of Christ, typified and revealed in the Old Testament. The genealogy itself can be considered a kind of abstract of the Old Testament, mentioning as it does all of the patriarchs and kings and even providing some historical notices such as "about the time they were carried away to Babylon" (verse 11). Since the Book of Matthew presents Christ as the King, there is a need to demonstrate the ancestry and lineage of the King, his antecedents and status. Luke also includes a genealogy which goes back to Adam, in accord with Luke's intention to show Christ's humanity. Matthew's genealogy begins with Abraham, since the kingdom is composed of members of the called people, both his descendants in the flesh and those in faith. A closer look at the genealogy reveals many interesting and significant facts. For example, in all the genealogies of the Old Testament, no woman is mentioned. Christ's genealogy, however, includes five women. Only one of these was a virgin, Mary, a descendant of the chosen people of whom Christ was born directly. All the rest – Tamar, Rahab, Ruth and Bathsheba were (apparently) Gentiles, all of whom were married more than once, three of whom were in fact quite sinful: Tamar committing incest, Rahab being a harlot, and Bathsheba committing adultery. Their inclusion in the line of Christ shows that Christ is also the kingly savior of typical sinners.

The genealogy is divided into three periods: from Abraham to David, from David to the Babylonian Exile, from the Exile to Christ. In sum, there are forty-two generations from Abraham to Christ, a number which corresponds with the forty-two stations in the wilderness through which the Children of Israel wandered before entering the Promised Land. This correspondence hints that Christ is the rest and satisfaction of the good land after a long period of trials and sufferings.

And Eliud begat Eleazar; and Eleazar begat Matthan; and Matthan begat Jacob;

And Jacob begat Joseph the husband of Mary, of whom was born Jesus, who is called Christ.

So all the generations from Abraham to David are fourteen generations; and from David until the carrying away into Babylon are fourteen generations; and from the carrying away into Babylon unto Christ are fourteen generations.

Now the birth of Jesus Christ was on this wise: When as his mother Mary was espoused to Joseph, before they came together, she was found with child of the Holy Ghost.

(1:15–18)

Now when Jesus was born in Bethelehem of Judaea in the days of Herod the king, behold, there came wise men from the east to Jerusalem,

Saying, Where is he that is born King of the Jews? for we have seen his star in the east, and are come to worship him.

When Herod the king had heard these things, he was troubled, and all Jerusalem with him.

And when he had gathered all the chief priests and scribes of the people together, he demanded of them where Christ should be born.

(2:1–4)

2. A view of Judea with Bethlehem and Herodium in the Judean Desert in the background.

Judea is the Latin form of Judah, and, in the New Testament, refers to the southern part of Palestine during the period of Roman hegemony. After the return from the Babylonian Exile, most of the returnees settled in the kingdom of Judah and during the Persian period the territory was called Yehud (Ezra 5:1; 8). The name Judea appears in the Hellenistic period.

Bethlehem is situated in the hilly part of Judea, bordering on the desert, while Herodium, rising southwest of Bethlehem, is in the Judean desert.

Bethlehem was the birthplace of David where Samuel anointed him as the future king of Israel.

3

4

5

6

Then Herod, when he had privily called the wise men, inquired of them diligently what time the star appeared.

And he sent them to Bethlehem, and said, Go and search diligently for the young child; and when ye have found him, bring me word again, that I may come and worship him also.

When they had heard the king, they departed; and, lo, the star, which they saw in the east, went before them, till it came and stood over where the young child was.   (2:7–9)

When he arose, he took the young child and his mother by night, and departed into Egypt:

And was there until the death of Herod: that it might be fulfilled which was spoken of the Lord by the prophet, saying, Out of Egypt have I called my son.

Then Herod, when he saw that he was mocked of the wise men, was exceeding wroth, and sent forth, and slew all the children that were in Bethlehem, and in all the coasts thereof, from two years old and under, according to the time which he had diligently inquired of the wise men.

Then was fulfilled that which was spoken by Jeremy the prophet, saying,

In Rama was there a voice heard, lamentation, and weeping, and great mourning, Rachel weeping for her children, and would not be comforted, because they are not.

But when Herod was dead, behold, an angel of the Lord appeareth in a dream to Joseph in Egypt,

Saying, Arise, and take the young child and his mother, and go into the land of Israel: for they are dead which sought the young child's life.

And he arose, and took the young child and his mother, and came into the land of Israel.

But when he heard that Archelaus did reign in Judaea in the room of his father Herod, he was afraid to go thither: notwithstanding, being warned of God in a dream, he turned aside into the parts of Galilee:

And he came and dwelt in a city called Nazareth: that it might be fulfilled which was spoken by the prophets, He shall be called a Nazarene.

(2:14–23)

3. Head found in Egypt, believed to represent Herod, king of Judea.

Known as Herod the Great, he was a courageous soldier, an energetic administrator and one of the greatest builders in antiquity. He was a faithful vassal of Rome. Toward the end of his long reign (37 B.C.–4 B.C.), the complex demands of a vast family led Herod into difficulties regarding the succession to the throne, and it was then that he degenerated into a vicious, corrupt and much-feared tyrant. His cruelty became proverbial.

4. The Roman emperor Augustus.

Augustus (Gaius Octavius; 63 B.C.– A.D. 14) whose name was Octavian, succeeded Julius Caesar as the head of the Roman Empire. He was the first to be given the title Augustus by the Senate, in 27 B.C. Augustus extended the Roman Empire to the east and this included, among other territories, the kingdom of Judea where Herod ruled.

5. The flight to Egypt of the Holy Family, represented on a carved column in the Milk Grotto at Bethlehem.

Dreams were taken very seriously by almost all ancient peoples. In biblical times dreams were believed to be divine communication. There are many dreams throughout the Old Testament (as for example in Genesis 20:3; 31:10–11).

Sometimes dreams are symbolic, as those of Joseph (Genesis 37:5ff.), or of Pharaoh's butler and baker (Genesis 41ff.), or of Pharaoh himself, (Genesis 41:1, 5), and many others.

6. Path in Sinai.

The journey undertaken by Joseph, Mary and the infant Jesus must have been extremely difficult, as it led them through the Negev and the Sinai Desert.

7. The Cave of the Innocent Children in Bethlehem. It was named after the children of Bethlehem who fell victim to Herod's paranoid fear and cruelty. There is no suggestion, however, that these children were ever buried here.

7

8. A view of Galilee and Nazareth.

At Herod's death, Augustus divided his kingdom among the king's three sons: Archelaus was appointed to rule over Judea, Idumea and Samaria. He had inherited his father's character and like him led a reign of terror. The second son, Herod Antipas (called by his family name, Herod, by the evangelists and not to be confused with his father Herod the Great), became the ruler of Galilee, including Nazareth.

9. The Wilderness of Judea.
The preaching of the New Testament "gospel of peace" (Acts 10:36–37) actually began with John the Baptist. He did his preaching not in the holy city of Jerusalem or in its Temple, where the religious and cultured people worshipped in their traditional way, but in the wilderness, away from the old customs and religion. John's message was "Repent ye, for the kingdom of heaven is at hand."

9

10

10. Fragment of the so-called Thanksgiving Scroll, one of the documents found at Qumran.
This scroll contains a series of poems written by members of the sect which expressed their gratitude to God; its contents are of great importance for a proper understanding of their philosophy.
Study of the scrolls proved that the documents from these caves came from the library of a Jewish community which lived there between the 1st century B.C. and the 1st century A.D. Some scholars believe that this settlement was established by the Essenes, although others prefer the term "Dead Sea Sect." In view of his teachings, which resemble those of the sect, it is believed that John the Baptist may have been, at some time, a member of the Dead Sea Sect.

11. Qumran, where the famous Dead Sea Scrolls were found in caves and ancient ruins in the Wilderness of Judea.

In those days came John the Baptist, preaching in the wilderness of Judaea,

And saying, Repent ye: for the kingdom of heaven is at hand.

For this is he that was spoken of by the prophet Esaias, saying, The voice of one crying in the wilderness, Prepare ye the way of the Lord, make his paths straight.

And the same John had his raiment of camel's hair, and a leathern girdle about his loins; and his meat was locusts and wild honey.

Then went out to him Jerusalem, and all Judaea, and all the region round about Jordan,

And were baptized of him in Jordan, confessing their sins.

But when he saw many of the Pharisees and Sadducees come to his baptism, he said unto them, O generation of vipers, who hath warned you to flee from the wrath to come?

Bring forth therefore fruits meet for repentance:

And think not to say within yourselves, We have Abraham to our father: for I say unto you, that God is able of these stones to raise up children unto Abraham.

And now also the axe is laid unto the root of the trees: therefore every tree which bringeth not forth good fruit is hewn down, and cast into the fire.

I indeed baptize you with water unto repentance: but he that cometh after me is mightier than I whose shoes I am not worthy to bear: he shall baptize you with the Holy Ghost, and with fire:

Whose fan is in his hand, and he will throughly purge his floor, and gather his wheat into the garner; but he will burn up the chaff with unquenchable fire.

12. The Jordan River.

13. Palm-trees in the oasis of Jericho. It is thought that the honey often mentioned in the Old Testament was a thick syrup made from either grapes or dates and it may well be that date honey was what John the Baptist ate. Although the Wilderness of Judea is a barren desert, there are oases in the region with plenty of date palms bearing abundant fruit. The date is one of the seven choice agricultural species of the Promised Land (Deuteronomy 8:8).

13

Then cometh Jesus from Galilee to Jordan unto John, to be baptized of him.

But John forbad him, saying, I have need to be baptized of thee, and comest thou to me?

And Jesus answering said unto him, Suffer it to be so now: for thus it becometh us to fulfil all righteousness. Then he suffered him.

And Jesus, when he was baptized, went up straightway out of the water: and, lo, the heavens were opened unto him, and he saw the Spirit of God descending like a dove, and lighting upon him:

And lo a voice from heaven, saying, This is my beloved Son, in whom I am well pleased.

(3:1–17)

14. The baptism of Christ, depicted in an 18th-century painting over the altar in the Armenian Monastery adjacent to the Church of the Annunciation in Bethlehem.

14

15

15. A short distance from Jericho, at 1200 feet below sea level, stands a convent dedicated to St. John the Baptist.
On the site of the present convent once stood a Byzantine basilica. It was destroyed by the Persians in 614, and rebuilt in 1128 by the Byzantine emperor Manuel Comnenus I. It was reconstructed in 1882, and renovated by the Greek Orthodox Patriarchate of Jerusalem in 1954. In Arabic, the Greek monastery is known as "Qasr el Yahud," the Castle of the Jews, as, according to tradition, it was at this spot that the Children of Israel led by Joshua crossed the Jordan into the Land of Canaan.

Then was Jesus led up of the Spirit into the wilderness to be tempted of the devil.

And when he had fasted forty days and forty nights, he was afterward an hungred.

And when the tempter came to him, he said, If thou be the Son of God, command that these stones be made bread.

But he answered and said, It is written, Man shall not live by bread alone, but by every word that proceedeth out of the mouth of God. (4:1–4)

Again, the devil taketh him up into an exceeding high mountain, and sheweth him all the kingdoms of the world, and the glory of them;

And saith unto him, All these things will I give thee, if thou wilt fall down and worship me.

(4:8–9)

16

20

17

18

16. Tradition identifies the Mountain of Quarantal, overlooking the oasis of Jericho, as the one on which the Temptation took place.

It was first settled in the 4th century by Greek monks led by St. Hariton. They lived in the caves in the vicinity, and built a monastery which was destroyed by the Persian invaders in the 7th century. In the 12th century the Crusaders attempted to resettle the place; the Knights Templars built a fortress on the hill top. In the 19th century Ethiopian monks lived in its ruins. In 1874 the mountain was acquired by the Greek Orthodox Church which undertook the construction of the present monastery. It was completed in 1905.

17. Perched on a steep mountainside, the Monastery of Quarantal takes its name from "quarantena," forty, commemorating the forty days and nights that Jesus fasted in the desert. The monastery appears to be part of the mountain.

18. The steps leading to the Monastery of Quarantal, seen from the highest point of the monastery.

19. Some of the caves in the mountainside where the monks lived.

The Judean Desert provides an ideal setting for the ascetic quest of perfection and solitude, and came in time to be considered a veritable "nursery of souls." Since John the Baptist preached in the wilderness, Jesus was tempted there and even Paul went away to "Arabia" for three years after his conversion, some were led to emulate their experiences in hope of obtaining some spiritual benefit. In fact, by the latter half of the 5th century, the center of monasticism shifted from Egypt to the Holy Land. Hermits took up residence in caves such as these in the harsh climate of the desert, and were unremitting in their fasts, drinking water sparingly, competing with one another in feats of endurance.

20. The monastery contains the traditional grotto, now a little chapel with a stone, believed to be the spot where Jesus sat when he fasted forty days.

19

21. The Greek Orthodox monastery at Capernaum (or Capharnaum). It stands on the shore of the Sea of Galilee. 21

And leaving Nazareth, he came and dwelt in Capernaum, which is upon the sea coast, in the borders of Zabulon and Nephthalim:

That it might be fulfilled which was spoken by Esaias the prophet, saying,

The land of Zabulon, and the land of Nephthalim, by the way of the sea, beyond Jordan, Galilee of the Gentiles;

The people which sat in darkness saw great light; and to them which sat in the region and shadow of death light is sprung up.

From that time Jesus began to preach, and to say, Repent: for the kingdom of heaven is at hand.

And Jesus, walking by the sea of Galilee, saw two brethren, Simon called Peter, and Andrew his brother, casting a net into the sea: for they were fishers.

And he saith unto them, Follow me, and I will make you fishers of men.

And they straightway left their nets, and followed him.

(4:13–20)

22. A view of the Sea of Galilee.

22

And Jesus went about all Galilee, teaching in their synagogues, and preaching the gospel of the kingdom, and healing all manner of sickness and all manner of disease among the people.

And his fame went throughout all Syria: and they brought unto him all sick people that were taken with divers diseases and torments, and those which were possessed with devils, and those which were lunatick, and those that had the palsy; and he healed them.

And there followed him great multitudes of people from Galilee, and from Decapolis, and from Jerusalem, and from Judaea, and from beyond Jordan.

(4:23–25)

23. The landscape in Galilee in the north of the Holy Land is green and peaceful. Cereals and fruit trees grow abundantly; the hills are thickly wooded.

The western shore of the Sea of Galilee was governed by Herod Antipas, Herod the Great's second son. The population was mainly Jewish. Herod Antipas founded Tiberias on the remains of biblical Rakkath (Joshua 19:35). It was named after the then reigning Roman emperor Tiberius and was declared the capital of Galilee. It enjoyed a measure of autonomy and the mixed population coexisted peacefully. The main source of income was fishing.

24 & 25. Fishing boats and nets on the shore of the Sea of Galilee.

26. The Sermon on the Mount, which may be described as the constitution of the kingdom of Heaven, was given on a hill overlooking the north shore of the Sea of Galilee, known as the Mount of Beatitudes. The church that now stands on the summit was built by the Order of St. Francis in 1938. It is octagonal in shape to commemorate the Eight Beatitudes, one of which is inscribed on each of the windows. The altar is topped by a dome with glittering gold mosaic, and encompassed by an open arched ambulatory.

27. A view of the Sea of Galilee from the Mount of Beatitudes.

The Sea of Galilee, or Lake Kinneret, is at times deep blue, placid, without a ripple, dotted with little sailing and fishing boats. At other times the whole landscape has a dreamlike character, the water is light green, almost white, and the mountains in the background seem to float in a soft mist. But this serene lake is also subject to sudden and violent storms: in no time dark clouds gather, the whole lake is shaken by violent spasms and high, menacing waves put the fishermen's lives in danger.

The name "Kinneret" (Chinnereth) for the Sea of Galilee is first mentioned in the Old Testament as the "sea of Chinneroth" (Joshua 12:3) or the "sea of Chinnereth" (Joshua 13:27), but the precise source or meaning of the name is not known. "Kinnor" means harp in Hebrew, and for some the lake owes its name to its harp-like shape. For others the music of its waters resembles the sound of a harp.

Matthew and Mark call it the Sea of Galilee or simply the Sea; John, the Sea of Tiberias (John 6:1). As for Luke, he calls it the Lake or the Lake of Gennesareth (Luke 5:1).

Lying about 690 feet below the level of the Mediterranean Sea, Lake Kinneret is flanked by the mountains of Galilee on the west and by the Golan Heights on the east.

Some of Christianity's most revered sites are to be found on its shores.

And seeing the multitudes, he went up into a mountain: and when he was set, his disciples came unto him:

And he opened his mouth, and taught them, saying.

Blessed are the poor in spirit: for theirs is the kingdom of heaven.

Blessed are they that mourn: for they shall be comforted.

Blessed are the meek: for they shall inherit the earth.

Blessed are they which do hunger and thirst after righteousness: for they shall be filled.

Blessed are the merciful: for they shall obtain mercy.

Blessed are the pure in heart: for they shall see God.

Blessed are the peacemakers: for they shall be called the children of God.

Blessed are they that are persecuted for righteousness' sake: for their's is the kingdom of heaven.

(5:1–10)

Think not that I am come to destroy the law, or the prophets: I am not come to destroy, but to fulfil.

For verily I say unto you, Till heaven and earth pass, one jot or one tittle shall in no wise pass from the law, till all be fulfilled.

Whosoever therefore shall break one of these least commandments, and shall teach men so, he shall be called the least in the kingdom of heaven: but whosoever shall do and teach them, the same shall be called great in the kingdom of heaven. For I say unto you, That except your righteousness shall exceed the righteousness of the scribes and Pharisees, ye shall in no case enter into the kingdom of heaven.

Ye have heard that it was said by them of old time, Thou shalt not kill; and whosoever shall kill shall be in danger of the judgment:

But I say unto you, That whosoever is angry with his brother without a cause shall be in danger of the judgment: and whosoever shall say to his brother, Raca, shall be in danger of the council: but whosoever shall say,

Thou fool, shall be in danger of hell fire.

(5:17–22)

Beware of false prophets, which come to you in sheep's clothing, but inwardly they are ravening wolves.

Ye shall know them by their fruits. Do men gather grapes of thorns, or figs of thistles?

Even so every good tree bringeth forth good fruit; but a corrupt tree bringeth forth evil fruit.

A good tree cannot bring forth evil fruit, neither can a corrupt tree bring forth good fruit.

Every tree that bringeth not forth good fruit is hewn down, and cast into the fire.

Wherefore by their fruits ye shall know them.

(7:15–20)

28

28. Section of the Habakkuk Commentary from Qumran, giving Habakkuk 2:5. A "tittle" refers to any small mark which distinguishes one letter from another, such as an uncrossed "t" which may be mistaken for an "l." "Jot" refers to the smallest letter in the Hebrew and Greek alphabets, *yod* (Greek: *iota*). This verse from the Qumran Habakkuk Commentary is especially illustrative of the difference a "jot or tittle" can make: the Hebrew text reads "but gathereth unto him all nations," that is, "the proud man" is the active subject, whereas the Qumran text reads "all nations will be gathered unto him," with the nations as the passive subject. This different reading (and meaning) is due simply to the presence or absence of one small "jot!"

29. Terracotta group of two wolves tearing at a ram, from Boeotia, 6th century B.C. False prophets are likened here to voracious wolves, in a passage which has given the proverbial saying "a wolf in sheep's clothing." Jesus' criterion for detecting false prophets: "by their fruits ye shall know them," is similar to one of those given by Jeremiah (Jeremiah 23). Jeremiah attacks three types of false prophets: those who have dreams and present them as the word of God, thus misleading the people; plagiarizers, who "steal my words every one from his neighbor," claiming that they have had direct revelation, and those who concoct their own "prophecies" from their own words, "that use their tongues, and say, He saith" (verse 31). Furthermore, if a prophet is of questionable moral character – a drunkard (Isaiah 8:27–28), an adulterer or liar (Jeremiah 23:14), or one who prophesies for a living, telling the people what they want to hear (Micah 3:11) – such a "corrupt tree" cannot be expected to bear wholesome fruit.

30. Fragment of cloth from the 1st century found in the Judean Desert.
Christ here appraises his forerunner, John the Baptist, now imprisoned, asking rhetorically if the people had gone to John expecting to see a person in soft raiment. Such persons are to be found in the houses of kings, but John was not like them. Jesus identifies John with the "messenger" prophesied in Malachi 3:1, where the messenger refers to the prophet Elijah, and to be sure, in verse 14 here, Christ says "if ye will receive it, this is Elias, [i.e. Elijah], which was for to come."
John is characterized here as "more than a prophet" and "there hath not risen a greater than John the Baptist." This refers to the fact that, in the New Testament view, all the prophets prior to John the Baptist prophesied that a Messiah was coming, but John testified (as opposed to prophesied) that Christ was come.

31. Pillar at the site of the ancient synagogue at Chorazin, in the hills above Capernaum, in Galilee.

32. Ruins at the synagogue.
It seems that a town existed at the site, but, according to Eusebius, it was already in ruins by the 4th century. Built of black basalt, the synagogue had doors facing Jerusalem and rows of pillars running parallel to the other three walls. The remains found show that it had a profusion of decorative carving in Byzantine style.

And as they departed, Jesus began to say unto the multitudes concerning John, What went ye out into the wilderness to see? A reed shaken with the wind?

But what went ye out for to see? A man clothed in soft raiment? behold, they that wear soft clothing are in kings' houses.

But what went ye out for to see? A prophet? yea, I say unto you, and more than a prophet.

For this is he, of whom it is written, Behold, I send my messenger before thy face, which shall prepare thy way before thee.

(11:7-10)

Then began he to upbraid the cities wherein most of his mighty works were done, because they repented not:

Woe unto thee, Chorazin! woe unto thee, Bethsaida! for if the mighty works, which were done in you, had been done in Tyre and Sidon, they would have repented long ago in sackcloth and ashes.

(11:20–21)

33. Wheat harvest in Galilee.

34. The sign at the entrance to "The Synagogue."
The beginnings of the synagogue, the Jewish house of worship, are obscure. It probably originated during the Babylonian Exile as an institution for public worship and instruction soon after the destruction of Solomon's Temple in 586 B.C. In the time of Jesus the synagogue was the center of religious and civic activity in Jewish communities outside Jerusalem, and it was in a synagogue that Jesus received his religious education, and probably found his first followers.

35. The door leading to "The Synagogue" in Nazareth, perhaps the one mentioned in the New Testament. This door is part of the remains of a synagogue, now inside the Greek Catholic church near the Basilica of the Annunciation. What is left of the synagogue consists of eighty stone steps, as well as some column bases, which have been dated to the 6th century A.D.

34

At that time Jesus went on the sabbath day through the corn; and his disciples were an hungred, and began to pluck the ears of corn, and to eat.

But when the Pharisees saw it, they said unto him, Behold, thy disciples do that which is not lawful to do upon the sabbath day.

But he said unto them, Have ye not read what David did, when he was an hungred, and they that were with him;

How he entered into the house of God, and did eat the shewbread, which was not lawful for him to eat, neither for them which were with him, but only for the priests?

Or have ye not read in the law, how that on the sabbath days the priests in the temple profane the sabbath, and are blameless?

But I say unto you, That in this place is one greater than the temple.

But if ye had known what this meaneth, I will have mercy, and not sacrifice, ye would not have condemned the guiltless.

For the Son of man is Lord even of the sabbath day.

(12:1–8)

And he said unto them, What man shall there be among you, that shall have one sheep, and if it fall into a pit on the sabbath day, will he not lay hold on it, and lift it out?

How much then is a man better than a sheep? Wherefore it is lawful to do well on the sabbath days.

(12:11–12)

And it came to pass, that when Jesus had finished these parables, he departed thence.

And when he was come into his own country, he taught them in their synagogue, insomuch that they were astonished, and said, Whence hath this man this wisdom, and these mighty works?

Is not this the carpenter's son? is not his mother called Mary? and his brethren, James, and Joses, and Simon, and Judas?

And his sisters, are they not all with us? Whence then hath this man all these things?

And they were offended in him. But Jesus said unto them, A prophet is not without honour, save in his own country, and in his own house.

And he did not many mighty works there because of their unbelief.

(13:53–58)

And Jesus went forth, and saw a great multitude, and was moved with compassion toward them, and he healed their sick.

And when it was evening, his disciples came to him, saying, This is a desert place, and the time is now past; send the multitude away, that they may go into the villages, and buy themselves victuals.

But Jesus said unto them, They need not depart; give ye them to eat.

And they say unto him, We have here but five loaves, and two fishes.

He said, Bring them hither to me. And he commanded the multitude to sit down on the grass, and took the five loaves, and the two fishes, and looking up to heaven, he blessed, and brake, and gave the loaves to his disciples, and the disciples to the multitude.

And they did all eat, and were filled: and they took up of the fragments that remained twelve baskets full.

And they that had eaten were about five thousand men, beside women and children.   (14:14–21)

36. A baker's stall displaying fresh bread and cakes; detail from a wall painting from "the house of the baker" at Pompeii, 1st century (Museo Nazionale, Naples).

The miracle of the feeding of the five thousand is an answer to a basic human need. Thus a basic need of daily life becomes the occasion of a miraculous sign full of spiritual significance. The disciples of Jesus wanted to send the crowds away to go buy food for themselves, that is to go out and do something to take care of their needs. Jesus told them, however, to "give" the multitude something to eat. The miracle demonstrates the real need of the followers of Christ – the proper food to satisfy their hunger. This food, of course, is not only physical but spiritual, and is mentioned many times in the New Testament. In the book of John, Jesus refers to himself as "the true bread from heaven" given by the Father: "For the bread of God is he which cometh down from heaven, and giveth life unto the world" (John 6:33). Jesus is thus "the bread of life," and "he that eateth me, even he shall live by me" (verses 35, 57). The matter of eating is central also in the Lord's Supper, which is essentially a feast, just like the Passover meal, full of symbolic significance.

Revelation 7:16 says, speaking of the heavenly kingdom and in fulfillment of the prophecy of Isaiah 49:10: "They shall hunger no more, neither thirst any more."

37. The Banias in the vicinity of Caesarea Philippi.

The Sea of Galilee is fed by fresh-water springs that rise in the surrounding Hermon range and flow down to the lake in the form of rivers. In ancient times, these springs were often regarded as sacred. The Banias (Arabic pronunciation of Paneas) is one of these. The spring came out of the mouth of the cave itself, a fact that caused the place to be regarded with special reverence. Perhaps because of the many shepherds who inhabited the region, the site was dedicated to the worship of Pan, the god of the shepherds and all

36

When Jesus came unto the coasts of Caesarea Philippi, he asked his disciples, saying, Whom do men say that I the Son of man am?

And they said, Some say that thou art John the Baptist: some, Elias; and others, Jeremias, or one of the prophets.

He saith unto them, But whom say ye that I am?

And Simon Peter answered and said, Thou art the Christ, the Son of the living God.

And Jesus answered and said unto him, Blessed art thou, Simon Barjona: for flesh and blood hath not revealed it unto thee, but my Father which is in heaven.

And I say also unto thee, That thou art Peter, and upon this rock I will build my church; and the gates of hell shall not prevail against it.

And I will give unto thee the keys of the kingdom of heaven: and whatsoever thou shalt bind on earth shall be bound in heaven: and whatsoever thou shalt loose on earth shall be loosed in heaven. (16:13–19)

wild things. Accordingly, the Greeks named this place "Paneas." Many shrines were built on the cliffs and caves of the mountainside. During the period of Roman rule in the Holy Land, Herod the Great received the nearby city from Augustus. His son Philip made it the capital of his tetrarchy and called it Caesarea, in honor of the Roman emperor. It came to be known as Caesarea Philippi.

Roman designs and inscriptions carved in the niches hewn in the rock are shown here. They are the remains of an ancient temple dedicated to Pan.

38. Roman designs and inscriptions carved in the rock on either side of one of the niches hewn out of the rock at Banias.

39 & 40. During Roman rule, some towns and cities were allowed to mint their own coins: shown here is a coin from Paneas adorned with the head of the god Pan and an image of the god's pipe.

37

39

38

40

And after six days Jesus taketh Peter, James, and John his brother, and bringeth them up into an high mountain apart,

And was transfigured before them: and his face did shine as the sun, and his raiment was white as the light.

And, behold, there appeared unto them Moses and Elias talking with him.

Then answered Peter, and said unto Jesus, Lord, it is good for us to be here: if thou wilt, let us make here three tabernacles; one for thee, and one for Moses, and one for Elias.

While he yet spake, behold, a bright cloud overshadowed them: and behold a voice out of the cloud, which said, This is my beloved Son, in whom I am well pleased: hear ye him.

And when the disciples heard it, they fell on their face, and were sore afraid.

And Jesus came and touched them, and said, Arise, and be not afraid.

And when they had lifted up their eyes, they saw no man, save Jesus only.

(17:1–8)

41. The impressive peak of Mount Hermon, rising more than 6000 feet above the plain, is visible from a distance of more than 60 miles. Some scholars believe it to be the "high mountain apart" where the Transfiguration took place.

42. Facade of the Franciscan basilica at Mount Tabor. In the church garden can be seen ruins of the earlier structures.
The Gospel does not mention the name of the mountain of the Transfiguration of Jesus, but according to a very old tradition which, according to Origen (c. 184–254), goes back to Apostolic days, it was upon Mount Tabor that Jesus Christ was transfigured. Churches to commemorate the event were built from an early period. A Byzantine basilica was erected on the mountain top. It was destroyed in the 7th century, rebuilt by the Crusaders, and again razed by the Mamelukes in the 13th century. The present basilica was built by the Franciscans in the 1920's (as well as a monastery nearby). Not far from the basilica is the Greek Orthodox church of St. Elias (Elijah). Adjoining the church is a convent. St. Elias was built upon the ruins of an ancient church mentioned by the historians of the Crusades. In the center of the flat mountain top an ancient oratory called "Descendentibus" has been restored. It recalls the words which Jesus spoke to the Apostles: "Tell the vision to no man till the Son of man be risen from the dead" (Matthew 17:9).

43. Interior of the church of the Transfiguration in the Franciscan church atop Mount Tabor, with a mosaic depicting the Transfiguration.

Deuteronomy 34:5–6 relates how Moses died and God hid his body. 1 Kings 2:11 tells how Elijah was taken by God into heaven. It is suggested that God did these two things purposely so that Moses and Elijah might appear with Christ on the mount of his Transfiguration. Revelation 11:3–4 also presents them as the two witnesses in the great tribulation. Moses represents the Law and Elijah the prophet, as the constituents of the Old Testament revelation. According to Luke 9:31, the subject of their conversation was Christ's death (Luke 24:25–27; 1 Corinthians 15:3), no doubt according to the prophecies of the Old Testament.

44. Mount Tabor. It stands out in the landscape and can be seen from a distance, just like Mount Hermon.

45. The village of Bethphage, on the slopes of the Mount of Olives in the immediate vicinity of Jerusalem.

The ass, or donkey, is the most commonly employed beast of burden in the domestic scenes of both the Old and the New Testament, as it has been up to modern times. The young ass or colt is referred to several times, as in the prophecy of Zechariah 9:9.

The riding upon an ass signifies not only the lowly and humble state in which the Lord willingly entered the city, but may conversely point to his kingly position. This can be learned from 1 Kings 1:33 and 38: David commanded, "Cause Solomon my son to ride upon mine own mule, and bring him down to Gihon," where he was to be anointed king of Israel.

And when they drew nigh unto Jerusalem, and were come to Bethphage, unto the mount of Olives, then sent Jesus two disciples, Saying unto them, Go into the village over against you, and straightway ye shall find an ass tied, and a colt with her: loose them, and bring them unto me.

And if any man say ought unto you, ye shall say, The Lord hath need of them; and straightway he will send them.

All this was done, that it might be fulfilled which was spoken by the prophet, saying,

Tell ye the daughter of Sion, Behold, thy King cometh unto thee, meek, and sitting upon an ass, and a colt the foal of an ass.

And the disciples went, and did as Jesus commanded them,

And brought the ass, and the colt, and put on them their clothes, and they set him thereon.

And a very great multitude spread their garments in the way; others cut down branches from the trees, and strawed them in the way.

And the multitudes that went before, and that followed, cried, saying, Hosanna to the Son of David: Blessed is he that cometh in the name of the Lord; Hosanna in the highest.

And when he was come into Jerusalem, all the city was moved, saying, Who is this?

And the multitude said, This is Jesus the prophet of Nazareth of Galilee.

(21:1–11)

46

47

46. A view of the Mount of Olives from Bethphage. According to Ezekiel, here the glory of God would be made manifest: "And the glory of the Lord went up from the midst of the city, and stood upon the mountain which is on the east side of the city," (Ezekiel 11:23). Zechariah also prophesied that "his feet shall stand that day upon the mount of Olives, which is before Jerusalem on the east" (Zechariah 14:4).

From Jerusalem the view to the east is blocked by the Mount of Olives rising some three hundred feet above the city. At various points there are magnificent views of the Old City and east across the Judean Desert to the Jordan Valley and the Mountains of Moab.

Jesus was familiar with the Mount of Olives because when in the Jerusalem area, he stayed with his friends at Bethany and each day he walked over the hill to the city and returned at nightfall: "In the day time he was teaching in the temple and at night he went out, and abode in the mount that is called the mount of Olives" (Luke 21:37).

47. The annual procession which marks the beginning of the Holy Week for the Latin Church in Jerusalem. The procession crosses the Kidron Valley and enters the walls of Jerusalem through St. Stephen's Gate. Nuns carry palm fronds and sing "Hosanna to the Son of David."

The word "Hosanna" is a Greek form of the Hebrew prayer formula *"Hoshia-na"* which means "please save." Other Hebrew words which have passed through Greek into the vocabulary of the New Testament are "Amen" – "let it be so," and "Hallelujah" – "praise the Lord." The cry of Hosanna in Psalm 118:25 (verse 26 of this Psalm is quoted in verse 9 here): "Save now, I beseech thee, O Lord", and the palm branches suggest the Feast of Tabernacles, when the people marched in procession carrying and waving branches of palm, myrtle and willow, crying "Hosanna." In fact, the seventh day of the Feast is known as "Hoshana Rabbah" – the Great Hoshana. Such processions were not necessarily restricted to the Feast of Tabernacles only and might spontaneously take place on any particularly joyous occasion, as related in the Book of Maccabees. In Revelation 7:9 the 144,000 stand before the throne and the Lamb "clothed with white robes, and palms in their hands."

Then went the Pharisees, and took counsel how they might entangle him in his talk.

And they sent out unto him their disciples with the Herodians, saying, Master, we know that thou art true, and teachest the way of God in truth, neither carest thou for any man: for thou regardest not the person of men.

Tell us therefore, What thinkest thou? Is it lawful to give tribute unto Caesar, or not? But Jesus perceived their wickedness, and said, Why tempt ye me, ye hypocrites?

Shew me the tribute money. And they brought unto him a penny.

And he saith unto them, Whose is this image and superscription?

They say unto him, Caesar's. Then saith he unto them, Render therefore unto Caesar the things which are Caesar's, and unto God the things that are God's.

When they had heard these words, they marvelled, and left him, and went their way.   (22:15–22)

Then spake Jesus to the multitude, and to his disciples,

Saying, The scribes and the Pharisees sit in Moses' seat;

48. A stone bust of the Roman emperor Tiberius who succeeded Augustus in A.D. 14. (Archaeology Museum, Istanbul).

These verses present the attempt of the Pharisees to ensnare Jesus in his talk so that they might have a good excuse to get rid of him. For this purpose they joined forces with the "Herodians", the people who sided with King Herod's policies of winning the Jews to the Greek and Roman way of life, and with the Sadducees. Their question was really an "entangling" one since to give tribute to Caesar was opposed by all the Jews, both on religious and political grounds. If Jesus said that it was lawful to give tribute to Caesar he would offend all the Jews and arouse both their religious and nationalistic opposition. If he said it was not lawful, the now-allied Herodians would have good grounds to accuse him before the Roman government. Jesus, by asking them to "shew me the tribute money" first of all, proved to them that they were using the Roman coins bearing the image of Caesar. His answer to the Pharisees was to pay tribute to Caesar according to Caesar's government regulations, and to pay the half-shekel to God, according to Exodus 30:11–16, and all the tithes of the Old Testament, according to the law of God.

All therefore whatsoever they bid you observe, that observe and do; but do not ye after their works: for they say, and do not.

For they bind heavy burdens and grievous to be borne, and lay them on men's shoulders; but they themselves will not move them with one of their fingers.

But all their works they do for to be seen of men: they make broad their phylacteries, and enlarge the borders of their garments, And love the uppermost rooms at feasts, and the chief seats in the synagogues,

And greetings in the markets, and to be called of men, Rabbi, Rabbi.

But be not ye called Rabbi: for one is your Master, even Christ; and all ye are brethren.

And call no man your father upon the earth: for one is your Father, which is in heaven.

Neither be ye called masters: for one is your Master, even Christ.

But he that is greatest among you shall be your servant.

And whosoever shall exalt himself shall be abased; and he that shall humble himself shall be exalted.   (23:1–12)

49

49. Phylactery found at the Qumran Caves in the Dead Sea region, dating from the first half of the first century.

Phylacteries, or *tefillin* in Hebrew, are two black leather boxes, containing scriptural passages, bound by black leather strips on the left arm and on the head, and worn by observant Jews for the morning services on all days of the year except Sabbaths and holidays. The practice is based on the biblical injunction to take these words (referring to the Law) "and thou shalt bind them for a sign upon thine hand, and they shall be as frontlets between thine eyes" (Deuteronomy 6:4–9; Exodus 13:1–10).

The *tefillin* capsule shown here opened is the only known example of the head *tefillin* of the period, found together with the portions of its text. The scriptural passages were written on slips of parchment, folded and tied, and they include the text of the Ten Commandments, which differs slightly from the later accepted text.

50. An interesting find among the remains of the synagogue of Chorazin is a seat carved out of a single basalt stone, in the form of an armchair. It may have been "Moses' seat" referred to in Matthew 23:2.

51. Facade of the Temple, from a reconstructed model.

The model of Herod's Temple shown here was planned by the late Professor Avi-Yonah of the Hebrew University, and now stands in the grounds of the Holyland Hotel in Jerusalem.

The Temple was the central building for the worship of God in ancient Israel. The First Temple was built by King Solomon on Mount Moriah (Temple Mount), in Jerusalem, and it served as a religious center for the Israelites until its destruction by Nebuchadnezzar. The ruler of Babylon, after besieging Jerusalem for two years, captured the city in 586 B.C., destroyed the Temple and exiled a large part of the population to Babylon.

Following the call of Cyrus, king of Persia, to the Jews to return to their homeland (538 B.C.), the Temple was rebuilt by the returnees, but it was a small and simple structure compared with the First Temple. Later, major reconstructions were carried out, notably during the period of Herod.

God's care for Jerusalem or for Israel is thrice compared to the care of a mother bird for her young. In Isaiah 31:5: "As birds flying, so will the Lord of hosts defend Jerusalem; defending also he will deliver it, and passing over he will preserve it." In Deuteronomy 32:11–12: "As an eagle stirreth up her nest, fluttereth over her young, spreadeth abroad her wings, taketh them, beareth them on her wings: So the Lord alone did lead him, and there was no strange god with him." In Psalm 91:4: "He shall cover thee with his feathers and under his wings shalt thou trust."

The prophecy against Jerusalem was fulfilled in A.D. 70, when Titus destroyed Jerusalem with the Roman army.

52. The so-called *Judaea capta* coin, showing a Roman soldier near a palm tree (the palm was a common symbol of Judea). The soldier is guarding a Jewish woman, who is shown sitting on a pile of weapons and weeping. The inscription reads "Judaea capta" (Judea captured).

Each time the Roman army achieved an important victory, the Romans would issue coins in commemoration of their latest conquest. The victory that the Romans achieved in Judea in A.D. 70 was a particularly important one because, although Judea was rather a small nation, yet the Jews had fought longer and more stubbornly for their independence than most other subject people. Thus, not only did the Romans issue a series of victory coins to commemorate the conquest of Judea, but they also made the series one of their largest issues of coins.

51

52

O Jerusalem, Jerusalem, thou that killest the prophets, and stonest them which are sent unto thee, how often would I have gathered thy children together, even as a hen gathereth her chickens under her wings, and ye would not! Behold, your house is left unto you desolate.

For I say unto you, Ye shall not see me henceforth, till ye shall say, Blessed is he that cometh in the name of the Lord. (23:37–39)

And Jesus went out, and departed from the temple: and his disciples came to him for to shew him the buildings of the temple.

And Jesus said unto them, See ye not all these things? verily I say unto you, There shall not be left here one stone upon another, that shall not be thrown down. (24:1–2)

But of that day and hour knoweth no man, no, not the angels of heaven, but my Father only. But as the days of Noe were, so shall also the coming of

53. Grain mill from the Second Temple period.
In this part of the prophecies concerning the last days, believers are warned to watch and be ready. "In the field" and "grinding at the mill" signify working for a living. Although the believers need to watch and be ready, and should not be overly caught up with the necessities of this life, they still work for a living. To be "taken" is to be raptured, as a sign of the Lord's coming.

the Son of man be. For as in the days that were before the flood they were eating and drinking, marrying and giving in marriage, until the day that Noe entered into the ark,

And knew not until the flood came, and took them all away; so shall also the coming of the Son of man be.

Then shall two be in the field; the one shall be taken, and the other left.

Two women shall be grinding at the mill; the one shall be taken, and the other left. Watch therefore: for ye know not what hour your Lord doth come.

But know this, that if the goodman of the house had known in what watch the thief would come, he would have watched, and would not have suffered his house to be broken up.

Therefore be ye also ready: for in such an hour as ye think not the Son of man cometh. (24:36–44)

Then shall the kingdom of heaven be likened unto ten virgins, which took their lamps, and went forth to meet the bridegroom.

And five of them were wise, and five were foolish.

They that were foolish took their lamps, and took no oil with them:

But the wise took oil in their vessels with their lamps.

While the bridegroom tarried, they all slumbered and slept.

And at midnight there was a cry made, Behold, the bridegroom cometh; go ye out to meet him.

Then all those virgins arose, and trimmed their lamps.

And the foolish said unto the wise, Give us of your oil; for our lamps are gone out.

But the wise answered, saying, Not so; lest there be not enough for us and you: but go ye rather to them that sell, and buy for yourselves.

And while they went to buy, the bridegroom came; and they that were ready went in with him to the marriage: and the door was shut.

Afterward came also the other virgins, saying, Lord, Lord, open to us.

But he answered and said, Verily I say unto you, I know you not.

Watch therefore, for ye know neither the day nor the hour wherein the

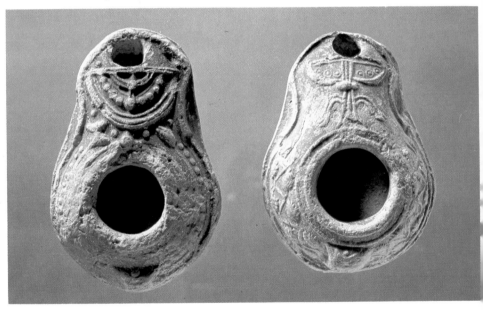

54. Two oil lamps from the Second Temple period.

The parable of the ten virgins is a call for watchfulness: "Watch therefore, for ye know neither the day nor the hour wherein the Son of man cometh." The parable indicates the responsibility of all believers to be "filled with oil," to be prudent or wise. It also indicates that no one can be "full" for others, but each must "buy" for himself. "Buy" indicates that having an adequate supply of oil (which symbolizes the Spirit) requires that a price be paid. "Gone out" in verse 8 means actually "going out" – the foolish virgins' lamps did not go out altogether, but they realized their supply was inadequate. Only those who are "ready" gain entrance to the marriage feast (not simply "marriage"; see Revelation 19:9; 1 Thessalonians 4:17), to which the foolish virgins are denied entrance. "Marriage feast" is not salvation, but a reward for the wise and ready virgins.

Son of man cometh.

For the kingdom of heaven is as a man travelling into a far country, who called his own servants, and delivered unto them his goods.

And unto one he gave five talents, to another two, and to another one; to every man according to his several ability; and straightway took his journey.

Then he that had received the five talents went and traded with the same, and made them other five talents.

And likewise he that had received two, he also gained other two.

But he that had received one went and digged in the earth, and hid his lord's money.

After a long time the lord of those servants cometh, and reckoneth with them.

And so he that had received five talents came and brought other five talents, saying Lord, thou deliveredst unto me five talents: behold, I have gained beside them five talents more.

His lord said unto him, Well done, good and faithful servant; thou hast been faithful over a few things, I will make thee ruler over many things: enter thou into the joy of thy lord.

He also that had received two talents came and said, Lord, thou deliveredst unto me two talents: behold, I have gained two other talents beside them.

His lord said unto him, Well done, good and faithful servant; thou hast been faithful over a few things, I will make thee ruler over many things: enter thou into the joy of thy lord.

Then he which had received the one talent came and said, Lord, I knew thee that thou art an hard man, reaping where thou hast not sown, and gathering where thou hast not strawed:

And I was afraid, and went and hid thy talent in the earth: lo, there thou hast that is thine.

55. Hoard of gold coins from Roman times. "Usury" in the Authorized Version did not yet have the later meaning of exorbitant interest and means simply "interest." The Old Testament forbade the charging of interest on loans by one Hebrew to another (Exodus 22:25, Deuteronomy 23:19ff., Leviticus 25:35–38). The loans mentioned in the Old Testament, however, are not advances for trading capital, but solely for the relief of a poor fellow Hebrew temporarily in distress who would otherwise be forced to sell himself as a slave. Lending in the Old Testament is thus an act of brotherly love, and not a commercial venture.

Conditions changed greatly, however, in New Testament times. The rise of urban commerce made capital necessary for many trading concerns. Jesus refers twice, here and in Luke 19:2, to the investment of money with "bankers" in order to gain "interest." The rate of interest in Israel is unknown but in the Greco-Roman world it was generally quite high.

The talent was one of the largest denominations of money in New Testament times, some venturing the estimation that it was worth about a thousand dollars of today. The significance of the talents and the interest gained by their investment is of course a parable of another aspect of the kingdom of heaven.

"Exchangers", or money-lenders, are mentioned in the Old Testament at the beginning of David's kingdom, and the Book of Proverbs warns several times about the dangers of making pledges and to be careful to cover risks by demanding collateral. The exchangers or bankers mentioned here, like those of modern times, undertook the charge of deposits of money for the use of which they paid interest. The opposite of going to the bankers is to hoard money. The apocryphal book of Ecclesiasticus or Ben Sira mentions money hoarders who put it "under a stone."

His lord answered and said unto him, Thou wicked and slothful servant, thou knewest that I reap where I sowed not, and gather where I have not strawed:

Thou oughtest therefore to have put my money to the exchangers, and then at my coming I should have received mine own with usury.

Take therefore the talent from him, and give it unto him which hath ten talents.

For unto every one that hath shall be given, and he shall have abundance: but from him that hath not shall be taken away even that which he hath.

And cast ye the unprofitable servant into outer darkness: there shall be weeping and gnashing of teeth.

When the Son of man shall come in his glory, and all the holy angels with him, then shall he sit upon the throne of his glory:

And before him shall be gathered all nations: and he shall separate them one from another, as a shepherd divideth his sheep from the goats:

And he shall set the sheep on his right hand, but the goats on the left.

Then shall the King say unto them on his right hand, Come, ye blessed of my Father, inherit the kingdom prepared for you from the foundation of the world:

For I was an hungred, and ye gave me meat: I was thirsty, and ye gave me drink: I was a stranger, and ye took me in:

Naked, and ye clothed me: I was sick, and ye visited me: I was in prison, and ye came unto me.

Then shall the righteous answer him, saying, Lord, when saw we thee an hungred, and fed thee? or thirsty, and gave thee drink?

56. A shepherd and his mixed flock near Bethlehem.
The pastoral scene of a shepherd and his flock is used to portray the coming judgement on the nations. The "sheep" are the believers in Christ, who will "inherit the kingdom prepared for you from the foundation of the world," whereas the goats are the unbelievers and are accursed and cast into everlasting fire.

57. Pottery imitation of an *alabastron*, an alabaster vessel for perfumes, 1st century B.C. (Israel Department of Antiquities, Jerusalem).
Various sorts of perfumed oils and ointments were in general use in antiquity because of the great exposure to sunlight, and because there was no soap. The most aromatic oils, the kind called "precious," were prepared with vegetable oils to which were added aromatic plant ingredients from distant lands. Because they were very expensive, such unguents were kept in vessels with narrow openings, from which they were poured drop by drop. One of these vessels was the so-called *alabastron*, an elongated drop-shaped container, usually made of alabaster (a translucent whitish stone). Oils were used for certain rituals and mainly for funerary and cosmetic purposes.

When saw we thee a stranger, and took thee in? or naked, and clothed thee?

Or when saw we thee sick, or in prison, and came unto thee?

And the King shall answer and say unto them, Verily I say unto you, Inasmuch as ye have done it unto one of the least of these my brethren, ye have done it unto me.

Then shall he say also unto them on the left hand, Depart from me, ye cursed, into everlasting fire, prepared for the devil and his angels:

For I was an hungred, and ye gave me no meat: I was thirsty, and ye gave me no drink.

(25:1–42)

And these shall go away into everlasting punishment: but the righteous into life eternal.

(25:46)

Now when Jesus was in Bethany, in the house of Simon the leper,

There came unto him a woman having an alabaster box of very precious ointment, and poured it on his head, as he sat at meat.

But when his disciples saw it, they had indignation, saying, To what purpose is this waste?

For this ointment might have been sold for much, and given to the poor.

When Jesus understood it, he said unto them, Why trouble ye the woman? for she hath wrought a good work upon me.

For ye have the poor always with you; but me ye have not always.

For in that she hath poured this ointment on my body, she did it for my burial.

Verily I say unto you, Wheresoever this gospel shall be preached in the whole world, there shall also this, that this woman hath done, be told for a memorial of her.

(26:6–13)   **58.** A general view of Bethany.

59

60

61

63

62

59–62. Walking through the old streets of Jerusalem today on the way to Mount Zion.

63. Model of private dwellings in Jerusalem at the time of Herod.

64. The Cenacle on Mount Zion in Jerusalem, believed to be the place where Jesus partook of the Passover feast with his disciples.
The building is typical of 12th-century Crusader architecture, as the Gothic arches and capitals of the pillars demonstrate. The room contains a prayer niche facing Mecca, built in 1928 by the Moslems, as it was then transformed into a mosque.
After the Crusader conquest in 1099, the Christian knights built a church at this site, the Church of St. Mary of Zion, with the present Cenacle in its southern wing.
The tradition concerning the Cenacle goes back to the early 5th century. The room is also associated with the events related in the Acts of the Apostles (1:13) concerning the descent of the Spirit on the Apostles at Pentecost.
The Passover was, and still is, celebrated on the 15th day of Nisan. Since the Jews measure the day from sundown to sundown, the

Now the first day of the feast of unleavened bread the disciples came to Jesus, saying unto him, Where wilt thou that we prepare for thee to eat the passover?

And he said, Go into the city to such a man, and say unto him, The Master saith, My time is at hand; I will keep the passover at thy house with my disciples.

And the disciples did as Jesus had appointed them: and they made ready the passover.

Now when the even was come, he sat down with the twelve.

And as they did eat, he said, Verily I say unto you, that one of you shall betray me.

And they were exceeding sorrowful, and began every one of them to say unto Him, Lord, is it I?

And he answered and said, He that dippeth his hand with me in the dish, the same shall betray me.

The Son of man goeth as it is written of him: but woe unto that man by whom the Son of man is betrayed! it had been good for that man if he had not been born.

Then Judas, which betrayed him, answered and said, Master, is it I? He said unto him, Thou hast said.

celebration begins on the night of the 14th, after sunset. It lasts one week. Pilgrims flocked from all over the country to Jerusalem several days before the feast to purify themselves at the Temple. A lamb or sheep was sacrificed by each family and then roasted and eaten at the evening meal. After the destruction of the Temple (A.D. 70), the sacrifice of the paschal lamb came to an end.

The celebration was a family affair, which took place in the home – as it does today.

Before partaking of the meal the story of the Exodus is told as prescribed in Exodus 13:8. The head of the family or one of the celebrants introduces the festival. He holds a goblet of wine in his hand and recites the benediction in which God is praised for giving the festivals to Israel, for creating the produce of the Vine, anniversaries for rejoicing, and "this feast-day of Passover, the season of our freedom, a holy convocation in memorial of our departure from Egypt...."

In addition to the roasted lamb, bitter herbs – in memory of the ordeals suffered by the Jews in Egypt – are consumed as well as unleavened bread in memory of the bread baked in haste before leaving Egypt.

The observances also include washing of the hands before breaking the unleavened bread and reciting Grace before Meals: ".... Blessed art Thou.... who bringest forth bread...."

And as they were eating, Jesus took bread, and blessed it, and brake it, and gave it to the disciples, and said, Take, eat; this is my body.

And he took the cup, and gave thanks, and gave it to them, saying, Drink ye all of it;

For this is my blood of the new testament, which is shed for many for the remission of sins.

But I say unto you, I will not drink henceforth of this fruit of the vine, until that day when I drink it new with you in my Father's kingdom.

And when they had sung an hymn, they went out into the mount of Olives.

65. This silver chalice, known as "The Chalice of Antioch," dates from about the 4th or 5th century A.D.

The term 'chalice' was originally reserved to designate the cup containing the wine used in the Eucharist. The earlier Christian chalices were made of glass, but from the 5th century they came to be made of gold or silver, and were richly ornamented. The chalice was a theme of poetry and romances, and was known as the Holy Grail in the Middle Ages. According to legend, the Holy Grail, which was believed to be the cup used by Jesus Christ at the Last Supper, and later to be in the possession of Joseph of Arimathea, was still extant and possessed spiritual qualities which could bring mystical benefits to its beholders. In the 13th century the search for the Holy Grail characterized the knights who aimed to reach perfection.

The cup shown here was once claimed to be the Holy Grail. (It is now at the Metropolitan Museum of Art, New York.)

66. The Church of the Agony (or Church of All Nations) stands in the Garden of Gethsemane. The mosaic on the facade depicts Jesus as the link beween Man and his Creator, with the whole of humanity raising their eyes in hope. Above his head appear the Greek letters Alpha and Omega, as it is said in Revelation 1:8: "I am Alpha and Omega, the Beginning and the Ending, saith the Lord." The site was first consecrated as that from which the Roman guards led Jesus away, by the Byzantine Christians in the 5th century, who built a church here. The present church was built in 1909. It owes its name – "Church of All Nations" – to the fact that men of all nations contributed to its construction.

Then saith Jesus unto them, All ye shall be offended because of me this night: for it is written, I will smite the shepherd, and the sheep of the flock shall be scattered abroad.

But after I am risen again, I will go before you into Galilee.

Peter answered and said unto him, Though all men shall be offended because of thee, yet will I never be offended.

Jesus said unto him, Verily I say unto thee, That this night, before the cock crow, thou shalt deny me thrice.

Peter said unto him, though I should die with thee, yet will I not deny thee. Likewise also said all the disciples.

Then cometh Jesus with them unto a place called Gethsemane, and saith unto the disciples, Sit ye here, while I go and pray yonder.

And he took with him Peter and the two sons of Zebedee, and began to be sorrowful and very heavy.

Then saith he unto them, My soul is exceeding sorrowful, even unto death: tarry ye here, and watch with me.

And he went a little further, and fell on his face, and prayed, saying, O my Father, if it be possible, let this cup pass from me: nevertheless not as I will, but as thou wilt.

And he cometh unto the disciples, and findeth them asleep, and saith unto Peter, what, could ye not watch with me one hour?

Watch and pray, that ye enter not into temptation: the spirit indeed is willing, but the flesh is weak.

He went away again the second time, and prayed, saying, O my Father,

67. This olive tree in the Garden of Gethsemane is said to be as much as two thousand years old.

68. An oil-press dating from the 15th century.
The name Gethsemane means "place of the oil press," Hebrew *gat* meaning "press" and *shemen* meaning "oil." Jerome, who translated the Bible into Latin, explained the name as meaning "valley of fatness," that is, *gei* meaning "valley" and *shamen* "fatness," thus identifying it with the "fat valleys" mentioned in Isaiah 28:1. Oil in the Old Testament is a symbol of the Spirit (Zechariah 12) and the context here refers not only to the physical characteristics of the place of Jesus' prayer but also to the pressing. The Lord was pressed here to pour out the oil, the Spirit.

67

68

69. View of the Church of St. Peter in Gallicantu (cock-crow) on present-day Mount Zion. Inside the church are ancient rock-cut structures, cellars, stables and cisterns, dating from Herodian times. The edifice, according to tradition, marks the site where Peter heard the crow of the cock after denying the Lord three times, as prophesied. Some think that the church is built over the remains of the high priest Caiaphas' house.

The church was built in 1931. Its walls are decorated with mosaics which depict the events supposed to have taken place at the site. Underneath the church is shown the place where Jesus was imprisoned. During the excavations of the foundations of the building, remains were uncovered including ancient mosaic floors. One of these floors contains the words of Psalm 121:8: "The Lord will preserve thy going out and thy coming in, both now and forever more" in Greek.

The Church of Gallicantu is situated in what was known as the "upper city" in ancient times, overlooking the "lower city," the biblical city of David. The balcony of the church offers a magnificent view of the city of David and the three valleys delineating Jerusalem.

if this cup may not pass away from me, except I drink it, thy will be done.

And he came and found them asleep again: for their eyes were heavy.

And he left them, and went away again, and prayed the third time, saying the same words.

Then cometh he to his disciples, and saith unto them, Sleep on now, and take your rest: behold, the hour is at hand, and the Son of man is betrayed into the hands of sinners.

Rise, let us be going: behold, he is at hand that doth betray me.

(26:17–46)

Now Peter sat without in the palace: and a damsel came unto him, saying, Thou also wast with Jesus of Galilee.

But he denied before them all, saying, I know not what thou sayest.

And when he was gone out into the porch, another maid saw him, and said unto them that were there, This fellow was also with Jesus of Nazareth.

And again he denied with an oath, I do not know the man.

And after a while came unto him they that stood by, and said to Peter, Surely thou also art one of them; for thy speech bewrayeth thee.

Then began he to curse and to swear, saying, I know not the man. And immediately the cock crew.

And Peter remembered the word of Jesus, which said unto him, before the cock crow, thou shalt deny me thrice. And he went out, and wept bitterly.

(26:69–75)

70. The remains of the ancient staircase which led down from the upper city to the lower city. By this stepped road Jesus descended from Mount Zion, across the Kidron Valley to Gethsemane.

71. A stone bearing the name of Pontius Pilate was found in Caesarea. It bears a dedicatory inscription by Pontius Pilate procurator of Judea in honor of the emperor Tiberius Caesar.

When the morning was come, all the chief priests and elders of the people took counsel against Jesus to put him to death:

And when they had bound him, they led him away, and delivered him to Pontius Pilate the governor.

(27:1–2)

When he was set down on the judgment seat, his wife sent unto him, saying, Have thou nothing to do with that just man: for I have suffered many things this day in a dream because of him.

But the chief priests and elders persuaded the multitude that they should ask Barabbas, and destroy Jesus.

The governor answered and said unto them, Whether of the twain will ye that I release unto you? They said, Barabbas.

72. Detail of the extensive section of Roman pavement excavated near the Ecce Homo Arch within the Convent of the Sisters of Zion, known as *Lithostratos* or "the pavement," thought to be the site of Jesus' trial before Pilate. The pavement is made of massive blocks of stones. In some parts the pavement has been roughened for the passage of animals and chariots, who would otherwise slip on the smooth stones. The paved area was on a raised-up place with the ground falling steeply to the east and west. It was in close proximity, if not actually within, the Roman fortress of Antonia north of the Temple Mount.

73. Pitcher and bowl found in a house in Pompeii, destroyed in A.D. 79.

In the Old Testament, washing the hands was prescribed by the Law in connection with purity. In connection with murder, the Law prescribed that in case someone slain was found and it was impossible to ascertain who the murderer was, the elders of the city were to slaughter a young cow at a place with running water and wash their hands over the young cow, to assert their innocence in regard to the murder and say "Our hands have not shed this blood, neither have our eyes seen it. Be merciful, O Lord unto thy people Israel, whom thou hast redeemed, and lay not innocent blood unto thy people of Israel's charge. And the blood shall be forgiven them. So shalt thou put away the guilt of innocent blood from among you, when thou shalt do that which is right in the sight of the Lord." (Deuteronomy 21:1–9).

After Pilate's examination of Jesus, and apparently coming to the conclusion that he had no real reason to condemn him (being no party to the religious motivations of Jesus' accusers), he makes a series of attempts to release Jesus without giving too much offense to the Jews, not desiring to stir up any turmoil in the province under his jurisdiction. Firstly, hearing that Jesus came from Galilee (according to Luke) he sends him to Herod Antipas who was in Jerusalem at that time for the feast. This act served to reconcile the enmity between the two governors by Pilate's courtesy in recognizing Herod's jurisdiction. But when the latter failed to get any reply or a miracle out of Jesus, he sent him back to Pilate. Pilate then sought to release a prisoner in honor of the Passover, as was the custom. Lastly, even after washing his hands of the responsibility of condemning an innocent man to death, he hoped to satisfy the anger of the accusers by having him scourged (Luke 23:16–22). But Pilate's superstitious fear having been aroused by his wife's dream (verse 19), he again questioned Jesus. What decided the issue was, in the end, the priests' cry, "If thou let this man go, thou art not Caesar's friend." The threat that the provincials under his rule would accuse him at Rome of treason was the factor which finally decided the outcome of the events.

The events dealing with Pilate illustrate the danger in the strict supervision which the Roman Caesars Augustus and Tiberius maintained over the government of the provinces: it enabled the provincials to intimidate a weak governor. The Imperial government also misjudged the difficulty and complexity involved in governing the Jewish population of Judea, and sent as procurators second-rate men, mostly, as Pilate was, nominees of Imperial favorites, and who were for the most part expecting to be promoted out of their undesirable positions from the moment they were appointed.

Pilate saith unto them, What shall I do then with Jesus which is called Christ? They all say unto him, Let him be crucified.

And the governor said, Why, what evil hath he done? But they cried out the more, saying, Let him be crucified.

When Pilate saw that he could prevail nothing, but that rather a tumult was made, he took water, and washed his hands before the multitude, saying, I am innocent of the blood of this just person: see ye to it.

Then answered all the people, and said, His blood be on us, and on our children.

Then released he Barabbas unto them: and when he had scourged Jesus, he delivered him to be crucified.

Then the soldiers of the governor took Jesus into the common hall, and gathered unto him the whole band of soldiers.

And they stripped him, and put on him a scarlet robe.

74. "The Disrobing of Christ," by El Greco, one of the greatest artists of the Renaissance.

75. In the Via Dolorosa (the Way of the Cross) in the Old City of Jerusalem is the Fifth Station of the Cross. Here Simon of Cyrene helped Jesus to carry his cross.

And when they had platted a crown of thorns, they put it upon his head, and a reed in his right hand: and they bowed the knee before him, and mocked him, saying, Hail, King of the Jews.

And they spit upon him, and took the reed, and smote him on the head.

And after that they had mocked him, they took the robe off from him, and put his own raiment on him, and led him away to crucify him.

And as they came out, they found a man of Cyrene, Simon by name: him they compelled to bear his cross.

And when they were come unto a place called Golgotha, that is to say, a place of a skull,

They gave him vinegar to drink mingled with gall: and when he had tasted thereof, he would not drink.

And they crucified him, and parted his garments, casting lots: that it might be fulfilled which was spoken by the prophet, They parted my garments among them, and upon my vesture did they cast lots.

And sitting down they watched him there.

And set up over his head his accusation written, This is Jesus the King of the Jews

(27:19–37)

76. & 77. The so-called Golgotha or "Gordon's Calvary" Garden Tomb.

The Garden Tomb lies beneath a rise which supposedly resembles a human skull – Golgoltha in Aramaic. It is believed by Protestants to be the true burial place of Jesus, rather than the Holy Sepulcher revered by the Roman Catholics and the Greek Orthodox.

It is also known as Gordon's Calvary, after the renowned British general, Charles Gordon, who visited Jerusalem in 1883 and became convinced that this was the true tomb of Jesus.

The site was acquired in 1894 and the Garden Tomb Association, with headquarters in London, England, was formed "for the preservation of the Tomb and Garden outside the walls of Jerusalem, believed by many to be the Sepulcher and garden of Joseph of Arimathea . . . that it might be kept sacred as a quiet spot . . .".

Identification of many sites related to the New Testament is dependent upon an assessment regarding the line of the walls of Jerusalem at the time of Jesus. For almost a century past debates on this question have not come up with a definite answer. The subject is important to the position of Calvary for no one questions that the Crucifixion was outside the City.

The discovery of a tomb in this vicinity was not sensational as many other tombs had been found in the area. When, however, an unusual sepulcher is seen to be adjacent to an ancient place of execution and in the setting of a vineyard garden, it is thought-provoking.

Furthermore it was in a garden, hewn out of the rock, a rich man's tomb (Matthew 27:60); the Disciples could look into the tomb from the outside (John 20:5); the tomb was closed by rolling a great stone over the entrance (Matthew 27:60); there was room for a number of persons (Luke 24:1–4); it was a new tomb and not a renovated old sepulcher (John 19:41).

In 1970 the late Dame Kathleen Kenyon – the renowned archaeologist – stated that it was a typical tomb of about the first century A.D. However convincing these arguments may seem to some, other archaeologists and scholars believe it unwise to reject the traditional sites of Calvary and the Holy Sepulcher, as there is also much evidence in their favor.

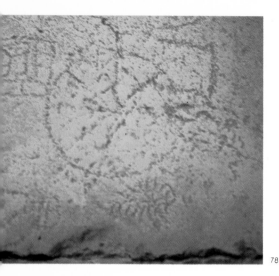

78. Carving in the pavement at the Lithostratos, cut by Roman soldiers for playing games of chance.
Among their games, the soldiers played the Game of the King, with which the Roman guards are believed to have amused themselves during Jesus' trial. The soldiers would choose a dummy king, address him by all the titles worthy of such rank, and give him full liberty to indulge his desires and instincts. They then would torture and kill him.

79. Roman legionaries, depicted on Trajan's Column in Rome.

When the even was come, there came a rich man of Arimathaea, named Joseph, who also himself was Jesus' disciple:

He went to Pilate, and begged the body of Jesus. Then Pilate commanded the body to be delivered. And when Joseph had taken the body, he wrapped it in a clean linen cloth,

And laid it in his own new tomb, which he had hewn out in the rock: and he rolled a great stone to the door of the sepulchre, and departed.

And there was Mary Magdalene, and the other Mary, sitting over against the sepulchre.

Now the next day, that followed the day of the preparation, the chief priests and Pharisees came together unto Pilate,

Saying, Sir, we remember that that deceiver said, while he was yet alive, After three days I will rise again.

Command therefore that the sepulchre be made sure until the third day, lest his disciples come by night, and steal him away, and say unto the people, He is risen from the dead: so the last error shall be worse than the first. Pilate said unto them, Ye have a watch: go your way, make it as sure as ye can.

So they went, and made the sepulchre sure, sealing the stone, and setting a watch. (27:57–66)

In the end of the sabbath, as it began to dawn toward the first day of the week, came Mary Magdalene and the other Mary to see the sepulchre.

And, behold, there was a great earthquake: for the angel of the Lord descended from heaven, and came and rolled back the stone from the door, and sat upon it.

His countenance was like lightning, and his raimant white as snow: And for fear of him the keepers did shake, and became as dead men.

And the angel answered and said unto the women, Fear not ye: for I know that ye seek Jesus, which was crucified. He is not here: for he is risen, as he said. Come, see the place where the Lord lay.

And go quickly, and tell his disciples that he is risen from the dead; and, behold, he goeth before you into Galilee; there shall ye see him: lo, I have told you. (28:1–7)

80. The "Tomb of Joseph of Arimathea" inside the Church of the Holy Sepulcher.
Joseph of Arimathea was a wealthy and God-fearing Jew and a member of the Sanhedrin. He became a follower of Jesus but kept his faith secret for fear of the hostility of his colleagues. He took no part in Jesus' condemnation but neither is it said that he spoke against it, probably not having been present at that meeting. After the crucifixion he was evidently struck with remorse and got up the courage to go and beg Pilate for the body.
It was common for friends of the crucified to purchase their bodies and give them a decent burial. Otherwise the body might have been left on the cross for the carrion-birds.

81. The women and the angel at the Sepulcher; gold embossed 11th-century relief from Aachen Cathedral, Germany.
Once again the angel tells the women that the resurrected Christ will appear to them not in Jerusalem, the holy city of Jewish religion, but in Galilee, where he also began his ministry.

The beginning of the gospel of Jesus Christ, the Son of God;

As it is written in the prophets, Behold, I send my messenger before thy face, which shall prepare thy way before thee.

The voice of one crying in the wilderness, Prepare ye the way of the Lord, make his paths straight.

John did baptize in the wilderness, and preach the baptism of repentance for the remission of sins.

And there went out unto him all the land of Judaea, and they of Jerusalem, and were all baptized of him in the river of Jordan, confessing their sins.

And John was clothed with camel's hair, and with a girdle of a skin about his loins; and he did eat locusts and wild honey;

And preached, saying, There cometh one mightier than I after me, the latchet of whose shoes I am not worthy to stoop down and unloose.

I indeed have baptized you with water: but he shall baptize you with the Holy Ghost.

And it came to pass in those days, that Jesus came from Nazareth of Galilee, and was baptized of John in Jordan.

And staightway coming out of the water, he saw the heavens opened, and the Spirit like a dove descending upon him:

And there came a voice from heaven, saying, Thou art my beloved Son, in whom I am well pleased.

(1:1–11)

82. The Wilderness of Judea extends from the eastern shore of the Dead Sea to the heights of Jerusalem, Bethlehem and Hebron to the west.

83. The Judean Desert with Herodium rising in the background.

84. The Jordan River, a narrow, straight stream at some points, broadens or meanders capriciously at others.
Originating in the northeastern corner of the Holy Land, where its headstreams meet at the foot of Mount Hermon, the Jordan flows south and enters the Sea of Galilee. In the last ten miles before reaching the Sea of Galilee, the Jordan falls from 200 feet above sea level to 700 feet below sea level. Before entering the Sea the river spreads into a small delta. It continues its course southward again and at last spills into the Dead Sea, having covered a distance of some 125 miles.
The importance of the Jordan and its sanctity go back to early biblical times. Elijah miraculously divided its waters, and so did Elisha; Naaman, the leprous captain, bathed seven times in the river and "he was clean" (II Kings 5:14). John the Baptist preached repentance and baptised followers in the Jordan.
The symbol of ritual immersion was common to many ancient religions, even before biblical times. It was the most common method of purification, but it is not to be confused with washing for the sake of cleanliness, which was required in any case before purification. At the time of Jesus such rites were observed by the Dead Sea Sect with its fanatical concern for ritual purity. The symbolic significance of baptism in the New Testament is to mark a break with the sinful past, and embark on a new way of life.

85. The spot traditionally believed to be the place of the baptism of Jesus.
The site is in the lower part of the Jordan, near its fall into the Dead Sea, and a short distance from Jericho. Here the Jordan is quite narrow and shallow, sometimes no more than a stream.

83

84

85

And they went into Capernaum; and straightway on the sabbath day he entered into the synagogue, and taught.

And they were astonished at his doctrine: for he taught them as one that had authority, and not as the scribes.

(1:21–22)

And again he entered into Capernaum, after some days; and it was noised that he was in the house.

And straightway many were gathered together, insomuch that there was no room to receive them, no, not so much as about the door: and he preached the word unto them.

And they come unto him, bringing one sick of the palsy, which was borne of four.

And when they could not come nigh unto him for the press, they uncovered the roof where he was: and when they had broken it up, they let down the bed wherein the sick of the palsy lay.

When Jesus saw their faith, he said unto the sick of the palsy, Son, thy sins be forgiven thee.

86. Remains of the synagogue of Capernaum in the Galilee.

Capernaum – in Hebrew, Kefar Nahum (Village of Nahum) – was an important Galilean town in ancient times on the northern shore of the Sea of Galilee. It is not known who was the Nahum for whom the town was named. In the Middle Ages it was believed that the reference was to the prophet Nahum of the Bible, and some even claimed that his tomb was to be found in the place. Today, Capernaum is a heap of ruins, but the remains of its ancient synagogue are among the most interesting relics in Israel. It was traditionally identified as the synagogue in which Jesus preached, as described in the New Testament. More recent studies point to a later period – the end of the 2nd century, or even later. Nevertheless, it is very likely that Jesus preached in a synagogue very much like the one whose vestiges are shown here.

The site has been definitely identified as the town of Capernaum, mentioned by Josephus and in the New Testament. According to Josephus this village was in the center of the fertile valley of Ginnosar, and in the New Testament it is mentioned as Jesus' "own city" and center of activity. Peter the fisherman was also active in the area. The Talmud mentions the "sectarians" who lived at Capernaum.

Excavations in Capernaum began in the middle of the 19th century and have been renewed several times since then. Since 1921 Franciscan monks have excavated the site and own most of the surroundings.

The synagogue was a rectangular structure, oriented north-south, and composed of two main parts: an arched prayer-hall and a court, or atrium, surrounded by a three-sided portico. In front of the building is a broad square with steps leading to the doors of the synagogue. The building itself was constructed of hewn stones which were brought here from afar. They glimmer in their whiteness against the dark basalt background surrounding Capernaum. Its walls were decorated inside and out with stone carvings of flora and fauna and geometric designs. The interior of the structure, some portions of which have been preserved, was apparently plastered and painted. The builders took special pains to beautify the facade of the building which faced Jerusalem.

Most of the decorations of the synagogue were found outside the building and only a few, such as the Corinthian capitals which supported the roof and parts of the decorated lintels, were left in place. Among these are friezes from the facade and smaller ones which graced the inner walls. The lintels over the doors and windows were also richly decorated.

But there were certain of the scribes sitting there, and reasoning in their hearts,

Why doth this man thus speak blasphemies? who can forgive sins but God only?

And immediately when Jesus perceived in his spirit that they so reasoned within themselves, he said unto them, Why reason ye these things in your hearts?

Whether is it easier to say to the sick of the palsy, Thy sins be forgiven thee; or to say, Arise, and take up thy bed, and walk?

But that ye may know that the Son of man hath power on earth to forgive sins, (he saith to the sick of the palsy,)

I say unto thee, Arise, and take up thy bed, and go thy way into thine house.

And immediately he arose, took up the bed, and went forth before them all; insomuch that they were all amazed, and glorified God, saying, We never saw it on this fashion.

(2:1–12)

87

87. Wall painting from Dura-Europos, Mesopotamia, depicting the miracle of the "man sick of the palsy." In this painting the paralyzed man, now healed, carries on his back a bed consisting of a metal or wooden framework formed by a crisscross of ropes.

The church at Dura-Europos is the oldest known Christian chapel found in a private house. It recalls Paul's epistles to Philemon: "And to our beloved Apphia, and Archippus our fellow-soldier, and to the church in thy house" (Philemon 2). In all probability such "churches" were not usually so richly decorated, and were probably simply the private homes of the early Christians, where the meetings of the early Church were held.

88

88. Interior of the Capernaum synagogue, showing two parallel rows of columns along the length of the main hall, and stone benches along the wall. In the area of the synagogue the remains of an octagonal church were found – probably of the 5th or 6th century – as well as fragments of a mosaic floor.

89. Capitals of two columns at the synagogue of Capernaum.

89

And it came to pass, that, as Jesus sat at meat in his house, many publicans and sinners sat also together with Jesus and his disciples: for there were many, and they followed him.

And when the scribes and Pharisees saw him eat with publicans and sinners, they said unto his disciples, How is it that he eateth and drinketh with publicans and sinners?

When Jesus heard it, he saith unto them, They that are whole have no need of the physician, but they that are sick: I came not to call the righteous, but sinners to repentance.

And the disciples of John and of the Pharisees used to fast: and they come and say unto him, Why do the disciples of John and of the Pharisees fast, but thy disciples fast not?

And Jesus said unto them, Can the children of the bridechamber fast, while the bridegroom is with them? as long as they have the bridegroom with them, they cannot fast. But the days will come, when the bridegroom shall be taken away from them, and then shall they fast in those days.

90. Votive relief dedicated to Amphiarios, from the sanctuary of Oropos, 4th century B.C. (Archaeological Museum, Athens).

In biblical usage, health is frequently a reward for obedience to the divine will: "If thou wilt diligently hearken to the voice of the Lord thy God, and wilt do that which is right in his sight, and wilt give ear to his commandments, and keep all his statutes, I will put none of these diseases upon thee . . . for I am the Lord that healeth thee" (Exodus 15:26). John 9:2 shows that disease was popularly regarded as punishment for sins: "And his disciples asked him, saying, Master, who did sin, this man, or his parents, that he was born blind?" Recovery was thus regarded as a token of divine forgiveness, and the priest's role was related to that of the physician.

Physicians as such are not mentioned in the Old Testament until the time of the monarchy, but prior to that time priests diagnosed the various forms of leprosy (Leviticus 13:2ff.). The prophets, too, were appealed to for medical advice, as in the case of Hezekiah and Isaiah (I Kings 20). In the New Testament, Luke is called a physician in Colossians 4:14. Visiting the sick is a pious act in the Bible (2 Kings 13:14, 20:1), and is counted by Jesus among the acts of ministry in Matthew 25:36: "I was sick, and ye visited me".

No man also seweth a piece of new cloth on an old garment: else the new piece that filled it up taketh away from the old, and the rent is made worse.

And no man putteth new wine into old bottles: else the new wine doth burst the bottles, and the wine is spilled, and the bottles will be marred: but new wine must be put into new bottles.

And it came to pass, that he went through the corn fields on the sabbath day; and his disciples began, as they went, to pluck the ears of corn.

And the Pharisees said unto him, Behold, why do they on the sabbath day that which is not lawful?

And he said unto them, Have ye never read what David did, when he had need, and was an hungred, he, and they that were with him?

How he went into the house of God in the days of Abiathar the high priest, and did eat the shewbread, which is not lawful to eat but for the priests, and gave also to them which were with him? And he said unto them, The sabbath was made for man, and not man for the sabbath:

Therefore the Son of man is Lord also of the sabbath. (2:15–28)

91. Detail from the arch of Titus commemorating the sacking and burning of the Temple of Jerusalem in A.D. 70. The detail shows Titus' soldiers carrying away the shewbread table as booty.

The shewbread (an archaic form of showbread) or "bread of the Presence" in the Old Testament, was the bread displayed in the Holy Place of the Temple, as prescribed in Exodus 25:30: "And thou shalt set upon the table shewbread before me alway." The shewbread consisted of twelve loaves arranged on a table in two rows of six each (Leviticus 24:5ff). The bread was changed every Sabbath, and the priests ate that which had been on display. The twelve loaves represented the twelve tribes of Israel, and were a symbolic acknowledgement that God was the source of Israel's life and nourishment. Jesus refers to the incident related in the Bible (I Sam. 21:1–6) when David, fleeing from Saul, requested bread for himself and his hungry men from Ahimelech the high priest. As he had nothing else to hand, the high priest gave David loaves of the shewbread that had been replaced.

92. The mustard plant (*Sinapis nigra*). The seed of this plant is used metaphorically both in the New Testament and in rabbinic writings for anything that is very small. The fast-growing plant grows wild all over the Holy Land, but it is also cultivated, sometimes reaching a great height, up to three meters or so. It bears a profusion of tiny seeds of which birds are particularly fond.

Whereas Matthew reveals the mysteries of the Kingdom of Heaven (which came in a specific way in Christ and was heralded by John the Baptist) in a number of special parables, the parables in Mark and in the other gospels speak of the kingdom of God, referring to God's rule in a more general way, from past eternity to future eternity. The parable of the mustard seed has often been misunderstood to refer to the greatness of the Gospel. In fact, "greatness" is seldom something positive in the New Testament, and since the "fowls of the air" in the preceding parable of the sower refer to the Evil One, Satan (4:4,15) the "fowls of the air" here must also refer to something negative, namely, the evil persons and things which find lodging in the abnormal "greatness" of the mustard plant. Jesus employed the particularly fitting metaphor of the mustard seed, an annual herb which, once sprouted, quickly outgrows all other herbs of the field and was never meant to be a tree (Matthew 13:32), to give expression to this aspect of the kingdom of God.

And he said, Whereunto shall we liken the kingdom of God? or with what comparison shall we compare it?

It is like a grain of mustard seed, which, when it is sown in the earth, is less than all the seeds that be in the earth:

But when it is sown, it groweth up, and becometh greater than all herbs, and shooteth out great branches; so that the fowls of the air may lodge under the shadow of it.

And with many such parables spake he the word unto them, as they were able to hear it.

But without a parable spake he not unto them: and when they were alone, he expounded all things to his disciples.

And the same day, when the even was come, he saith unto them, Let us pass over unto the other side.

93. Fishermen on the Sea of Galilee in the early evening.

94. Fishing boats on the Sea of Galilee at dusk.

And when they had sent away the multitude, they took him even as he was in the ship. And there were also with him other little ships.

And there arose a great storm of wind, and the waves beat into the ship, so that it was now full.

And he was in the hinder part of the ship, asleep on a pillow: and they awake him, and say unto him, Master, carest thou not that we perish?

And he arose, and rebuked the wind, and said unto the sea, Peace, be still. And the wind ceased, and there was a great calm.

And he said unto them, Why are ye so fearful? how is it that ye have no faith?

And they feared exceedingly, and said one to another, What manner of man is this, that even the wind and the sea obey him?

(4:30–41)

95. Dark clouds hanging over the usually placid Sea of Galilee, threatening a sudden storm.

And they came over unto the other side of the sea, into the country of the Gadarenes.

And when he was come out of the ship, immediately there met him out of the tombs a man with an unclean spirit,

Who had his dwelling among the tombs; and no man could bind him, no, not with chains:

Because that he had been often bound with fetters and chains, and the chains had been plucked asunder by him, and the fetters broken in pieces: neither could any man tame him.

And always, night and day, he was in the mountains, and in the tombs, crying, and cutting himself with stones.

But when he saw Jesus afar off, he ran and worshipped him,

And cried with a loud voice, and said, What have I to do with thee, Jesus, thou Son of the most high God? I adjure thee by God, that thou torment me not.

For he said unto him, Come out of the man, thou unclean spirit.

And he asked him, What is thy name? And he answered, saying, My name is Legion: for we are many.

And he besought him much that he would not send them away out of the country.

96. A general view of Kursi, a prominence on the eastern shore of the Sea of Galilee a few miles north of Capernaum.

Now there was there nigh unto the mountains a great herd of swine feeding.

And all the devils besought him, saying, Send us into the swine, that we may enter into them.

And forthwith Jesus gave them leave. And the unclean spirits went out, and entered into the swine: and the herd ran violently down a steep place into the sea, (they were about two thousand;) and were choked in the sea.

And they that fed the swine fled, and told it in the city, and in the country. And they went out to see what it was that was done.

And they come to Jesus, and see him that was possessed with the devil, and had the legion, sitting, and clothed, and in his right mind: and they were afraid.

And they that saw it told them how it befell to him that was possessed with the devil, and also concerning the swine.

And they began to pray him to depart out of their coasts.

And when he was come into the ship, he that had been possessed with the devil prayed him that he might be with him.

Howbeit Jesus suffered him not, but saith unto him, Go home to thy friends, and tell them how great things the Lord hath done for thee, and hath had compassion on thee.

97. Remains of a 6th-century church on the eastern shore of the Sea of Galilee, where the Golan range juts into the Sea. Here, it is believed, Jesus healed the possessed man and caused the demons to enter the Gadarene swine.

Some hold that "Gadarene" refers to the people of the town of Gadara. Other scholars disagree with this, as Gadara lies far from the shore.

Remains of a Byzantine church at Kursi have recently been excavated. The ruins of a tower and of a small chapel built in the rock were brought to light. On the walls are frescoes and painted crosses. Parts of a mosaic with some of the patterns rendered in pieces of colored glass have also been found.

The care with which the chapel was planned and built leads one to believe that it commemorated the site where Jesus performed the miracle of healing the two demoniacs.

98. – 100. Details of the mosaic pavement. Most of it is in simple geometric design, but some medallions of the lateral aisles of the church contain representations of the flora and fauna of the area, cups and baskets. Very few depict animals.

7

99

8

100

101. One of the cities of the Decapolis, a region in which Jesus spent some time, was located in the Valley of Beth-shean shown here. The valley climbs gently to the west from the Jordan, merging gradually with the Jezreel Valley running to the coast.

101

And he departed, and began to publish in Decapolis how great things Jesus had done for him: and all men did marvel.
(5:1–20)

102. & 103. Remains of the Roman theater at Beth-shean renamed Scythopolis.

Scythopolis belonged to a confederation of ten Hellenistic cities known as the Decapolis (ten cities). These ten cities had become centers of Hellenistic culture and organization, following Alexander the Great's conquest in 333 B.C. When Pompey conquered and reorganized the area in 63 B.C. the ten cities were given Roman protection and a special status. They were allowed to mint their own coins, and granted a measure of self-rule, while owing allegiance to Rome – represented by the Syrian provincial government. These ten cities prospered and flourished in this period. In the New Testament, the term Decapolis often refers to the regions in which these cities were situated: in the northern Jordan Valley and Transjordan.

Beth-shean played an important role in biblical times. The history of the city from the time when it was a city of Solomon's empire, until the 3rd century B.C. when it reappears as Scythopolis, is obscure. The town contains two distinct sites: the ancient biblical remains excavated on the high tel or mound, and an impressive Roman theater, built about A.D. 200, with seating for five thousand spectators.

102

104. Remains at Susita, or Hippos, another city of the Decapolis, on the east shore of the Sea of Galilee.

The Greek name Hippos (horse) is a translation of the Aramaic Susita. The city sits on a high promontory jutting out between two wadis. The flat top is connected with the Golan mountains by a narrow neck of land. With much imagination people saw in this topography the shape of a horse, hence its name. Augustus gave the city to Herod, governor of Judea, but the citizens submitted to his rule unwillingly, and after his death Hippos reverted to the Roman province of Syria.

Hippos prospered in the Roman and Byzantine period due to its location on the Roman road linking Scythopolis with Damascus. Remains of a 5th-century cathedral show that it was destroyed by an earthquake, since all the columns lie pointing in the same direction.

105. A view from Hippos overlooking the surrounding environs.

106. Remains of a Roman temple at Gerasa, modern Jerash, a short distance from Rabath Ammon (Philadelphia). The temple is dated by an inscription to A.D. 163. Built on a high podium, it was surrounded by columns, and there was a smaller temple nearby.

Later tradition attributes the foundation of the city to Alexander the Great. The city was conquered by the Hasmonean Alexander Jannaeus and freed by Pompey who made it a member of the Decapolis. The Hellenistic-Roman-Byzantine city was one of the largest and most important in this area.

107. Remains of Roman columns at Gadara, identified with Umm Keis in the Transjordan. In Hellenistic times it was one of the centers of Greek culture in this area.

Like Gerasa it was conquered by the Hasmonean Alexander Jannaeus and freed by Pompey in 63 B.C., immediately rebuilt and made a member of the Decapolis.

And a certain woman, which had an issue of blood twelve years,

And had suffered many things of many physicians, and had spent all that she had, and was nothing bettered, but rather grew worse, When she had heard of Jesus, came in the press behind, and touched his garment.

For she said, If I may touch but his clothes, I shall be whole.

And straightway the fountain of her blood was dried up; and she felt in her body that she was healed of that plague.

And Jesus, immediately knowing in himself that virtue had gone out of him, turned him about in the press, and said, Who touched my clothes?

And his disciples said unto him, Thou seest the multitude thronging thee, and sayest thou, Who touched me?

And he looked round about to see her that had done this thing.

But the woman fearing and trembling, knowing what was done in her, came and fell down before him, and told him all the truth.

And he said unto her, Daughter, thy faith hath made thee whole; go in peace, and be whole of thy plague. (5:25–34)

108. Woman touching Jesus' mantle, detail from a 4th-century sarcophagus (Musée Lapidaire Chrétien, Arles, France).

108

And he called unto him the twelve, and began to send them forth by two and two; and gave them power over unclean spirits;

And commanded them that they should take nothing for their journey, save a staff only; no scrip, no bread, no money in their purse:

But be shod with sandals; and not put on two coats.

And he said unto them, In what place soever ye enter into an house, there abide till ye depart from that place.

And whosoever shall not receive you, nor hear you, when ye depart thence, shake off the dust under your feet for a testimony against them. Verily I say unto you, It shall be more tolerable for Sodom and Gomorrha in the day of judgment, than for that city.

And they went out, and preached that men should repent.

And they cast out many devils, and anointed with oil many that were sick, and healed them.

And king Herod heard of him; (for his name was spread abroad:) and he said, That John the Baptist was risen from the dead, and therefore mighty

109. Sandal from the 1st century A.D., found in the excavations at the fortress of Masada, which was built by Herod the Great near the Dead Sea. Masada was the last stronghold of resistance to the Romans after the fall of Jerusalem and the destruction of the Temple in A.D. 70.

works do shew forth themselves in him.

Others said, That it is Elias. And others said, That it is a prophet, or as one of the prophets.

But when Herod heard thereof, he said, It is John, whom I beheaded: he is risen from the dead.

For Herod himself had sent forth and laid hold upon John and bound him in prison for Herodias' sake, his brother Philip's wife: for he had married her. For John had said unto Herod, It is not lawful for thee to have thy brother's wife.

Therefore Herodias had a quarrel against him, and would have killed him; but she could not:

For Herod feared John, knowing that he was a just man and an holy, and observed him; and when he heard him, he did many things, and heard him gladly.

And when a convenient day was come, that Herod on his birthday made a supper to his lords, high captains, and chief estates of Galilee;

And when the daughter of the said Herodias came in, and danced, and pleased Herod and them that sat with him, the king said unto the damsel, Ask of me whatsoever thou wilt, and I will give it thee.

And he sware unto her, Whatsoever thou shalt ask of me, I will give it thee, unto the half of my kingdom.

And she went forth, and said unto her mother, What shall I ask? And she said, The head of John the Baptist.

And she came in straightway with haste unto the king, and asked, saying, I will that thou give me by and by in a charger the head of John the Baptist.

And the king was exceeding sorry; yet for his oath's sake, and for their sakes which sat with him, he would not reject her.

And immediately the king sent an executioner, and commanded his head to be brought: and he went and beheaded him in the prison,

And brought his head in a charger, and gave it to the damsel: and the damsel gave it to her mother.

And when his disciples heard of it, they came and took up his corpse, and laid it in a tomb.

(6:7–29)

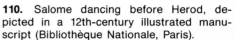

110. Salome dancing before Herod, depicted in a 12th-century illustrated manuscript (Bibliothèque Nationale, Paris).
This scene is believed to have taken place at Machaerus, in southern Perea, the present-day al-Mukawir, a ruin east of the Jordan. Here stood a fortress erected by the Hasmonean king Alexander Yannai (Jannaeus) (c. 126–76 B.C.). According to tradition, John the Baptist was executed here on the orders of Herod Antipas, (c. 21 B.C–A.D. 39), the son of Herod the Great, who was Tetrarch of Galilee and Perea. Herod Antipas divorced his first wife in order to marry Herodias, the wife of his brother Herod Philip. This union aroused the anger of the people because Jewish law forbade a man to marry his brother's divorced wife. John boldly denounced the marriage to Herod's face. The ruler took John's rebuke as lèse-majesté, and had John arrested. Herod's first wife had been a Nabataean princess and espousing her cause had political implications: Herod feared local support for a possible action on the part of the Nabataean king. Herod was also apprehensive of the considerable response John had stirred up among the people.

111. The tomb at the traditional burial site of John the Baptist at Samaria.
After the Roman conquest of Palestine, Samaria was given to Herod the Great who reconstructed it magnificently, and renamed it Sebaste. The town's decline began in the 3rd century, and when it was captured by the Crusaders led by Tancred the Norman in 1099, it was a small village.
Sebaste had been the seat of an early bishopric from the beginning of the 4th century, and was renowned as a place of pilgrimage, due to an ancient tradition that the body of John the Baptist, who was beheaded at Machaerus (east of the Dead Sea), had been brought here by his disciples. It was said that the body was burned by the Roman emperor Julian the Apostate in the 4th century and its ashes were scattered, but John's head was saved because it had already been taken to Alexandria, and from there to Constantinople, and subsequently to Poitou in France. It was also said that one of his fingers was saved from burning and likewise, according to some accounts, his arm. The tomb was located in the cave in which the prophets Elisha and Obadiah were also supposedly buried, as well as, according to some sources, Elisabeth and Zachariah – John the Baptist's parents.
Before the arrival of the Crusaders a Greek monastery stood on this site. Between 1150 and 1160 the Crusaders built a church on the ruins of the ancient structure. It was described as one of the most magnificent churches in the Holy Land, surpassed only by the Holy Sepulcher in Jerusalem.
In 1187 Sebaste was captured by Saladin and the church became a mosque.

Then came together unto him the Pharisees, and certain of the scribes, which came from Jerusalem.

And when they saw some of his disciples eat bread with defiled, that is to say, with unwashen, hands, they found fault.

For the Pharisees, and all the Jews, except they wash their hands oft, eat not, holding the tradition of the elders.

And when they come from the market, except they wash, they eat not. And many other things there be, which they have received to hold, as the washing of cups, and pots, brasen vessels, and of tables.

112. Ritual washing of the hands, in a miniature from the so-called *Barcelona Haggadah*; Spain, 14th century (British Museum, London).

The origin of the ritual is not clear. It seems that the custom spread from the priests who washed their hands before eating the consecrated food to the pious among the laity, and finally became a rabbinic ordinance. The Pharisees insisted upon the strict observance of the Law and adherence to tradition. The Pharisees were a Jewish religious and political movement during the Second Temple period, whose members maintained the validity of the so-called Oral Law (i.e. the Mishnah — the authoritative interpretation of the Written Law) in addition to the Written Law (Pentateuch). They attempted to imbue the masses with a spirit of holiness based on a scrupulous observance of the Law by spreading religious teaching.

After the destruction of Jerusalem in A.D. 70, the movement as such gradually disappeared, because the majority of the Jewish people accepted its tenets.

While the Pharisees, as a whole, set high ethical standards for themselves, not all lived up to them. The leaders were aware of the hypocrites and the mindless followers among their number, who are described in the Talmud as "sore spots," or "plagues of the Pharisaic party."

Then the Pharisees and scribes asked him, Why walk not thy disciples according to the tradition of the elders, but eat bread with unwashen hands?

He answered and said unto them, Well hath Esaias prophesied of you hypocrites, as it is written, This people honoureth me with their lips, but their heart is far from me.

Howbeit in vain do they worship me, teaching for doctrines the commandments of men.

For laying aside the commandment of God, ye hold the tradition of men, as the washing of pots and cups: and many other such like things ye do.

And he said unto them, Full well ye reject the commandment of God, that ye may keep your own tradition.

For Moses said, Honour thy father and thy mother; and, Whoso curseth father or mother, let him die the death:

But ye say, If a man shall say to his father or mother, It is Corban, that is to say, a gift, by whatsoever thou mightest be profited by me; he shall be free.

And ye suffer him no more to do ought for his father or his mother;

Making the word of God of none effect through your tradition, which ye have delivered: and many such like things do ye.

(7:1–13)

113. Drawing of two doves and an inscription on the fragment of a stone jar found at the southwest corner of the Temple walls in Jerusalem; Herodian period, 1st century B.C. (Israel Department of Antiquities, Jerusalem). The inscription reads "Korban" which means in Hebrew "sacrifice offering," or "oblation."

And from thence he arose, and went into the borders of Tyre and Sidon, and entered into an house, and would have no man know it: but he could not be hid.

For a certain woman, whose young daughter had an unclean spirit, heard of him, and came and fell at his feet:

The woman was a Greek, a Syrophenician by nation; and she besought him that he would cast forth the devil out of her daughter.

But Jesus said unto her, Let the children first be filled: for it is not meet to take the children's bread, and to cast it unto the dogs.

And she answered and said unto him, Yes, Lord: yet the dogs under the table eat of the children's crumbs.

And he said unto her, For this saying go thy way; the devil is gone out of thy daughter.

And when she was come to her house, she found the devil gone out, and her daughter laid upon the bed.

And again, departing from the coasts of Tyre and Sidon, he came unto the sea of Galilee, through the midst of the coasts of Decapolis.

114. Terracotta dog holding a piece of bread between his teeth; from Boeotia, 6th century B.C. (Louvre, Paris).
When Jesus went to the coast of Tyre and Sidon, the Gentiles of the region had an opportunity to come into contact with him. When approached by the woman of Canaan, who called him "Lord, son of David," the disciples wanted to send her away, and Jesus said that he was sent only to the lost sheep of the house of Israel. When she persisted in asking for help and worshipped him, Jesus answered in a figurative way, referring to himself as bread, the real spiritual nourishment of his people, and to the woman as a dog. According to Leviticus 11:26, a dog is an unclean animal, and at the time of Jesus the Jews considered the pagans as "dogs." The woman, however, was not offended at Jesus' words, but admitted that she was a heathen dog, and that Christ, having been rejected by the "children" – that is the traditional religionists referred to in the first part of the chapter – became as crumbs under the table as a portion to the Gentiles.

115. Remains of the circus at Tyre where horse and chariot racing took place in Roman times.

116. Remains of Roman columns at Tyre. The city of Tyre is very ancient. In biblical times friendly relations existed between Tyre and Israel, notably during the reigns of David and Solomon, and the Tyrians also supplied timber for the building and reconstruction of the Temple (I Kings 5, Ezra 3:7; Nehemia 13:16).

In 332 B.C. Alexander the Great destroyed the city, but it was rebuilt, and in the first century it was an important port in the eastern Mediterranean. In 64 B.C. Pompey conquered it and proclaimed its autonomy and it was an important and flourishing commercial center throughout the Roman period.

And they bring unto him one that was deaf, and had an impediment in his speech; and they beseech him to put his hand upon him.

And he took him aside from the multitude, and put his fingers into his ears, and he spit, and touched his tongue;

And looking up to heaven, he sighed, and saith unto him, Ephphatha, that is, Be opened.

And straightway his ears were opened, and the string of his tongue was loosed, and he spake plain.

And he charged them that they should tell no man: but the more he charged them, so much the more a great deal they published it;

And were beyond measure astonished, saying, He hath done all things well: he maketh both the deaf to hear, and the dumb to speak.

(7:24–37)

115

116

In those days the multitude being very great, and having nothing to eat, Jesus called his disciples unto him, and saith unto them,

I have compassion on the multitude, because they have now been with me three days, and have nothing to eat:

And if I send them away fasting to their own houses, they will faint by the way: for divers of them came from far.

And his disciples answered him, From whence can a man satisfy these men with bread here in the wilderness?

And he asked them, How many loaves have ye? And they said, Seven.

And he commanded the people to sit down on the ground: and he took the seven loaves, and gave thanks, and brake, and gave to his disciples to set before them; and they did set them before the people.

And they had a few small fishes: and he blessed, and commanded to set them also before them.

So they did eat, and were filled: and they took up of the broken meat that was left seven baskets.

And they that had eaten were about four thousand: and he sent them away.

And straightway he entered into a ship with his disciples, and came into the parts of Dalmanutha.

And the Pharisees came forth, and began to question with him, seeking of him a sign from heaven, tempting him.

And he sighed deeply in his spirit, and saith, Why doth this generation seek after a sign? verily I say unto you, There shall no sign be given unto this generation.

And he left them, and entering into the ship again departed to the other side.

(8:1–13)

117. Mosaic from the Church of the Multiplication of the Loaves and Fishes.

The present structure was built recently, incorporating the beautiful mosaic floor remaining from a church built in the middle of the 5th century. This mosaic of two fish flanking a basket of loaves is found on the floor in front of the altar.

The remains of a 4th-century church lie beneath the present floor of the church, which stands at Tabgha, on the shore of the Sea of Galilee, near Capernaum.

The name Tabgha comes from an Arabic mispronunciation of Heptapegon, meaning "seven springs," which were to be seen here according to Egeria, a nun who visited the Holy Land in A.D. 384, and left the following description of the site: "Not far away from Capernaum are some stone steps where the Lord stood. And in the same place by the sea is a grassy field with plenty of hay and many palm-trees. By them are seven springs, each flowing strongly. And this is the field where the Lord fed the people with the five loaves and the two fishes. In fact the stone on which the Lord placed the bread has now been made into an altar ... Past the walls of this church goes the public highway on which the Apostle Matthew had his place of custom. Near there on a mountain is the cave to which the Savior climbed and spoke the Beatitudes." Thus, according to the 4th-century source, several episodes in the life of Jesus are located there: when Jesus conferred on Peter the responsibility of leadership (John 21), the multiplication of the loaves and fishes, the Sermon on the Mount and the post-Resurrection appearance.

117

118. Snow-capped Mount Hermon. It is thought to be the site of the Transfiguration, even though most scholars agree that it is more likely to have taken place on Mount Tabor.

And he said unto them, Verily I say unto you, That there be some of them that stand here, which shall not taste of death, till they have seen the kingdom of God come with power.

And after six days Jesus taketh with him Peter, and James, and John, and leadeth them up into an high mountain apart by themselves: and he was transfigured before them.

And his raiment became shining, exceeding white as snow; so as no fuller on earth can white them.

And there appeared unto them Elias with Moses: and they were talking with Jesus.

And Peter answered and said to Jesus, Master, it is good for us to be here: and let us make three tabernacles; one for thee, and one for Moses, and one for Elias.

For he wist not what to say; for they were sore afraid.

And there was a cloud that overshadowed them: and a voice came out of the cloud, saying, This is my beloved Son: hear him.

And suddenly, when they had looked round about, they saw no man any more, save Jesus only with themselves.

And as they came down from the mountain, he charged them that they should tell no man what things they had seen, till the Son of man were risen from the dead.

And they kept that saying with themselves, questioning one with another what the rising from the dead should mean.

And they asked him, saying, Why say the scribes that Elias must first come?

And he answered and told them, Elias verily cometh first, and restoreth all things; and how it is written of the Son of man, that he must suffer many things, and be set at nought.

But I say unto you, That Elias is indeed come, and they have done unto him whatsoever they listed, as it is written of him.

(9:1–13)

119. The village of Dabburiya on the slopes of Mount Tabor. It has been identified as the Deberath mentioned in I Chronicles 6:72, and it is traditionally identified as the place where Jesus left nine of his disciples waiting while he ascended Mount Tabor with Peter, James and John.

119

120. Ascension of the prophet Elijah; Verdun altar, 1180 (Klosterneuberg Abbey, Austria). In Deuteronomy 34:5–6 we read how Moses died and God hid his body, and in I Kings 2:11 we are told how Elijah was taken by God into heaven in a fiery chariot. Christian tradition has it that God wanted Moses and Elijah to appear with Christ at the Transfiguration. In Revelation 11:3–4 the two are witnesses in the great tribulation. Moses represents the Law, and Elijah the prophets. According to Luke 9:31, the subject of their conversation was Christ's death (Luke 24:25–27, I Corinthians 15:3).

120

And when they came nigh to Jerusalem, unto Bethphage and Bethany, at the mount of Olives, he sendeth forth two of his disciples,

And saith unto them, Go your way into the village over against you: and as soon as ye be entered into it, ye shall find a colt tied, whereon never man sat; loose him, and bring him.

And if any man say unto you, Why do ye this? say ye that the Lord hath need of him; and straightway he will send him hither.

And they went their way, and found the colt tied by the door without in a place where two ways met; and they loose him.

And certain of them that stood there said unto them, What do ye, loosing the colt?

And they said unto them even as Jesus had commanded: and they let them go.

And they brought the colt to Jesus, and cast their garments on him; and he sat upon him.

121. A short distance from Jerusalem, on the eastern slope of the Mount of Olives on the way to Jericho, lies the small village of Bethany. Today it is known as al-Azarieh, i.e., "the place of Lazarus", in Arabic.
Though the village is poor, olive, fig and almond trees make the surroundings pleasant. Bethany was the home of Martha, Mary and Lazarus, who were the beloved friends of Jesus, and here Jesus performed the miracle of Lazarus' resurrection.
Higher up the slope on which the village now stands is a field known as the House of Simon the Leper. Excavations have revealed no buildings, but the rock is honeycombed with caves, pits, cisterns and graves; their contents reveal that this area had been occupied since the 6th century B.C., and also in the Roman, Byzantine and medieval periods.

122. The entry of Jesus into Jerusalem, depicted on a page from the illuminated Book of Psalms belonging to Queen Melisande. In the background is a palm tree and a gate in the city wall.
Queen Melisande, to whom the psalter belonged, was the wife of Fulk of Anjou, the Crusader king of Jerusalem in 1131. She played an important part in the affairs of the Crusader states.

122

And many spread their garments in the way: and others cut down branches off the trees, and strawed them in the way.

And they that went before, and they that followed, cried, saying, Hosanna; Blessed is he that cometh in the name of the Lord:

Blessed be the kingdom of our father David, that cometh in the name of the Lord: Hosanna in the highest.

And Jesus entered into Jerusalem, and into the temple: and when he had looked round about upon all things, and now the eventide was come, he went out unto Bethany with the twelve.

And on the morrow, when they were come from Bethany, he was hungry:

And seeing a fig tree afar off having leaves, he came, if haply he might find any thing thereon: and when he came to it, he found nothing but leaves; for the time of figs was not yet.

And Jesus answered and said unto it, No man eat fruit of thee hereafter for ever. And his disciples heard it.

123. A familiar scene near Bethany.

124. "Banker," shown on a Roman relief. The ancient laws of Judaism prescribed that every man over 20 had to pay a tax to the Temple in Jerusalem. This tax, which amounted to a half-shekel of silver, could be paid only with silver coins. For this reason, money-changers carried on their business near the Temple, making a small profit each time they exchanged bronze for silver coins. Furthermore, people from foreign countries came to the Temple for the holidays and exchanged their foreign currency for money that would be acceptable in the local markets.

And they come to Jerusalem: and Jesus went into the temple, and began to cast out them that sold and bought in the temple, and overthrew the tables of the moneychangers, and the seats of them that sold doves;

And would not suffer that any man should carry any vessel through the temple.

And he taught, saying unto them, Is it not written, My house shall be called of all nations the house of prayer? but ye have made it a den of thieves.

(11:1–17)

125. & 126. A Tyrian shekel.
When the Romans occupied the Holy Land
the most important coin in use was the shekel
minted in the city of Tyre. The people of the
Holy Land did not accept Roman coins as le-
gitimate currency until long after the Roman
conquest. Even when they did, the old coins
continued to be used alongside the new ones.
The Tyrian shekel was accepted as the principal currency, and the proper coin for payment
of the Temple tax. On one side of the coin was
a portrait of the Greek demi-god Hercules,
who was associated with Melkart, the patron
god of Tyre. On the other side, the Tyrians
copied the eagle that characterised the Greek
coins of the time. Between the eagle's feet is
depicted the prow of a ship, symbolizing the
maritime character of Tyre. A mint mark – a
small club, the favorite weapon of Hercules,
also appears on the coin.

127. & 128. Coins minted by two procurators
of Judea: one of Valerius Gratius in A.D. 16;
the other of Ambilus, procurator from A.D.
9–12.

*And he said unto them in his doctrine, Beware of the scribes, which love
to go in long clothing, and love salutations in the marketplaces,*

*And the chief seats in the synagogues, and the uppermost rooms at
feasts:*

*Which devour widows' houses, and for a pretence make long prayers:
these shall receive greater damnation.*

*And Jesus sat over against the treasury, and beheld how the people cast
money into the treasury: and many that were rich cast in much.*

*And there came a certain poor widow, and she threw in two mites, which
make a farthing.*

129. Corner of the zealot synagogue at Herod's fortress of Masada, showing the steps used as seats by the congregants.
The writings of the Qumran sect give explicit directions for the seating order according to rank in the assemblies of the sect.
In the rabbinic schools of the Talmudic period a similar practice prevailed, where more advanced students were seated in the first rows, and sometimes demoted or promoted according to their merit.

And he called unto him his disciples, and saith unto them, Verily I say unto you, That this poor widow hath cast more in, than all they which cast into the treasury:

For all they did cast in of their abundance; but she of her want did cast in all that she had, even all her living. (12:38–44)

And as he went out of the temple, one of his disciples saith unto him, Master, see what manner of stones and what buildings are here!

And Jesus answering said unto him, Seest thou these great buildings? there shall not be left one stone upon another, that shall not be thrown down. (13:1–2)

130. The stones of the Western (or Wailing) Wall in Jerusalem, believed to be the last remnant of the Temple after its destruction by the Romans in A.D. 70. It came to symbolise the Jews' lost freedom, an historical tragedy whose anniversary has been observed every year since then as a day of mourning by Jews all over the world.
The Western Wall was not actually part of the Temple itself – which was completely destroyed by the Romans – but one of the four retaining walls which King Herod built to support the enlarged plateau on which the Temple stood.

131

And being in Bethany in the house of Simon the leper, as he sat at meat, there came a woman having an alabaster box of ointment of spikenard very precious; and she brake the box, and poured it on his head.

And there were some that had indignation within themselves, and said, Why was this waste of the ointment made?

For it might have been sold for more than three hundred pence, and have been given to the poor. And they murmured against her.

And Jesus said, Let her alone; why trouble ye her? she hath wrought a good work on me.

For ye have the poor with you always, and whensoever ye will ye may do them good: but me ye have not always.

She hath done what she could: she is come aforehand to anoint my body to the burying.

Verily I say unto you, Wheresoever this gospel shall be preached throughout the whole world, this also that she hath done shall be spoken of for a memorial of her.   (14:3–9)

And they came to a place which was named Gethsemane: and he saith to his disciples, Sit ye here, while I shall pray.

132

And he taketh with him Peter and James and John, and began to be sore amazed, and to be very heavy;

And saith unto them, My soul is exceeding sorrowful unto death: tarry ye here, and watch.

And he went forward a little, and fell on the ground, and prayed that, if it were possible, the hour might pass from him.

And he said, Abba, Father, all things are possible unto thee; take away this cup from me: nevertheless not what I will, but what thou wilt.

And he cometh, and findeth them sleeping, and saith unto Peter, Simon, sleepest thou? couldest not thou watch one hour?

Watch ye and pray, lest ye enter into temptation. The spirit truly is ready, but the flesh is weak.

And again he went away, and prayed, and spake the same words.

And when he returned, he found them asleep again, (for their eyes were heavy,) neither wist they what to answer him.

And he cometh the third time, and saith unto them, Sleep on now, and take your rest: it is enough, the hour is come; behold, the Son of man is betrayed into the hands of sinners.

(14:32–41)

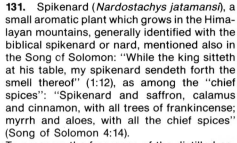

131. Spikenard (*Nardostachys jatamansi*), a small aromatic plant which grows in the Himalayan mountains, generally identified with the biblical spikenard or nard, mentioned also in the Song of Solomon: "While the king sitteth at his table, my spikenard sendeth forth the smell thereof" (1:12), as among the "chief spices": "Spikenard and saffron, calamus and cinnamon, with all trees of frankincense; myrrh and aloes, with all the chief spices" (Song of Solomon 4:14).

To preserve the fragrance of the distilled essence, a light reddish-colored liquid, it was sealed in small alabaster bottles. The great value of spikenard (John 12:3) may be due to its remote source in India.

According to the Talmud, spikenard was one of the 11 spices from which the incense in the Temple was prepared. Rabbinic literature also mentions *polyaton* oil, referring to the Latin name for the spikenard leaves (*foliatum*) as one of the forbidden luxuries after the destruction of the Temple.

132. A general view of the Garden of Gethsemane.

133

133. Olive trees at the Garden of Gethsemane. Most of these trees are hundreds of years old.

And straightway in the morning the chief priests held a consultation with the elders and scribes and the whole council, and bound Jesus, and carried him away, and delivered him to Pilate.

And Pilate asked him, Art thou the King of the Jews? And he answering said unto him, Thou sayest it.

And the chief priests accused him of many things: but he answered nothing.

And Pilate asked him again, saying, Answerest thou nothing? behold how many things they witness against thee.

But Jesus yet answered nothing; so that Pilate marvelled.

Now at that feast he released unto them one prisoner, whomsoever they desired.

And there was one named Barabbas, which lay bound with them that had made insurrection with him, who had committed murder in the insurrection.

And the multitude crying aloud began to desire him to do as he had ever done unto them.

But Pilate answered them, saying, Will ye that I release unto you the King of the Jews?

For he knew that the chief priests had delivered him for envy.

134. A reconstruction of the Antonia fortress.

Tradition places the residence of the procurator in the Antonia fortress, at the northwestern corner of the Temple Mount, with underground stairs and passages connecting it with the Temple. Excavations in this area have brought to light a courtyard paved with stone slabs which apparently occupied the center of the Antonia fortress. The fortress, which comprised a palace, courtyards, bath house and cisterns, was known as the Citadel. It was fortified by Herod and renamed Antonia in honor of Marc Antony.

134

135

136

But the chief priests moved the people, that he should rather release Barabbas unto them.

And Pilate answered and said again unto them, What will ye then that I shall do unto him whom ye call the King of the Jews?

And they cried out again, Crucify him.

Then Pilate said unto them, Why, what evil hath he done? And they cried out the more exceedingly, Crucify him.

And so Pilate, willing to content the people, released Barabbas unto them, and delivered Jesus, when he had scourged him, to be crucified.

And the soldiers led him away into the hall, called Praetorium; and they call together the whole band.

And they clothed him with purple, and platted a crown of thorns, and put it about his head,

And began to salute him, Hail, King of the Jews!

And they smote him on the head with a reed, and did spit upon him, and bowing their knees worshipped him.

And when they had mocked him, they took off the purple from him, and put his own clothes on him, and led him out to crucify him.

And they compel one Simon a Cyrenian, who passed by, coming out of the country, the father of Alexander and Rufus, to bear his cross.

And they bring him unto the place Golgotha, which is being interpreted, The place of a skull.

And they gave him to drink wine mingled with myrrh: but he received it not.

And when they had crucified him, they parted his garments, casting lots upon them, what every man should take.

135. The Praetorium – Pilate's judgement hall.
The "Gabatha" (Pavement), as it is called in John 19:13, now stands in the grounds of the convent of Notre Dame de Sion in the Old City of Jerusalem.

136. The Pillar of Flagellation, believed to be a fragment of the one to which Jesus was tied when he was flagellated by the Romans. It is now in the Franciscan Church of the Apparition.

And it was the third hour, and they crucified him.

And the superscription of his accusation was written over, The King of the Jews.

And with him they crucify two thieves; the one on his right hand, and the other on his left.

And the scripture was fulfilled, which saith, And he was numbered with the transgressors.

And they that passed by railed on him, wagging their heads, and saying, Ah, thou that destroyest the temple, and buildest it in three days,

Save thyself, and come down from the cross.

Likewise also the chief priests mocking said among themselves with the scribes, He saved others; himself he cannot save.

Let Christ the King of Israel descend now from the cross, that we may see and believe. And they that were crucified with him reviled him.

And when the sixth hour was come, there was darkness over the whole land until the ninth hour.

And at the ninth hour Jesus cried with a loud voice, Saying, Eloi, Eloi, lama sabachthani? which is, being interpreted, My God, my God, why hast thou forsaken me?

And some of them that stood by, when they heard it, said, Behold, he calleth Elias.

And one ran and filled a spunge full of vinegar, and put it on a reed, and gave him to drink, saying, Let alone; let us see whether Elias will come to take him down.

And Jesus cried with a loud voice, and gave up the ghost.

And the veil of the temple was rent in twain from the top to the bottom.

(15:1–38)

And when the sabbath was past, Mary Magdalene, and Mary the mother

137. The Monastery of the Cross: it owes its name to the belief that the tree from which the Cross was made grew on the wooded slopes of the valley where it stands. Nowadays this valley is surrounded by the new city of Jerusalem. Inside the church, the monks point to an opening in the floor where, it is believed, the actual tree grew.

It is not known precisely who built the first Monastery of the Cross. Some say that it was the 5th-century Georgian king Tatian. Others ascribe it to Constantine and Helena, who built so many other edifices in the Holy Land. It is first mentioned in Greek documents in the 6th century. Pilgrims began to visit the Monastery of the Cross during Crusader times, and they all describe it as beautiful. The monastery was partly destroyed in the 13th century by the Moslems and converted into a mosque, but was restored to the Georgians in the 14th century.

The monastery changed ownership in the 17th century, when it was turned over to the Greek Orthodox Church. Until 1903 the monastery served as a theological seminary, and in recent years has been used as a hospice.

The monastery was built like a fortress to protect its monks from the marauding Bedouin. Its medieval appearance is emphasized by the modern structures surrounding it today.

of James, and Salome, had bought sweet spices, that they might come and anoint him.

And very early in the morning the first day of the week, they came unto the sepulchre at the rising of the sun.

And they said among themselves, Who shall roll us away the stone from the door of the sepulchre?

And when they looked, they saw that the stone was rolled away: for it was very great.

And entering into the sepulchre, they saw a young man sitting on the right side, clothed in a long white garment; and they were affrighted.

And he saith unto them, Be not affrighted: Ye seek Jesus of Nazareth, which was crucified: he is risen; he is not here: behold the place where they laid him.

But go your way, tell his disciples and Peter that he goeth before you into Galilee: there shall ye see him, as he said unto you.

And they went out quickly, and fled from the sepulchre; for they trembled and were amazed: neither said they any thing to any man; for they were afraid.

Now when Jesus was risen early the first day of the week, he appeared first to Mary Magdalene, out of whom he had cast seven devils.

And she went and told them that had been with him, as they mourned and wept.

And they, when they had heard that he was alive, and had been seen of her, believed not.

After that he appeared in another form unto two of them, as they walked, and went into the country.

And they went and told it unto the residue: neither believed they them.

(16:1–13)

138. Herod's family tomb in Jerusalem, with a circular stone at the entrance of the tomb. Its appearance matches Luke's words: "...and laid him in a sepulcher which was hewn out of a rock, and rolled a stone unto the door of the sepulcher."

Various devices were used in antiquity to protect family vaults from robbery. One of these, of which several examples have survived, was a cylindrical stone block placed in a sloping groove cut in the rock across the vault entrance, which was rolled upwards along the groove and secured by a wedge.

139. The picturesque village of Ein Karem (Vineyard Spring), now a suburb of Jerusalem, is traditionally identified as "the city in Judah," the hometown of Zacharias and Elisabeth, Mary's kinswoman, and the birthplace of John the Baptist.

Some scholars believe that the present-day village corresponds with biblical Beth-haccerem, mentioned in Jeremiah 6:1 where fires were lit to warn Jerusalem of advancing enemy forces.

The village clings to the slopes of the Judean hills among tapering cypresses.

Here stands the Church of the Visitation, commanding a breathtaking view of the valley below. On the way to the church a small mosque marks the Spring of Mary where, it is said, the Virgin stopped on her way to visit Elisabeth.

There was in the days of Herod, the king of Judaea, a certain priest named Zacharias, of the course of Abia: and his wife was of the daughters of Aaron, and her name was Elisabeth.

And they were both righteous before God, walking in all the commandments and ordinances of the Lord blameless.

And they had no child, because that Elisabeth was barren, and they both were now well stricken in years.

And it came to pass, that while he executed the priest's office before God in the order of his course,

According to the custom of the priest's office, his lot was to burn incense when he went into the temple of the Lord.

And the whole multitude of the people were praying without at the time of incense.

And there appeared unto him an angel of the Lord standing on the right side of the altar of incense.

And when Zacharias saw him, he was troubled, and fear fell upon him.

But the angel said unto him, Fear not, Zacharias: for thy prayer is heard; and thy wife Elisabeth shall bear thee a son, and thou shalt call his name John.

And thou shalt have joy and gladness; and many shall rejoice at his birth.

For he shall be great in the sight of the Lord, and shall drink neither wine nor strong drink; and he shall be filled with the Holy Ghost, even from his mother's womb.

And many of the children of Israel shall he turn to the Lord their God.

And he shall go before him in the spirit and power of Elias, to turn the hearts of the fathers to the children, and the disobedient to the wisdom of the just; to make ready a people prepared for the Lord.

(1:5–17)

140. Incense shovel found in the Bar Kokhba caves of the Judean Desert, 1st century A.D. Incense was used in the Temple service and offered daily. This was Zacharias' duty as a priest.

141. A general view of Nazareth, with the Church of the Annunciation in the center.
Nazareth is one of the oldest cities in the Holy Land. Its history goes back some three thousand years.
The town is scattered over the terraces of the hills above the Jezreel Valley. Present-day Nazareth is not in exactly the same place as it was in ancient times. The original town was destroyed, and rebuilt in the 12th and 13th centuries at a somewhat lower level. Its remarkable beauty has been often mentioned in the past, and Hieronymus (St. Jerome) refers to it in the 4th century as "the flower of Galilee."
All around Nazareth today there are groves of figs, pomegranates and other fruit.
The early Christians were often called Nazarenes, and both the Hebrew and Arabic words for Christians (*Notzri, Nasrani*) are derived from the town's name.

And in the sixth month the angel Gabriel was sent from God unto a city of Galilee, named Nazareth,

To a virgin espoused to a man whose name was Joseph, of the house of David; and the virgin's name was Mary.

142. The Church of the Annunciation at Nazareth.
Excavations conducted between 1955 and 1966 on the site of the Church of the Annunciation revealed the remains of a church with a mosaic pavement dating from c. A.D.450. Below the church were silos, vaulted cellars, cisterns and oil presses. There were also stuccoed and inscribed stones, as well as column bases. These are believed to be remnants of a Judeo-Christian synagogue.
The present church was built on the site of an ancient basilica of which it is told that when the Moslems seized Nazareth from the Crusaders in the 13th century, they decided to turn the church into a mosque. But then angels came down from heaven, raised the church and carried it far away beyond the seas. The church was finally set down in Dalmatia, in the Balkan mountains. Several years later it was transported to the Italian side of the Adriatic Sea. To this day, it is told, that the church still stands in the village of Loretto near Ancona. The village is also known as "Nazareth de Italia" and the church as the "Santa Casa" – the Holy House.

And the angel came in unto her, and said, Hail, thou that art highly favoured, the Lord is with thee: blessed art thou among women.

And when she saw him, she was troubled at his saying, and cast in her mind what manner of salutation this should be.

And the angel said unto her, Fear not, Mary: for thou hast found favour with God.

And, behold, thou shalt conceive in thy womb, and bring forth a son, and shalt call his name JESUS.

He shall be great, and shall be called the Son of the Highest: and the Lord God shall give unto him the throne of his father David:

And he shall reign over the house of Jacob for ever; and of his kingdom there shall be no end.

143. The Annunciation, painted by Simone Martini (1284–1344). Note the white lilies.

Then said Mary unto the angel, How shall this be, seeing I know not a man?

And the angel answered and said unto her, The Holy Ghost shall come upon thee, and the power of the Highest shall overshadow thee: therefore also that holy thing which shall be born of thee shall be called the Son of God.

And, behold, thy cousin Elisabeth, she hath also conceived a son in her old age: and this is the sixth month with her, who was called barren.

For with God nothing shall be impossible.

And Mary said, Behold the handmaid of the Lord; be it unto me according to thy word. And the angel departed from her.

144. The Madonna Lily (*lilium candidium*) grows near the mountaintops in the Holy Land, and particularly in the region of Nazareth. It is larger and more beautiful than the garden variety.
In many pictures showing the Angel Gabriel appearing before the Virgin, the angel carries a bunch of white lilies. The rarity of this beautiful flower in Israel today can perhaps be explained by the desire of pilgrims over the ages to pick the flowers with their bulbs, to take home as a living reminder of the Annunciation.

And Mary arose in those days, and went into the hill country with haste, into a city of Juda;

And entered into the house of Zacharias, and saluted Elisabeth.

And it came to pass, that when Elisabeth heard the salutation of Mary, the babe leaped in her womb; and Elisabeth was filled with the Holy Ghost:

And she spake out with a loud voice, and said, Blessed art thou among women, and blessed is the fruit of thy womb.

And whence is this to me, that the mother of my Lord should come to me?

For, lo, as soon as the voice of thy salutation sounded in mine ears, the babe leaped in my womb for joy.

And blessed is she that believed: for there shall be a performance of those things which were told her from the Lord.

And Mary said, My soul doth magnify the Lord,

And my spirit hath rejoiced in God my Saviour.

For he hath regarded the low estate of his handmaiden: for, behold, from henceforth all generations shall call me blessed.

For he that is mighty hath done to me great things; and holy is his name.

147. In the courtyard of the Church of the Visitation, inscribed on ceramic plaques in forty-two languages, are Mary's words rejoicing that she is to be the mother of the Lord. The Magnificat, as these words are called, are based on Hannah's Song of praise to the Lord after giving birth to Samuel (I Samuel 1:46–55).

148. Gold coin with portrait of Emperor Augustus, who ordered a census of the population for tax-collecting purposes.

149. A view of Bethlehem.
The quiet little town stands on a rocky prominence about 2200 feet above sea level and 4100 feet above the Dead Sea to the east. The hills slope down in a succession of terraces covered with vines, olive, almond and fig trees, to the valleys, which surround it on every side except the northwest.
Bethlehem means "House of Bread," and in spite of the nearby desert, the surrounding soil is fertile.
In the Old Testament it is also called Bethlehem Ephratah, and it was a peaceful, prosperous town.

That we should be saved from our enemies, and from the hand of all that hate us;

To perform the mercy promised to our fathers, and to remember his holy covenant;

The oath which he sware to our father Abraham,

That he would grant unto us, that we being delivered out of the hand of our enemies might serve him without fear,

In holiness and righteouness before him, all the days of our life.

And thou, child, shalt be called the prophet of the Highest: for thou shalt go before the face of the Lord to prepare his ways;

To give knowledge of salvation unto his people by the remission of their sins,

Through the tender mercy of our God; whereby the dayspring from on high hath visited us,

To give light to them that sit in darkness and in the shadow of death, to guide our feet into the way of peace.

And the child grew, and waxed strong in spirit, and was in the deserts till the day of his shewing unto Israel.

(1:26–80)

And it came to pass in those days, that there went out a decree from Caesar Augustus, that all the world should be taxed.

(And this taxing was first made when Cyrenius was governor of Syria.)

And all went to be taxed, every one into his own city.

And Joseph also went up from Galilee, out of the city of Nazareth, into Judaea, unto the city of David, which is called Bethlehem; (because he was of the house and lineage of David:)

To be taxed with Mary his espoused wife, being great with child.

And so it was, that, while they were there, the days were accomplished that she should be delivered.

And she brought forth her firstborn son, and wrapped him in swaddling clothes, and laid him in a manger; because there was no room for them in the inn.

And there were in the same country shepherds abiding in the field, keeping watch over their flock by night.

And, lo, the angel of the Lord came upon them, and the glory of the Lord shone round about them: and they were sore afraid.

And the angel said unto them, Fear not: for, behold, I bring you good tidings of great joy, which shall be to all people.

148

149

150

The decree of Caesar Augustus, commanding that a census be taken in all the provinces of the Roman Empire, brought Mary and Joseph from Nazareth to their native city.
For the early Christians, Bethlehem, as the birthplace of Jesus, appeared as the fulfillment of the prophet Micah's words: "But thou, Bethlehem Ephratah, though thou be little among the thousands of Judah, yet out of thee shall he come forth unto me that is to be ruler in Israel; whose goings forth have been from of old, from everlasting" (Micah 5:2).

150. The inn where Joseph and Mary would have stayed had there been room probably resembled the *khan* (inn) shown here, which is of more recent times.
The typical Middle Eastern inn consisted of a walled courtyard with only one entrance. Along the walls was a series of simple rooms for sheltering travellers and goods. The innkeepers supplied a few necessary provisions to travellers, and the animals were left in the large central court.

151. Bir-el-Kadismu (in Arabic), Well of Kathisma, or the Well of the Magi, on the way to Bethlehem.
A legend says that the water in the well at this spot suddenly burst out of the rock to quench the thirst of the Virgin Mary, when she stopped to rest. It is also associated with the appearance of the star that guided the Wise Men on their journey from the East (Matthew 2:9).

152. The ruins of the once famous Kathisma (place of rest) Monastery.
According to tradition, Mary rested in this place on the way to Bethlehem. About the middle of the 5th century a church stood here, dedicated to Mary. It was built by the pious and wealthy matron Hicelia.

For unto you is born this day in the city of David a Saviour, which is Christ the Lord.

And this shall be a sign unto you; Ye shall find the babe wrapped in swaddling clothes, lying in a manger.

And suddenly there was with the angel a multitude of the heavenly host praising God, and saying,

Glory to God in the highest, and on earth peace, good will toward men.

And it came to pass, as the angels were gone away from them into heaven, the shepherds said one to another, Let us now go even unto Bethlehem, and see this thing which is come to pass, which the Lord hath made known unto us.

And they came with haste, and found Mary, and Joseph, and the babe lying in a manger.

And when they had seen it, they made known abroad the saying which was told them concerning this child.

And all they that heard it wondered at those things which were told them by the shepherds.

But Mary kept all these things, and pondered them in her heart.

153. One of the sites identified as the Shepherds' Field.

There are many traditions concerning the exact site of the field where the shepherds received the first tidings of the Nativity, and several locations have been venerated by Christians at different periods. They are all east of Bethlehem, in a broad valley where to this day there are many flocks of sheep.

Every year, at midnight on Christmas Eve, these fields are crowded with thousands of pilgrims, singing Christmas hymns to celebrate the joyous event. *Gloria in Excelsis*, "Glory to God in the highest, and on earth peace, good will toward men," was sung here for the first time.

Archaeological exploration has uncovered an early church, dating from the 5th century, at one of the venerated sites.

154. The cave traditionally believed to be the Grotto of the Shepherds, under the Church of the Angels, built over the remains of the 5th-century church. The grotto is just east of the church, and contains an altar. It was believed to be the one inhabited by the Shepherds.

And the shepherds returned, glorifying and praising God for all the things that they had heard and seen, as it was told unto them.

And when eight days were accomplished for the circumcising of the child, his name was called JESUS, which was so named of the angel before he was conceived in the womb.

155. The Grotto of the Nativity.
In the Church of the Nativity at Bethlehem two flights of steps descend from either side of the great choir to the grotto, and meet before the Altar of the Nativity. The floor beneath the altar is covered with white marble, where, fitted into the paving, shines a silver star marking the traditional spot of Jesus' birth. To the right is the Manger hewn in the rock, where Mary laid the child.
There are many caves in Bethlehem and the vicinity. Joseph and Mary did not find room at the inn, and sought a secluded place for the birth. It was probably a house on the outskirts of the village. The local inhabitants still sometimes settle in a cave in the hillside and erect another room in front of it. A cave is warmer in winter and cooler in summer than an ordinary house, and if it is large enough, it can also be used for keeping animals at night. The manger was most likely used for storing fodder, rather than a place to which the animals came to feed.

156. The star which marks the spot where Jesus was born. An inscription above reads: "Hic de Virgine Maria Jesus Christus Natus Est" – Here Jesus Christ was born to the Virgin Mary. Seventeen lamps burn above the star night and day.
The mention of an extra-bright star in Matthew 2:1–4,9 has led to attempts to date the birth of Christ by means of astronomy. The appearance of such a star would naturally have attracted the attention of the ancient astronomers.
In 1603 and 1604 the great astronomer Kepler observed a conjunction of Jupiter and Saturn, made even more luminous by the addition of Mars in March, 1604. In the autumn of the same year he observed near these planets a new, fixed star of uncommon brilliance. By careful calculation he ascertained that a similar conjunction of Jupiter and Saturn in the sign of Pisces, with the later addition of Mars and most likely, an extraordinary star, took place around the time of Christ's birth.
In Jewish tradition such an occurrence was associated with the advent of a great king, on the basis of Balaam's prophecy in Numbers 24:17, and the messianic prophecies of Isaiah and Daniel.
Jewish astrologers traditionally ascribed a special significance to the conjunction of the planets Jupiter and Saturn in the sign of Pisces, and connected it with the advent of the Messiah. The Jewish scholar and commentator Abarbanel wrote fifty years before Kepler that such a conjunction took place three years before the birth of Moses, and predicted that it would reappear before the birth of the Messiah.

157. The Church of the Nativity in Bethlehem.
Like the Holy Sepulcher in Jerusalem, the birthplace of Jesus was identified by a pagan emperor: following the Jewish revolt led by

And when the days of her purification according to the law of Moses were accomplished, they brought him to Jerusalem, to present him to the Lord.

(As it is written in the law of the Lord, Every male that openeth the womb shall be called holy to the Lord;)

And to offer a sacrifice according to that which is said in the law of the Lord, A pair of turtledoves, or two young pigeons.

And, behold, there was a man in Jerusalem, whose name was Simeon; and the same man was just and devout, waiting for the consolation of Israel: and the Holy Ghost was upon him.

And it was revealed unto him by the Holy Ghost, that he should not see death, before he had seen the Lord's Christ.

And he came by the Spirit into the temple: and when the parents brought in the child Jesus, to do for him after the custom of the law,

Then took he him up in his arms, and blessed God, and said,

Lord, now lettest thou thy servant depart in peace, according to thy word:

For mine eyes have seen thy salvation,

Which thou hast prepared before the face of all people;

A light to lighten the Gentiles, and the glory of thy people Israel.

And Joseph and his mother marvelled at those things which were spoken of him.

And Simeon blessed them, and said unto Mary his mother, Behold, this child is set for the fall and rising again of many in Israel; and for a sign which shall be spoken against;

(Yea, a sword shall pierce through thy own soul also,) that the thoughts of many hearts may be revealed.

And there was one Anna, a prophetess, the daughter of Phanuel, of the tribe of Aser: she was of a great age, and had lived with an husband seven years from her virginity;

And she was a widow of about fourscore and four years, which departed not from the temple, but served God with fastings and prayers night and day.

And she coming in that instant gave thanks likewise unto the Lord, and spake of him to all them that looked for redemption in Jerusalem.

And when they had performed all things according to the law of the Lord, they returned into Galilee, to their own city Nazareth.

And the child grew, and waxed strong in spirit, filled with wisdom: and the grace of God was upon him.

Now his parents went to Jerusalem every year at the feast of the passover.

And when he was twelve years old, they went up to Jerusalem after the custom of the feast.

And when they had fulfilled the days, as they returned, the child Jesus tarried behind in Jerusalem; and Joseph and his mother knew not of it.

But they, supposing him to have been in the company, went a day's journey; and they sought him among their kinsfolk and acquaintance.

And when they found him not, they turned back again to Jerusalem, seeking him.

Bar-Kokhba against the Romans (A.D. 132–35), the emperor Hadrian was determined to suppress any Jewish-inspired messianic movement. All known Judeo-Christian holy places were paganized. In Bethlehem, over the grotto where Jesus is said to have been born, the Romans planted a grove dedicated to Adonis. However, by the 3rd century the Church Father Origen (c.185–c.254) wrote that he had visited this pagan grove and was shown the grotto where, according to the Gospels, Jesus was born, as well as the manger in which, wrapped in swaddling clothes, he was laid. The heathens themselves, he wrote, "tell everyone who would listen that in the said grotto a certain Jesus was born whom the Christians revered."

The present church is not very different in aspect from the original basilica built in the 4th century by Constantine and enlarged by Justinian (527–65). Part of the facade is covered by a fortress-like supporting wall.

158. The entrance to the Church of the Nativity.
The original church had three entrances, two of which have been walled up. The central and highest portal of Justinian's church was lowered during the Middle Ages; the trace of the pointed arch is still visible today. During the Ottoman era this arch was reduced further, to a low and narrow opening to prevent mounted horsemen from entering the church.

159. Interior of the Church of the Nativity.
With the exception of the roof and the floor, which have been replaced several times, the structure of the body of the church is as it was in the time of Justinian. The red limestone pillars, quarried near Bethlehem, may have stood in the 4th-century church, whose outer walls still stand. Crusader decorations adorn the upper part of the pillars with paintings of saints whose names appear in Latin or Greek. Some heraldic devices were engraved on the lower part of the pillars, dating from the 14th/15th century.

The only visible element of Constantine's church is the mosaic pavement of the nave below the present one. An opening has been left in the present floor to show the mosaic below.

160

160. View of a reconstruction of the Second Temple.

The "Doctors" of the Temple here refers to the rabbis, or learned teachers, interpreters of the Law. They were both moral teachers and judges. The Temple courts and outer halls were popular centers of learning, in some ways comparable to the Greek academy. Many of the teachings, rulings, sermons and dissertations of these rabbis were later collected and codified in the Jerusalem and Babylonian Talmuds. The first Jewish Christians also gathered here in the Temple courts to preach their gospel.

161. Beneath the southeastern corner of the Temple Mount, in the so-called Solomon's Stables, there is a chamber known for centuries as the Cradle of Jesus. This is believed to be where Mary rested the cradle of Jesus when she came to the Temple.

161

And it came to pass, that after three days they found him in the temple, sitting in the midst of the doctors, both hearing them, and asking them questions.

And all that heard him were astonished at his understanding and answers.

And when they saw him, they were amazed: and his mother said unto him, Son, why hast thou thus dealt with us? behold, thy father and I have sought thee sorrowing.

And he said unto them, How is it that ye sought me? wist ye not that I must be about my Father's business?

And they understood not the saying which he spake unto them.

And he went down with them, and came to Nazareth, and was subject unto them: but his mother kept all these sayings in her heart.

And Jesus increased in wisdom and stature, and in favour with God and man.

(2:1–52)

162. The Presentation of Christ at the Temple, depicted on a stone relief of the 12th century, at the church of Moissac, France.
This ceremony had a double purpose. It took place forty days after the birth of a male child, as according to the Law a woman was not allowed to enter the Temple "until the days of her purification were fulfilled... and when the days of her purification are fulfilled, for a son or for a daughter, she shall bring a lamb of the first year for a burnt offering... unto the door of the tabernacle of the congregation unto the priest..." (Leviticus 12:4–6). The child was

163

164

Now in the fifteenth year of the reign of Tiberius Caesar, Pontius Pilate being governor of Judaea, and Herod being tetrarch of Galilee, and his brother Philip tetrarch of Ituraea and of the region of Trachonitis, and Lysanias the tetrarch of Abilene,

Annas and Caiaphas being the high priests, the word of God came unto John the son of Zacharias in the wilderness.

And he came into all the country about Jordan, preaching the baptism of repentance for the remission of sins;

As it is written in the book of the words of Esaias the prophet, saying, The voice of one crying in the wilderness, Prepare ye the way of the Lord, make his paths straight.

Every valley shall be filled, and every mountain and hill shall be brought low; and the crooked shall be made straight, and the rough ways shall be made smooth;

And all flesh shall see the salvation of God.

Then said he to the multitude that came forth to be baptized of him, O generation of vipers, who hath warned you to flee from the wrath to come?

Bring forth therefore fruits worthy of repentance, and begin not to say within yourselves, We have Abraham to our father: for I say unto you, That God is able of these stones to raise up children unto Abraham.

And now also the ax is laid unto the root of the trees: every tree therefore which bringeth not forth good fruit is hewn down, and cast into the fire.

And the people asked him, saying, What shall we do then?

He answereth and saith unto them, He that hath two coats, let him impart to him that hath none; and he that hath meat, let him do likewise.

Then came also publicans to be baptized, and said unto him, Master, what shall we do?

And he said unto them, Exact no more than that which is appointed you.

And the soldiers likewise demanded of him, saying, And what shall we do? And he said unto them, Do violence to no man, neither accuse any falsely; and be content with your wages.

And as the people were in expectation, and all men mused in their hearts of John, whether he were the Christ, or not;

John answered, saying unto them all, I indeed baptize you with water; but one mightier than I cometh, the latchet of whose shoes I am not worthy to unloose: he shall baptize you with the Holy Ghost and with fire.

(3:1–16)

And Jesus himself began to be about thirty years of age, being (as was supposed) the son of Joseph, which was the son of Heli,

Which was the son of Matthat, which was the son of Levi, which was the son of Melchi, which was the son of Janna, which was the son of Joseph,

Which was the son of Mattathias, which was the son of Amos, which was the son of Naum, which was the son of Esli, which was the son of Nagge,

Which was the son of Maath, which was the son of Mattathias, which was the son of Semei, which was the son of Joseph, which was the son of Juda.

(3:23–26)

163. Bust of the Roman emperor Tiberius (A.D. 14–37).

164. "The Tetrarchs"; porphyry sculpture on St. Mark's Basilica, Venice; c. A.D. 300.
At the time of Jesus the term "tetrarchy" – literally, "rule of a quarter" – had lost its original meaning and described many small principalities in the eastern provinces of the Roman Empire.

165. Jesus and his ancestry; mosaic in the ceiling of the 14th-century Kariye Church in Istanbul.
Of the four gospels, only Matthew and Luke give the genealogies of Christ. Matthew's genealogy begins with Abraham, the father of the faith and of the chosen people, whereas Luke goes all the way back to Adam. Matthew's intention is to show Christ as the princely Savior of both the people and the faithful, whereas Luke seeks to show Christ as Son of Man, making his gospel one of universal salvation. Later, the idea of Christ as the second Adam was further developed by Paul (I Corinthians 13:45). Luke's universality can be seen in several places in his gospel. The infant Savior is greeted by Simeon as "A light to lighten the Gentiles, and the glory of thy people Israel" (2:31). John the Baptist, applying Isaiah's prophecy concerning the voice in the wilderness, quotes the prophet (Isaiah 52:10): "And all flesh shall see the salvation of God" (3:6). Only Luke records the mission of the Seventy Apostles, who represent the Gentile nations, just as the Twelve Apostles represent the twelve tribes of Israel.
Luke alone provides a real history of Jesus from infancy to boyhood and manhood, telling us that the child Jesus "grew, and waxed strong in spirit, filled with wisdom" (2:40), and describes the remarkable scene in the Temple where the twelve-year-old Jesus sat "in the midst of the doctors, both hearing them, and asking them questions" (2:46), as well as other details which underline the humanity of Jesus.

Which was the son of Melchi, which was the son of Addi, which was the son of Cosam, which was the son of Elmodam, which was the son of Er,

Which was the son of Jose, which was the son of Eliezer, which was the son of Jorim, which was the son of Matthat, which was the son of Levi,

Which was the son of Simeon, which was the son of Juda, which was the son of Joseph, which was the son of Jonan, which was the son of Eliakim,

Which was the son of Melea, which was the son of Menan, which was the son of Mattatha, which was the son of Nathan, which was the son of David,

Which was the son of Jesse, which was the son of Obed, which was the son of Booz, which was the son of Salmon, which was the son of Naasson,

Which was the son of Aminadab, which was the son of Aram, which was the son of Esrom, which was the son of Phares, which was the son of Juda,

Which was the son of Jacob, which was the son of Isaac, which was the son of Abraham, which was the son of Thara, which was the son of Nachor,

Which was the son of Saruch, which was the son of Ragau, which was the son of Phalec, which was the son of Heber, which was the son of Sala,

Which was the son of Cainan, which was the son of Arphaxad, which was the son of Sem, which was the son of Noe, which was the son of Lamech,

Which was the son of Mathusala, which was the son of Enoch, which was the son of Jared, which was the son of Maleleel, which was the son of Cainan, Which was the son of Enos, which was the son of Seth, which was the son of Adam, which was the son of God.   (3:28–38)

166. The southeast corner of the present Temple Mount, believed to be the "pinnacle of the temple."

167. Stones in the desert near Eilat, a geological formation resembling loaves of bread. In Luke, Jesus' temptation is to prove that he can withstand and overcome the Devil. Forty days is a period associated with testing and suffering, as in Deuteronomy 9:9, when Moses received the Law on Mount Sinai, and in 1 Kings 19:8 when Elijah went to Horeb.
In Luke 3:22, a voice came from heaven saying that Jesus was God's beloved son, and the Devil uses this to tempt him. If Jesus acted as the Son of God he would lose his standing to defeat the enemy as the Son of Man. The text suggests that often the thought of performing a miracle comes from the Devil. Jesus answers the tempter in the words of the Bible, and adds that he took the word of God as his "bread" and lived by it. The second temptation offers Jesus glory in this world, and again

And Jesus being full of the Holy Ghost returned from Jordan, and was led by the Spirit into the wilderness,

Being forty days tempted of the devil. And in those days he did eat nothing: and when they were ended, he afterward hungered.

And the devil said unto him, If thou be the Son of God, command this stone that it be made bread.

And Jesus answered him, saying, It is written, That man shall not live by bread alone, but by every word of God.

And the devil, taking him up into an high mountain, shewed unto him all the kingdoms of the world in a moment of time.

And the devil said unto him, All this power will I give thee, and the glory of them: for that is delivered unto me; and to whomsoever I will I give it.

If thou therefore wilt worship me, all shall be thine.

And Jesus answered and said unto him, Get thee behind me, Satan: for it is written, Thou shalt worship the Lord thy God, and him only shalt thou serve.

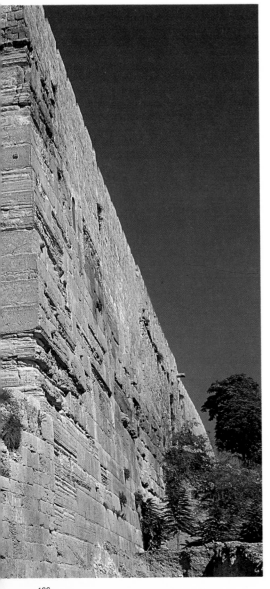

And he brought him to Jerusalem, and set him on a pinnacle of the temple, and said unto him, If thou be the Son of God, cast thyself down from hence: For it is written, He shall give his angels charge over thee, to keep thee:

And in their hands they shall bear thee up, lest at any time thou dash thy foot against a stone. And Jesus answering said unto him, It is said, Thou shalt not tempt the Lord thy God.

And when the devil had ended all the temptation, he departed from him for a season.

And Jesus returned in the power of the Spirit into Galilee: and there went out a fame of him through all the region round about.

Jesus defeats the enemy by the word (Deuteronomy 6:13). In the third temptation the Devil himself quotes the Scripture this time. But Jesus defeats the Devil with the simple statement taken from the Bible, "Thou shalt not tempt the Lord thy God."

168. & 169. Landscape in the Galilee, where Jesus wandered from village to village, preaching in the synagogues.

Now when he had left speaking, he said unto Simon, Launch out into the deep, and let down your nets for a draught.

And Simon answering said unto him, Master, we have toiled all the night, and have taken nothing: nevertheless at thy word I will let down the net.

And when they had this done, they inclosed a great multitude of fishes: and their net brake.

And they beckoned unto their partners, which were in the other ship, that they should come and help them. And they came, and filled both the ships, so that they began to sink.

When Simon Peter saw it, he fell down at Jesus' knees, saying, Depart from me; for I am a sinful man, O Lord.

For he was astonished, and all that were with him, at the draught of the fishes which they had taken:

And so was also James, and John, the sons of Zebedee, which were partners with Simon. And Jesus said unto Simon, Fear not; from henceforth thou shalt catch men.

And when they had brought their ships to land, they forsook all. and followed him. (5:4–11)

And when it was day, he called unto him his disciples: and of them he

175

175. Fish are plentiful in the Sea of Galilee. Among the varieties some are forbidden by Jewish dietary law. Only fish with fins and scales are permitted. This rules out catfish, eels, lampreys, rays, sharks and the crustacea (Leviticus 11:9–12). Jewish fishermen therefore separated the permitted fish from the rest (Matthew 13:47–48).
There is a quaint legend about one species of fish found here. On either side of its body there is a dark smudge, and it is said that this is the mark of the finger of St. Peter when he took a coin from the mouth of this fish to pay the Temple tax required by custom, and threw the fish back into the water (Matthew 17:27).

176. Zealot dwellings at the southeastern wall of Masada.
The disciple Simon, one of the original twelve, is designated here and in Acts 1:13 as a Zealot.
The Zealots were members of a political faction who believed themselves to be the agents of divine wrath and judgement against idolatry, apostasy or any transgression of the Law. The movement was especially strong in the Maccabean period, and later revived as one of the main parties in the Jewish revolt against Rome. Simon had probably been a member of the Zealots, which also held fervent messianic beliefs and expectations, before he became a disciple of Jesus.

chose twelve, whom also he named apostles;

Simon, (whom he also named Peter,) and Andrew his brother, James and John, Philip and Bartholomew,

Matthew and Thomas, James the son of Alphaeus, and Simon called Zelotes,

And Judas the brother of James, and Judas Iscariot, which also was the traitor. (6:13–16)

180. The Church of Mary Magdalene, in her birthplace, Migdal, or Magdala.
Magdala was one of the oldest towns in Galilee on the western shore of the Sea of Galilee. According to Josephus, Emperor Nero gave the town of Magdala to Agrippa II, who later renamed it Taricheae, a Latinized form of the Aramaic word for "drying and salting," a reference to the town's fishing industry.

181. View in the region of the Banias, where Caesarea Philippi was located, and where, according to Matthew 16:1 ff. and Mark 8:27–29, Peter's confession took place.
Caesarea Philippi was in the northern part of the Holy Land, at the foot of Mount Hermon, where the Transfiguration is believed to have taken place. It was far from the capital and Temple, with its priestly and rabbinical establishment. Jesus brought his disciples purposely to this place, in order to reveal to them something new concerning himself and the church (Matthew 16:18).

And it came to pass, as he was alone praying, his disciples were with him: and he asked them, saying, Whom say the people that I am?

They answering said, John the Baptist; but some say Elias; and others say, that one of the old prophets is risen again.

He said unto them, But whom say ye that I am? Peter answering said, The Christ of God.

And he straitly charged them, and commanded them to tell no man that thing;

Saying, The Son of man must suffer many things, and be rejected of the elders and chief priests and scribes, and be slain, and be raised the third day.

(9:18–22)

And Jesus answering said, A certain man went down from Jerusalem to Jericho, and fell among thieves, which stripped him of his raiment, and wounded him, and departed, leaving him half dead.

And by chance there came down a certain priest that way: and when he saw him, he passed by on the other side.

(10:30–31)

182. The way to Jericho.

But a certain Samaritan, as he journeyed, came where he was: and when he saw him, he had compassion on him,

And went to him, and bound up his wounds, pouring in oil and wine, and set him on his own beast, and brought him to an inn, and took care of him.

And on the morrow when he departed, he took out two pence, and gave them to the host, and said unto him, Take care of him; and whatsoever thou spendest more, when I come again, I will repay thee.

Which now of these three, thinkest thou, was neighbour unto him that fell among the thieves?

And he said, He that shewed mercy on him. Then said Jesus unto him, Go, and do thou likewise.　　　　　　　　　　　　　　　(10:33–37)

183. A small inn called "The Good Samaritan" on the way to Jericho.

184. The spire of the Pater Noster Church on the Mount of Olives, with the Judean Desert in the background.

The Church of the Pater Noster is built over two grottoes: one where Christ "revealed to his disciples inscrutable mysteries," and another called the Grotto of the Credo, where according to tradition, Jesus taught his disciples the Lord's Prayer (Matthew 6:9–13; Luke 11:2). The Emperor Constantine built a basilica above this grotto and named it Eleona ("of the olive trees" in Greek). The Church of Eleona was destroyed by the Persians in the 7th century. It was rebuilt by the Crusaders and destroyed several times. In 1856 a French noblewoman, the Princesse de la Tour d'Auvergne, arrived in Jerusalem; she bought the site of the Pater, and donated it to her country. She herself lived on the site for eight years in a wooden chalet brought from France. She then built the church and the cloister which were given to the Carmelite Sisters. The Princess retired to Florence but expressed the wish to be buried in the Pater Noster in the sarcophagus she herself had prepared in the cloister. Her wish was fulfilled in 1957.

And it came to pass, that, as he was praying in a certain place, when he ceased, one of his disciples said unto him, Lord, teach us to pray, as John also taught his disciples.

And he said unto them, When ye pray, say, our Father which art in heaven, Hallowed be thy name. Thy kingdom come. Thy will be done, as in heaven, so in earth.

Give us day by day our daily bread.

And forgive us our sins; for we also forgive every one that is indebted to us. And lead us not into temptation; but deliver us from evil.

And he said unto them, Which of you shall have a friend, and shall go unto him at midnight, and say unto him, Friend, lend me three loaves;

For a friend of mine in his journey is come to me, and I have nothing to set before him?

And he from within shall answer and say, Trouble me not: the door is now shut, and my children are with me in bed; I cannot rise and give thee.

I say unto you, Though he will not rise and give him, because he is his friend, yet because of his importunity he will rise and give him as many as he needeth.

And I say unto you, Ask, and it shall be given you; seek, and ye shall find; knock, and it shall be opened unto you.

For every one that asketh receiveth; and he that seeketh findeth; and to him that knocketh it shall be opened.

If a son shall ask bread of any of you that is a father, will he give him a stone? or if he ask a fish, will he for a fish give him a serpent?

Or if he shall ask an egg, will he offer him a scorpion?

If ye then, being evil, know how to give good gifts unto your children: how much more shall your heavenly Father give the Holy Spirit to them that ask him?

185. In the cloister of the monastery by the Pater Noster Church the Lord's Prayer is written in more than fifty languages.

186. An expelled demon coming out of a man's mouth; detail from an Italian 10th-century ivory tablet depicting the healing of the possessed (Hessisches Landesmuseum, Darmstadt, Germany).
Since it was believed that demons cannot rest in "dry places," this meant that their dwelling place was the sea. In Matthew, the verse "Even so shall it be also unto this wicked generation" is added, in the context of the rejection of Christ.

186

And he was casting out a devil, and it was dumb. And it came to pass, when the devil was gone out, the dumb spake; and the people wondered.

But some of them said, He casteth out devils through Beelzebub the chief of the devils.

And others, tempting him, sought of him a sign from heaven. But he, knowing their thoughts, said unto them, Every kingdom divided against itself is brought to desolation; and a house divided against a house falleth.

If Satan also be divided against himself, how shall his kingdom stand? because ye say that I cast out devils through Beelzebub.

And if I by Beelzebub cast out devils, by whom do your sons cast them out? therefore shall they be your judges.

But if I with the finger of God cast out devils, no doubt the kingdom of God is come upon you.

When a strong man armed keepeth his palace, his goods are in peace:

But when a stronger than he shall come upon him, and overcome him, he taketh from him all his armour wherein he trusted, and divideth his spoils.

He that is not with me is against me: and he that gathereth not with me scattereth.

When the unclean spirit is gone out of a man, he walketh through dry places, seeking rest; and finding none, he saith, I will return unto my house whence I came out.

And when he cometh, he findeth it swept and garnished.

Then goeth he, and taketh to him seven other spirits more wicked than himself; and they enter in, and dwell there: and the last state of that man is worse than the first. (11:1–26)

And when the people were gathered thick together, he began to say, This is an evil generation: they seek a sign; and there shall no sign be given it, but the sign of Jonas the prophet.

For as Jonas was a sign unto the Ninevites, so shall also the Son of man be to this generation.

The queen of the south shall rise up in the judgment with the men of this generation, and condemn them: for she came from the utmost parts of the earth to hear the wisdom of Solomon; and behold, a greater Solomon is here.

The men of Nineve shall rise up in the judgment with this generation, and shall condemn it: for they repented at the preaching of Jonas; and, behold, a greater than Jonas is here. No man, when he hath lighted a candle, putteth it in a secret place, neither under a bushel, but on a candlestick, that they which come in may see the light. The light of the body is the eye: therefore when thine eye is single, thy whole body also is full of light; but when thine eye is evil, thy body also is full of darkness.

Take heed therefore that the light which is in thee be not darkness.

If thy whole body therefore be full of light, having no part dark, the whole shall be full of light, as when the bright shining of a candle doth give thee light.

(11:29–36)

187. Jonah swallowed by the whale; bas-relief, 9th century (Archaeological Museum, Istanbul, Turkey).

In I Corinthians 1:22 Paul writes: "For the Jews require a sign," meaning a miraculous token substantiating what is preached. The "sign of Jonas" is mentioned also in Matthew 12 and Mark 8, and refers to the "sign" of Jesus' death and the "three days and three nights in the heart of the earth" (Matthew 12:40) corresponding with Jonah's days in the whale's belly. Thus Christ is the "greater Jonas." He is also the "greater Solomon," who will build the Temple of God, the Church, and to whom "the utmost parts of the earth" will come to hear the word of wisdom.

Consider the lilies how they grow: they toil not, they spin not; and yet I say unto you that Solomon in all his glory was not arrayed like one of these.

If then God so clothe the grass, which is to day in the field, and to morrow is cast into the oven; how much more will he clothe you, O ye of little faith?

(12:27–28)

And he spake this parable unto them, saying,

What man of you, having an hundred sheep, if he lose one of them, doth not leave the ninety and nine in the wilderness, and go after that which is lost, until he find it?

And when he hath found it, he layeth it on his shoulders, rejoicing.

And when he cometh home, he calleth together his friends and neighbours, saying unto them, Rejoice with me; for I have found my sheep which was lost.

I say unto you, that likewise joy shall be in heaven over one sinner that repenteth, more than over ninety and nine just persons, which need no repentance.

(15:3–7)

188

188. Wild flowers in the Holy Land.

189. The Good Shepherd; stone statuette, 4th century (Archaeological Museum, Istanbul).

190. & 191. Tree and fruit of the carob. The fruit of the carob tree was a source of food for the poor in ancient times and is so described in Jewish folklore. It is also known as St. John's Bread, because it was eaten by John the Baptist in the wilderness.

When the young prodigal had nothing left, and the country in which he was living was undergoing a terrible famine, he worked at feeding husks to swine, and would gladly have eaten the husks himself (Luke 15:16). These husks are pods of the carob tree which are green at first, but turn brown when ripe; they can also be dried in the sun. They contain a sweet syrup and have been used since antiquity for fattening cattle. But they are also fit for human consumption and quite nourishing. At one time the seeds of the carob (in Greek *keratea*) were used as standards of weight, and the word "carat" is derived from their name.

And he said, A certain man had two sons:

And the younger of them said to his father, Father, give me the portion of goods that falleth to me. And he divided unto them his living.

And not many days after the younger son gathered all together, and took his journey into a far country, and there wasted his substance with riotous living.

And when he had spent all, there arose a mighty famine in that land; and he began to be in want.

And he went and joined himself to a citizen of that country; and he sent him into his fields to feed swine.

And he would fain have filled his belly with the husks that the swine did eat: and no man gave unto him.

And when he came to himself, he said, How many hired servants of my father's have bread enough and to spare, and I perish with hunger!

I will arise and go to my father, and will say unto him, Father, I have sinned against heaven, and before thee,

190

And am no more worthy to be called thy son: make me as one of thy hired servants.

And he arose, and came to his father. But when he was yet a great way off, his father saw him, and had compassion, and ran, and fell on his neck, and kissed him.

And the son said unto him, Father, I have sinned against heaven, and in thy sight, and am no more worthy to be called thy son.

But the father said to his servants, Bring forth the best robe, and put it on him; and put a ring on his hand, and shoes on his feet:

And bring hither the fatted calf, and kill it; and let us eat, and be merry:

For this my son was dead, and is alive again; he was lost, and is found. And they began to be merry.   (15:11–24)

And when he was demanded of the Pharisees, when the kingdom of God should come, he answered them and said, The kingdom of God cometh not with observation: Neither shall they say, Lo here! or, lo there! for, behold, the kingdom of God is within you.

And he said unto the disciples, The days will come, when ye shall desire to see one of the days of the Son of man, and ye shall not see it.

And they shall say to you, See here; or, see there: go not after them, nor follow them.

For as the lightning, that lighteneth out of the one part under heaven, shineth unto the other part under heaven; so shall also the Son of man be in his day.

But first must he suffer many things, and be rejected of this generation.

And as it was in the days of Noe, so shall it be also in the days of the Son of man. They did eat, they drank, they married wives, they were given in marriage, until the day that Noe entered into the ark, and the flood came, and destroyed them all.

(17:20–27)

192. People drowning in the flood; detail of a Spanish illuminated manuscript of the 8th century (Library of the Cathedral, Gerona, Spain).

The time of the Lord's coming will be "as it was in the days of Noah." In the days of Noah people were preoccupied and befuddled by eating, drinking, marrying and being given in marriage, and with their commercial activities and household concerns, so much so that God's judgement – the flood – came upon them unawares. So it will be, acccording to the New Testament, when Christ comes to judge the world, and he warns the believers to be soberly aware of God's coming judgement on the corrupt world.

193

193. *Murex*: a shellfish from which was extracted a fluid used in making purple dye. A small gland in the neck of these creatures contains a minute amount of this fluid, making its extraction a costly process. Purple-dyed garments, therefore, were the mark of wealthy and important persons. *Murex* shells are found along the coasts of the Mediterranean Sea. Ancient Sidon and Tyre were famous for a purple or deep crimson dye known as Tyrian or Imperial purple. The Phoenician city of Tyre is mentioned in the Old Testament as a source of purple wool (Ezekiel 27:2,7,24).

194. The Pharisee and the publican; Byzantine mosaic of the 6th century at San Apollinare in Classe, Ravenna, Italy. The term publican derives from the Latin word designating members of the large Roman financial companies which farmed out the taxes of the provinces of the Roman Empire.

In order to save the expense of collecting taxes from the provinces, the privilege was sold at auction. The bidders were the Roman financial companies, who hired their own officials to do the work. This system gave rise to abuses, provincial governors being bribed to ignore extortion. The publicans mentioned in the Gospels, usually described as "sinners," were probably agents of the procurator of Judea, who also collected duty on exports. The Jews who served the Roman state in this way were held in contempt by their fellow-countrymen.

The Pharisees, on the other hand, represented traditional, rigid orthodoxy, which frequently degenerated into self-righteousness, confounding piety with narrow-minded adherence to the Law. They analyzed the Mosaic Law meticulously and were inclined to substitute casuistry for the living code. In the New Testament they are reproached for hypocrisy, though certain illustrious exceptions, such as Nicodemus, Gamaliel and his disciple, Paul, are also mentioned.

195. A purse shown in a detail of a wall painting found in the "banker's house" at Pompeii (Museo Nazionale, Naples).

There was a certain rich man, which was clothed in purple and fine linen, and fared sumptuously every day:

And there was a certain beggar named Lazarus, which was laid at his gate, full of sores,

And desiring to be fed with the crumbs which fell from the rich man's table: moreover the dogs came and licked his sores.

And it came to pass, that the beggar died, and was carried by the angels into Abraham's bosom: the rich man also died, and was buried;

And in hell he lift up his eyes, being in torments, and seeth Abraham afar off, and Lazarus in his bosom.

And he cried and said, Father Abraham, have mercy on me, and send Lazarus, that he may dip the tip of his finger in water, and cool my tongue; for I am tormented in this flame.

But Abraham said, Son, remember that thou in thy lifetime receivedst thy good things, and likewise Lazarus evil things: but now he is comforted, and thou art tormented.   (16:19–25)

And he spake this parable unto certain which trusted in themselves that they were righteous, and despised others:

Two men went up into the temple to pray; the one a Pharisee, and the other a publican.

The Pharisee stood and prayed thus with himself, God, I thank thee, that I am not as other men are, extortioners, unjust, adulterers, or even as this publican.

I fast twice in the week, I give tithes of all that I possess.

And the publican, standing afar off, would not lift up so much as his eyes unto heaven, but smote upon his breast, saying, God be merciful to me a sinner.

I tell you, this man went down to his house justified rather than the other: for every one that exalteth himself shall be abased; and he that humbleth himself shall be exalted.   (18:9–14)

And a certain ruler asked him, saying, Good Master, what shall I do to inherit eternal life?

And Jesus said unto him, Why callest thou me good? none is good, save one, that is, God.

Thou knowest the commandments, Do not commit adultery, Do not kill, Do not steal, Do not bear false witness, Honour thy father and thy mother.

And he said, All these have I kept from my youth up.

Now when Jesus heard these things, he said unto him, Yet lackest thou one thing: sell all that thou hast, and distribute unto the poor, and thou shalt have treasure in heaven: and come, follow me.

And when he heard this, he was very sorrowful: for he was very rich.

And when Jesus saw that he was very sorrowful, he said, How hardly shall they that have riches enter into the kingdom of God!

For it is easier for a camel to go through a needle's eye, than for a rich man to enter into the kingdom of God.

And they that heard it said, Who then can be saved?

And he said, The things which are impossible with men are possible with God.   (18:18–27)

196. A view from Bethphage, looking toward Jericho and the Judean Desert.

197. Jerusalem seen from the Mount of Olives, affording a wide view of the Temple Mount and the Old City.
Jerusalem is mentioned 144 times in the New Testament. It was the city of God's own choosing, where he chose to dwell in his Temple, but it had deteriorated, and was even described as a "den of thieves," whose inhabitants out of misguided religious zeal killed prophets and stoned apostles (Matthew 23:37). Nevertheless, Jesus had a special love and concern for Jerusalem, as indicated by his anguished cry "O Jerusalem Jerusalem."
In the Book of Revelation there is a marvelous picture of the New Jerusalem in which God will dwell with his people for eternity.
Josephus tells of a certain Jesus (not Jesus of Nazareth), son of Ananias, "an uncouth peasant" who during the Festival of Tabernacles came into the Temple courts and suddenly began to cry out, "A voice from the east, a voice from the west, a voice from the four winds, a voice against Jerusalem and the sanctuary, a voice against the bridegroom and the bride [compare Jeremiah 7:34ff], a voice against the whole people." He uttered his cry day and night throughout the city and provoked some of the leading citizens, who gave him a good beating. But he went on proclaiming his prophecy. The Roman governor had him flogged, but he continued to cry out at every stroke, writes Josephus, "Woe, woe to Jerusalem."
The leaders of the people, who could not be sure whether or not he was possessed by the Spirit of God, and therefore not punishable according to Jewish Law, had handed him over to the procurator, who released him because he regarded him as crazy and harmless. He continued his prophesying for seven years, until he was struck down by a stone hurled at him by some citizen.

And it came to pass, when he was come nigh to Bethphage and Bethany, at the mount called the mount of Olives, he sent two of his disciples,

Saying, Go ye into the village over against you; in the which at your entering ye shall find a colt tied, whereon yet never man sat: loose him, and bring him hither.

And if any man ask you, Why do ye loose him? thus shall ye say unto him, Because the Lord hath need of him.

And they that were sent went their way, and found even as he had said unto them.

And as they were loosing the colt, the owners thereof said unto them, Why loose ye the colt?

And they said, The Lord hath need of him.

And they brought him to Jesus: and they cast their garments upon the colt, and they set Jesus thereon.

And as he went, they spread their clothes in the way.

And when he was come nigh, even now at the descent of the mount of Olives, the whole multitude of the disciples began to rejoice and praise God with a loud voice for all the mighty works that they had seen;

Saying, Blessed be the King that cometh in the name of the Lord: peace in heaven, and glory in the highest.

And some of the Pharisees from among the multitude said unto him, Master, rebuke thy disciples.

And he answered and said unto them, I tell you that, if these should hold their peace, the stones would immediately cry out.

And when he was come near, he beheld the city, and wept over it,

Saying, If thou hadst known, even thou, at least in this thy day, the things which belong unto thy peace! but now they are hid from thine eyes.

For the days shall come upon thee, that thine enemies shall cast a trench about thee, and compass thee round, and keep thee in on every side,

And shall lay thee even with the ground, and thy children within thee; and they shall not leave in thee one stone upon another; because thou knewest not the time of thy visitation.

(19:29—44)

198. A fig tree in early summer, when it begins to put out bright green leaves.

In *The Jewish War*, Josephus tells of various signs and portents which deluded the people and led them to self-destruction: "Man is quickly persuaded in adversity, and when the deceiver actually holds out a prospect of release from the prevailing horrors, the sufferer falls wholly prey to these expectations." These "expectations" were apparently an indication of the messianic beliefs of the people, made all the more urgent by a sense of impending disaster. The warnings in the Gospels, and also later in the Epistles to the Thessalonians in particular, against the false prophets, show how successful some of these self-proclaimed messiahs were and what harm they could cause. The Zealots were especially susceptible, but as the promises remained unfulfilled and miracles did not materialize, the term "prophet" soon became derogatory.

Josephus mentions several miraculous portents which took place about the time of the destruction of the Temple. He introduces them by saying, "This is how the unhappy people were beguiled at this stage by charlatans and false messengers of God, while they disregarded and disbelieved the unmistakable portents that foreshadowed the coming desolation, and, as though thunderstruck, blind, senseless, paid no heed to the clear warning of God." He reports that a star that looked like a sword hung over the city. A light appeared in the middle of the night and shone about the Temple and the altar, so bright that it was like broad daylight, lasting for half an hour. One of the heavy gates of the inner sanctuary opened of its own accord. A cow brought for sacrifice gave birth to a lamb, and there were many other strange signs. Josephus comments that the "uninitiated" believed that the miraculous opening of the gate was "the best of omens, as they assumed that God had opened to them the gate of happiness. But wiser people realized that the security of the Temple was breaking down of its own accord, and that the opening of the gate was a gift to the enemy, and they interpreted this in their own minds as a portent of coming desolation."

199. The rock shown here is in the Chapel of the Agony in a grotto under the church of that name in the Garden of Gethsemane, where it is believed Jesus sweated blood. Here the disciples rested while Jesus prayed.

This was probably on the night preceding the Passover, which is known as *Leil Shimurim* in Hebrew, i.e., "a night of vigil," on which God once saved his people, who were commanded since to mark it each year by keeping watch throughout the night: "It is a night to be much observed unto the Lord for bringing them [the children of Israel] out from the land of Egypt: this is that night of the Lord to be observed of all the children of Israel in their generations." (Exodus 12:42).

200. The Garden of Gethsemane.

And there shall be signs in the sun, and in the moon, and in the stars; and upon the earth distress of nations, with perplexity; the sea and the waves roaring;

Men's hearts failing them for fear, and for looking after those things which are coming on the earth: for the powers of heaven shall be shaken.

And then shall they see the Son of man coming in a cloud with power and great glory.

And when these things begin to come to pass, then look up, and lift up your heads; for your redemption draweth nigh.

And he spake to them a parable; Behold the fig tree, and all the trees;

When they now shoot forth, ye see and know of your own selves that summer is now nigh at hand.

So likewise ye, when ye see these things come to pass, know ye that the kingdom of God is nigh at hand. Verily I say unto you, This generation shall not pass away, till all be fulfilled.

Heaven and earth shall pass away: but my words shall not pass away.

(21:25–33)

And he came out, and went, as he was wont, to the mount of Olives; and his disciples also followed him.

And when he was at the place, he said unto them, Pray that ye enter not into temptation.

And he was withdrawn from them about a stone's cast, and kneeled down, and prayed, Saying, Father, if thou be willing, remove this cup from me: nevertheless not my will, but thine, be done.

And there apeared an angel unto him from heaven, strengthening him.

And being in an agony he prayed more earnestly: and his sweat was as it were great drops of blood falling down to the ground.

And when he rose up from prayer, and was come to his disciples, he found them sleeping for sorrow,

And said unto them, Why sleep ye? rise and pray, lest ye enter into temptation.

(22:39–46)

201. Coin issued by Pontius Pilate (A.D. 26–36) with a *litus* (a bent staff), the symbol of his office, on the obverse; the reverse shows three ears of barley tied together.

Pontius Pilate was the Roman procurator of Judea. Tiberius appointed him in A.D. 26 and his rule lasted ten years.

At the outset of his rule as the emperor's representative, Pilate incurred the resentment of the Jews when his army, camped in Jerusalem for its winter quarters, brought into the city its standards bearing the imperial images. This offended the religious sensibilities of the Jews, who staged a mass protest before Pilate, who was then in Caesarea. Pilate also caused bitterness by his appropriation of Temple funds. When angry crowds demanded abandonment of the project, Pilate planted Roman soldiers among them, who fell upon the demonstrators and killed and injured many in the crowd. The procurator exercised full control of the province. Caesarea was the official residence of the Roman procurator, and the main body of Roman troops was stationed there, with a small detachment at Jerusalem. The procurator, however, resided in Jerusalem during the festivals – such as Passover – and brought military reinforcements with him.

And they were instant with loud voices, requiring that he might be crucified. And the voices of them and of the chief priests prevailed.

And Pilate gave sentence that it should be as they required.

And he released unto them him that for sedition and murder was cast into prison, whom they had desired; but he delivered Jesus to their will.

(23:23–25)

And there followed him a great company of people, and of women, which also bewailed and lamented him.

But Jesus turning unto them said, Daughters of Jerusalem, weep not for me, but weep for yourselves, and for your children.

For, behold, the days are coming, in the which they shall say, Blessed are the barren, and the wombs that never bare, and the paps which never gave suck.

Then shall they begin to say to the mountains, Fall on us; and to the hills, Cover us.

For if they do these things in a green tree, what shall be done in the dry?

And there were also two other, malefactors, led with him to be put to death. And when they were come to the place, which is called Calvary, there they crucified him, and the malefactors, one on the right hand, and the other on the left.

Then said Jesus, Father, forgive them; for they know not what they do. And they parted his raiment, and cast lots. And the people stood beholding. And the rulers also with them derided him, saying, He saved others; let him save himself, if he be Christ, the chosen of God.

And the soldiers also mocked him, coming to him, and offering him vinegar, And saying, If thou be the king of the Jews, save thyself.

And a superscription also was written over him in letters of Greek, and Latin, and Hebrew, This is the King of the Jews.

And one of the malefactors which were hanged railed on him, saying, If thou be Christ, save thyself and us.

But the other answering rebuked him, saying, Dost not thou fear God, seeing thou art in the same condemnation?

And we indeed justly; for we receive the due reward of our deeds: but this man hath done nothing amiss.

And he said unto Jesus, Lord, remember me when thou comest into thy kingdom.

And Jesus said unto him, Verily I say unto thee, To day shalt thou be with me in paradise.

(23:27–43)

202. Mourning women; 14th-century mosaic from the Kariye Church, Istanbul, Turkey.

203. Remains of the fortress built by the Knights Templars between 1150 and 1170, known as Le Toron des Chevaliers – Tower of the Knights, in old French – on the top of a hill a short distance northwest of Jerusalem. The name Le Toron has undergone interesting transformations. The Arabs pronounced it al-Atrun or al-Natrun, which means "guard" or "lookout." After the Crusader period the name Latrun took root. In the 14th century, the Christians, not knowing its French origin, thought it meant *Latro* (robber), hence the tradition that here was the home of "the good thief" (Boni latronis in Latin). A French Trappist monastery was built on the slope of the hill toward the end of the 19th century.

204. The church at Emmaus, built on the foundations of an old house, traditionally called the home of Cleophas.

Emmaus has been identified with the village of al-Qubeibeh a few miles away, where the Judean hills begin their gradual rise.

Excavations have revealed a Crusader church constructed over the remains of a Byzantine one, which, in turn was built over "an ancient room," believed to be the house of Cleophas. A Roman road led from Emmaus to Jerusalem. In the year 4 B.C. the Roman commander Cassius sold its inhabitants into slavery, and it became the center of an insurrection. In retaliation, the proconsul of Syria, Varus, set fire to the city. Several tombstones bearing the names of Roman soldiers have been found at the site. Excavations have also revealed foundations of thick walls dating to the 2nd and 3rd centuries B.C.; an aqueduct leading water from an adjacent spring to the town; oil and wine presses cut out of rock; the remains of a Roman villa of the 2nd or 3rd century, surrounded by porticoes along one side of the building. The earliest church found there is a 3rd-century basilica; Crusader structures were also found.

Near the church was discovered a Crusader village which straddled a Roman road leading to Jerusalem. The village consisted of one-room houses. The Frankish settlers who occupied the place were driven out by the Moslems at the end of the 12th century.

Many scholars doubt that al-Qubeibeh was the site of Emmaus, and believe that it was at Amwas, not far from Latrun.

And, behold, two of them went that same day to a village called Emmaus, which was from Jerusalem about threescore furlongs.

And they talked together of all these things which had happened.

And it came to pass, that, while they communed together and reasoned, Jesus himself drew near, and went with them.

But their eyes were holden that they should not know him.

And he said unto them, What manner of communication are these that ye have one to another, as ye walk, and are sad?

And the one of them, whose name was Cleopas, answering said unto him, Art thou only a stranger in Jerusalem, and hast not known the things which are come to pass there in these days?

And he said unto them, What things? And they said unto him, Concerning Jesus of Nazareth, which was a prophet mighty in deed and word before God and all the people:

And how the chief priests and our rulers delivered him to be condemned to death, and have crucified him.

But we trusted that it had been he which should have redeemed Israel: and beside all this, to day is the third day since these things were done.

Yea, and certain women also of our company made us astonished, which were early at the sepulchre;

205. Remains outside the house where Jesus met two of his disciples at Emmaus.

And when they found not his body, they came, saying, that they had also seen a vision of angels, which said that he was alive.

And certain of them which were with us went to the sepulchre, and found it even so as the women had said: but him they saw not.

Then he said unto them, O fools, and slow of heart to believe all that the prophets have spoken:

Ought not Christ to have suffered these things, and to enter into his glory?

And beginning at Moses and all the prophets, he expounded unto them in all the scriptures the things concerning himself.

And they drew nigh unto the village, whither they went: and he made as though he would have gone further.

But they constrained him, saying, Abide with us: for it is toward evening, and the day is far spent. And he went in to tarry with them.

And it came to pass, as he sat at meat with them, he took bread, and blessed it, and brake, and gave to them.

And their eyes were opened, and they knew him; and he vanished out of their sight.

And they said one to another, Did not our heart burn within us, while he talked with us by the way, and while he opened to us the scriptures?

And they rose up the same hour, and returned to Jerusalem, and found the eleven gathered together, and them that were with them,

Saying, The Lord is risen indeed, and hath appeared to Simon.

And they told what things were done in the way, and how he was known of them in breaking of bread.

And as they thus spake, Jesus himself stood in the midst of them, and saith unto them, Peace be unto you. But they were terrified and affrighted, and supposed that they had seen a spirit. And he said unto them, Why are ye troubled? and why do thoughts arise in your hearts?

Behold my hands and my feet, that it is I myself: handle me, and see; for a spirit hath not flesh and bones, as ye see me have.   (24:13–39)

And he said unto them, These are the words which I spake unto you, while I was yet with you, that all things must be fulfilled, which were written in the law of Moses, and in the prophets, and in the psalms, concerning me.

Then opened he their understanding, that they might understand the scriptures, And said unto them, Thus it is written, and thus it behoved Christ to suffer, and to rise from the dead the third day:

And that repentance and remission of sins should be preached in his name among all nations, beginning at Jerusalem. And ye are witnesses of these things.

And, behold, I send the promise of my Father upon you: but tarry ye in the city of Jerusalem, until ye be endued with power from on high.

And he led them out as far as to Bethany, and he lifted up his hands, and blessed them.

And it came to pass, while he blessed them, he was parted from them, and carried up into heaven.

And they worshipped him, and returned to Jerusalem with great joy:

And were continually in the temple, praising and blessing God. Amen.
(24:44–53)

206. The rock bearing what is said to be the footprint of Jesus, inside the Dome of the Ascension.

207. Dome of the Ascension, with Jerusalem in the background.

The Dome is built in the place traditionally believed to be where Christ ascended to heaven. A church was built here originally at the end of the 4th century, though it is not mentioned in historical sources until the 7th century. The original church was destroyed in the 10th century.

In the 12th century the Crusaders built a new church, whose general plan is preserved to this day. The church was built as a fortress and served as part of a chain of fortresses between Jerusalem and Jericho. It is octagonal in shape, with a guard tower and loopholes in the walls. The structure houses a stone bearing the reputed footprint of Jesus. Crusader inscriptions may still be seen today, with rich decoration of foliage, as well as capitals with griffins.

With the conquests of Saladin the site passed into the hands of the Moslems. They changed the building little, closing the dome, previously open at the top, and the space between pillars, and moving the stone with the footprint to the south.

Once a year the festival of the Ascension is celebrated at the site.

206

208. Tower of the Russian church commemorating the Ascension on the Mount of Olives.

The tower contains 214 steps and its summit commands a marvelous view of Jerusalem and its environs, the Judean Desert, the Dead Sea, the Jordan Valley and the mountains of Edom east of the Jordan.

When the church was being built the remains of ancient buildings were discovered, including those of an Armenian church from Byzantine times, 5th/6th centuries A.D. These remains include rich mosaics with old Armenian inscriptions.

In the beginning was the Word, and the Word was with God, and the Word was God.

The same was in the beginning with God.

All things were made by him; and without him was not any thing made that was made.

In him was life; and the life was the light of men.

And the light shineth in darkness; and the darkness comprehended it not.

There was a man sent from God, whose name was John.

The same came for a witness, to bear witness of the Light, that all men through him might believe.

He was not that Light, but was sent to bear witness of that Light.

That was the true Light, which lighteth every man that cometh into the world.

He was in the world, and the world was made by him, and the world knew him not.

He came unto his own, and his own received him not.

But as many as received him, to them gave he power to become the sons of God, even to them that believe on his name:

Which were born, not of blood, nor of the will of the flesh, nor of the will of man, but of God.

And the Word was made flesh, and dwelt among us, (and we beheld his glory, the glory as of the only begotten of the Father,) full of grace and truth.

John bare witness of him, and cried, saying, This was he of whom I spake, He that cometh after me is preferred before me: for he was before me.

And of his fulness have all we received, and grace for grace.

For the law was given by Moses, but grace and truth came by Jesus Christ.

No man hath seen God at any time; the only begotten Son, which is in the bosom of the Father, he hath declared him.   (1:1–18)

The next day John seeth Jesus coming unto him, and saith, Behold the Lamb of God, which taketh away the sin of the world.

This is he of whom I said, After me cometh a man which is preferred before me: for he was before me.

And I knew him not: but that he should be made manifest to Israel, therefore am I come baptizing with water.

And John bare record, saying, I saw the Spirit descending from heaven like a dove, and it abode upon him.

And I knew him not: but he that sent me to baptize with water, the same said unto me, Upon whom thou shalt see the Spirit descending, and remaining on him, the same is he which baptizeth with the Holy Ghost.

And I saw, and bare record that this is the Son of God.   (1:29–34)

The day following Jesus would go forth into Galilee, and findeth Philip, and saith unto him, Follow me.

Now Philip was of Bethsaida, the city of Andrew and Peter.

Philip findeth Nathanael, and saith unto him, We have found him, of whom Moses in the law, and the prophets, did write, Jesus of Nazareth, the son of Joseph.

209. John the Baptist dressed in goatskin, with a lamb in a medallion; detail from a carved ivory plaque, 6th century (Museo dell'Arcivescovado, Ravenna).
In the Gospel of John, the function of John the Baptist is hinted at by means of several key words which indicate his ministry. The first of these is the word "behold". First used in verse 14 in relation to the Transfiguration on the Mount (see also Matthew 17:1–3, 5; Luke 9:32; 2 Peter 1:16–18), it recurs in verse 29, where John the Baptist declares "Behold the Lamb of God." In verse 22, John says that he "saw" or "beheld", the Spirit descending from heaven like a dove." In verse 36 John again says to two of his disciples "Behold the Lamb of God".

210. The site of Bethsaida (House of the Fisherman), on the northeastern shore of the Sea of Galilee. It was a fisherman's village as its name implies. The site of the village itself has never been identified precisely.
Here Jesus healed the blind, as told in Mark 8:22; it was also one of the cities he reproached and even cursed (Matthew 8:22, Luke 10:13).

And Nathanael said unto him, Can there any good thing come out of Nazareth? Philip saith unto him, Come and see.

Jesus saw Nathanael coming to him, and saith of him, Behold an Israelite indeed, in whom is no guile!

Nathanael saith unto him, Whence knowest thou me? Jesus answered and said unto him, Before that Philip called thee, when thou wast under the fig tree, I saw thee.

Nathanael answered and saith unto him, Rabbi, thou art the Son of God; thou art the King of Israel.

Jesus answered and said unto him, Because I said unto thee, I saw thee under the fig tree, believest thou? thou shalt see greater things than these.

And he saith unto him, Verily, verily, I say unto you, Hereafter ye shall see heaven open, and the angels of God ascending and descending upon the Son of man. (1:43–51)

And the third day there was a marriage in Cana of Galilee; and the mother of Jesus was there: And both Jesus was called, and his disciples, to the marriage. And when they wanted wine, the mother of Jesus saith unto him, They have no wine. Jesus saith unto her, Woman, what have I to do with thee? mine hour is not yet come.

His mother saith unto the servants, Whatsoever he saith unto you, do it.

And there were set there six waterpots of stone, after the manner of the purifying of the Jews, containing two or three firkins apiece.

Jesus saith unto them, Fill the waterpots with water. And they filled them up to the brim.

And he saith unto them, Draw out now, and bear unto the governor of the feast. And they bare it.

When the ruler of the feast had tasted the water that was made wine, and knew not whence it was: (but the servants which drew the water knew;) the governor of the feast called the bridegroom,

And saith unto him, Every man at the beginning doth set forth good wine; and when men have well drunk, then that which is worse: but thou hast kept the good wine until now.

This beginning of miracles did Jesus in Cana of Galilee, and manifested forth his glory; and his disciples believed on him.

(2:1–11)

211. A general view of Cana (Kefar Kana as it is known today), in a small valley northeast of Nazareth in the Galilee.
The village, with its setting of olive and pomegranate trees, has not changed much since the time of Jesus.
The village was on the Nazareth-Tiberias road and has been identified with the Cana of the Gospels since Byzantine times.
A Jewish settlement existed there in the 15th-16th centuries. The village today numbers about 5000 inhabitants, most of whom are Christian, and the rest Moslem.

212. Two churches commemorate Jesus' first miracle at Cana: One is a Greek Orthodox church in which one can see a pitcher – with no claim to authenticity – recalling the miracle. The other church, in the center of the village, is a Franciscan one, built in 1879. It also has an old jar, believed to be a replica of the one used in the miracle. The chapel adjoining the Franciscan church stands on what is believed to be the site of the house of Nathanel. The church itself was built on the remains of a 4th-century synagogue, of which a mosaic floor has been unearthed.

Then cometh he to a city of Samaria, which is called Sychar, near to the parcel of ground that Jacob gave to his son Joseph.

Now Jacob's well was there. Jesus therefore, being wearied with his journey, sat thus on the well: and it was about the sixth hour.

There cometh a woman of Samaria to draw water: Jesus saith unto her, Give me to drink.

(For his disciples were gone away unto the city to buy meat.)

Then saith the woman of Samaria unto him, How is it that thou, being a Jew, askest drink of me, which am a woman of Samaria? for the Jews have no dealings with the Samaritans.

Jesus answered and said unto her, If thou knewest the gift of God, and who it is that saith to thee, Give me to drink; thou wouldest have asked of him, and he would have given thee living water.

The woman saith unto him, Sir, thou hast nothing to draw with, and the well is deep: from whence then hast thou that living water?

213. A view of Samaria, through which Jesus passed on his way from Galilee to Jerusalem.

213

214. View of Nablus (Shechem) and Mount Gerizim in Samaria. This is the religious center of the Samaritan sect.

The Samaritans were an Israelite sect in Second Temple times. Today there are only a few hundred of them left, mostly in Nablus – the biblical Shechem called Sychar in the New Testament. They recognize only the Pentateuch as the true Scripture.

When the king of Assyria conquered the Kingdom of Israel and its capital Samaria in 732 B.C., he took into captivity many of the leading citizens, and in their place settled people from five of his provinces. These people, who were pagan, mingled in Samaria with the Israelite inhabitants (II Kings 17:24), and in time they adopted the Mosaic law, without entirely giving up their own traditions.

In 586 B.C., the Kingdom of Judah, with its capital, Jerusalem, was conquered by Babylon and some of its population was exiled. After the return when Ezra and Nehemiah wanted to rebuild the Temple, the Samaritans, claiming to be of the faith of Moses, wanted to participate in the undertaking. But the religion of the Samaritans was suspect in the eyes of the returning priesthood, who rejected the Samaritans and refused their help. In retaliation the Samaritans made things as difficult as possible, resorting to various means to stop the construction of the Temple.

When the Samaritans found that they were barred from participating in the reconstruction of the Temple in Jerusalem, they built their own temple on Mount Gerizim, and set themselves apart from the mainstream of Judaism.

Samaria, as well as the temple on Mount Gerizim, was destroyed by Alexander the Great in 331 B.C. and rebuilt once again by John Hyrcanus in 108 B.C.

In 64 B.C. the Romans took Samaria, and in 27 B.C. Herod the Great began to develop the city. He renamed it Sebaste – a Greek form of the name Augustus – in honor of the Roman emperor.

The Samaritans prospered under Roman rule, and had enough influence in Rome to cause the dismissal of Pontius Pilate in A.D. 36, who had had a great number of Samaritans massacred on Mount Gerizim.

215. A view of Mount Gerizim from Mount Ebal.

The Samaritans hold Moses to have been God's only prophet, and Mount Gerizim His unique sanctuary. The Ten Commandments are counted as nine by the Samaritans who added a tenth of their own – the sanctity of Mount Gerizim.

Samaritan ritual law generally adheres to the biblical, as in the laws of the Sabbath and festivals. When praying, the Samaritans, like the Jews, wrap themselves in prayer shawls; like the Moslems they take off their shoes to enter the house of worship.

The Samaritan principal holy day is Passover, when the Samaritans sacrifice the paschal lamb on Mount Gerizim, where all the mem-

Art thou greater than our father Jacob, which gave us the well, and drank thereof himself, and his children, and his cattle?

Jesus answered and said unto her, Whosoever drinketh of this water shall thirst again:

But whosoever drinketh of the water that I shall give him shall never thirst; but the water that I shall give him shall be in him a well of water springing up into everlasting life.

The woman saith unto him, Sir, give me this water, that I thirst not, neither come hither to draw.

Jesus saith unto her, Go, call thy husband, and come hither.

The woman answered and said, I have no husband. Jesus said unto her, Thou hast well said, I have no husband:

For thou hast had five husbands; and he whom thou now hast is not thy husband: in that saidst thou truly.

The woman saith unto him, Sir, I perceive that thou art a prophet.

Our fathers worshipped in this mountain; and ye say, that in Jerusalem is the place where men ought to worship.

Jesus saith unto her, Woman, believe me, the hour cometh, when ye shall neither in this mountain, nor yet at Jerusalem, worship the Father.

Ye worship ye know not what: we know what we worship: for salvation is of the Jews.

But the hour cometh, and now is, when the true worshippers shall worship the Father in spirit and in truth: for the Father seeketh such to worship him.

God is a Spirit: and they that worship him must worship him in spirit and in truth.

The woman saith unto him, I know that Messias cometh, which is called Christ: when he is come, he will tell us all things.

Jesus saith unto her, I that speak unto thee am he.

And upon this came his disciples, and marvelled that he talked with the woman: yet no man said, What seekest thou? or, Why talkest thou with her?

The woman then left her waterpot, and went her way into the city, and saith to the men,

Come, see a man, which told me all things that ever I did: is not this the Christ?

Then they went out of the city, and came unto him.

(4:5–30)

216

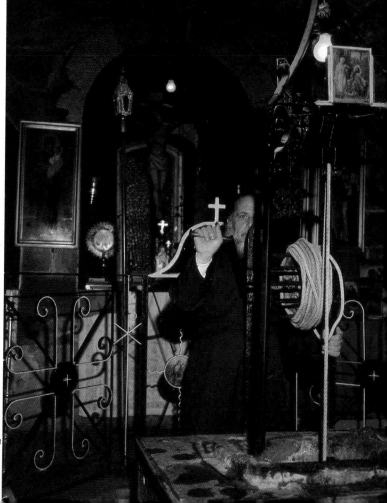
218

219

After this there was a feast of the Jews; and Jesus went up to Jerusalem.

Now there is at Jerusalem by the sheep market a pool, which is called in the Hebrew tongue Bethesda, having five porches.

In these lay a great multitude of impotent folk, of blind halt, withered, waiting for the moving of the water.

For an angel went down at a certain season into the pool, and troubled the water: whosoever then first after the troubling of the water stepped in was made whole of whatsoever disease he had.

And a certain man was there, which had an infirmity thirty and eight years.

When Jesus saw him lie, and knew that he had been now a long time in that case, he saith unto him, Wilt thou be made whole?

The impotent man answered him, Sir, I have no man, when the water is troubled, to put me into the pool: but while I am coming, another steppeth down before me.

Jesus saith unto him, Rise, take up thy bed, and walk.

And immediately the man was made whole, and took up his bed, and walked: and on the same day was the sabbath.

The Jews therefore said unto him that was cured, It is the sabbath day: it is not lawful for thee to carry thy bed.

He answered them, He that made me whole, the same said unto me, Take up thy bed, and walk.

(5:1–11)

bers of the community assemble and spend the entire week of Passover.

On the first day they gather around the altar. The high priest stands on a rock and reads the story of the Exodus from Egypt, while the sheep are being slaughtered according to ritual, one sheep for every family in the community. The meat is later roasted and eaten with bitter herbs and unleavened bread.

216. Samaritan high priest showing the Samaritan Pentateuch. The Scroll is eight hundred years old; it is written in gold letters in three parallel columns – in Hebrew, Aramaic and Arabic – and wound on two silver rollers.

217. An unfinished Greek Orthodox monastery built over Jacob's Well in Shechem (Nablus).

The Old Testament does not relate that Jacob dug a well there, but only that "he bought a parcel of a field, where he had spread his tent, at the hand of the children of Hamor, Shechem's father . . ." (Genesis 33:19).

218. Jacob's Well inside the Greek monastery, built in the 19th century, over the remains of several churches of the Byzantine period.

219. St Anne's Church.

North of the area of the Temple Mount, near the Gate of St. Stephen, was the Convent of St Anne. The convent is by the "Sheep Pool," or the Pool of Bethesda. Ever since the 4th century this has been shown as the dwelling of the parents of the Virgin Mary, Anne and Joachim. The present church was built in 1140. The building is not symmetrical, and was apparently erected on the foundations of the earlier Byzantine church.

Saladin converted the church into a Moslem theological college. The building was subsequently used for stabling and storage, and in 1856 it was given to the French government, by whom it was restored.

220. The Pool of Bethesda, near St. Stephen's Gate in Jerusalem. Nearby stands St. Anne's Church, built by the Crusaders.

The water of the pool was believed to have curative powers, and invalids used to throng to it. A Jewish legend mentions an angel who

But I have greater witness than that of John: for the works which the Father hath given me to finish, the same works that I do, bear witness of me, that the Father hath sent me.

And the Father himself, which hath sent me, hath borne witness of me. Ye have neither heard his voice at any time, nor seen his shape.

And ye have not his word abiding in you: for whom he hath sent, him ye believe not.

Search the scriptures; for in them ye think ye have eternal life: and they are they which testify of me.

And ye will not come to me, that ye might have life.

I receive not honour from men.

But I know you, that ye have not the love of God in you.

I am come in my Father's name, and ye receive me not: if another shall come in his own name, him ye will receive.

How can ye believe, which receive honour one of another, and seek not the honour that cometh from God only?

Do not think that I will accuse you to the Father: there is one that accuseth you, even Moses, in whom ye trust.

For had ye believed Moses, ye would have believed me: for he wrote of me.

But if ye believe not his writings, how shall ye believe my words?

(5:36–47)

entered the water from time to time, making it boil, guaranteeing a cure to any invalid who entered the bubbling pool. It is possible that the pool may have stemmed from a now-dry thermal spring.

221. Young woman reading; terracotta figurine from the Greek island of Lymnos 3rd-2nd century B.C. (Louvre, Paris).
The end of chapter 5 of the Gospel of John gives the Son of God's four-fold testimony: the testimony of John the Baptist (verses 31–35); the testimony of the Son's work (verse 36); the testimony of the Father (verses 37–38); and lastly the testimony of the Scriptures. Jesus points out that "searching the scriptures" is not the same as "coming to me," even though it is the Scriptures themselves which testify concerning the Lord.
Like Paul, who distinguishes between the dead letter and the living word, Jesus emphasizes the need to touch the life in the Scriptures to "come to me that ye might have life."

And as Jesus passed by, he saw a man which was blind from his birth.

And his disciples asked him, saying, Master, who did sin, this man, or his parents, that he was born blind?

Jesus answered, Neither hath this man sinned, nor his parents: but that the works of God should be made manifest in him.

I must work the works of him that sent me, while it is day: the night cometh, when no man can work.

As long as I am in the world, I am the light of the world.

When he had thus spoken, he spat on the ground, and made clay of the spittle, and he anointed the eyes of the blind man with the clay,

And said unto him, Go, wash in the pool of Siloam, (which is by interpretation, Sent.) He went his way therefore, and washed, and came seeing.

The neighbours therefore, and they which before had seen him that he was blind, said, Is not this he that sat and begged?

Some said, This is he: others said, He is like him: but he said, I am he.

Therefore said they unto him, How were thine eyes opened?

He answered and said, A man that is called Jesus made clay, and anointed mine eyes, and said unto me, Go to the pool of Siloam, and wash: and I went and washed, and I received sight.

(9:1–11)

222. Another famous pool in Jerusalem: the Pool of Siloam, south of the city. The pool is fed by the Gihon spring through a channel cut in the rock by King Hezekiah, as described in the Second Book of the Kings (20:20), and in the Second Book of the Chronicles (32:4). Ancient traditions ascribe therapeutic properties to the waters of Siloam to this day. The Moslems still consider the pool as a holy place, as the Christians once did. On Fridays, men, women and children come and pour water over themselves in hope of being healed of some sickness. Jews also visit here at the Feast of Tabernacles.

And it was at Jerusalem the feast of the dedication, and it was winter.
And Jesus walked in the temple in Solomon's porch.

Then came the Jews round about him, and said unto him, How long dost
thou make us to doubt? If thou be the Christ, tell us plainly.

Jesus answered them, I told you, and ye believed not: the works that I do
in my Father's name, they bear witness of me.

But ye believe not, because ye are not of my sheep, as I said unto you.
My sheep hear my voice, and I know them, and they follow me:

And I give unto them eternal life; and they shall never perish, neither
shall any man pluck them out of my hand.

My Father, which gave them me, is greater than all; and no man is able
to pluck them out of my Father's hand.

I and my Father are one.

Then the Jews took up stones again to stone him. (10:22–31)

Now a certain man was sick, named Lazarus, of Bethany, the town of
Mary and her sister Martha.

(It was that Mary which anointed the Lord with ointment, and wiped
his feet with her hair, whose brother Lazarus was sick.)

Therefore his sisters sent unto him, saying, Lord, behold, he whom thou
lovest is sick.

When Jesus heard that, he said, This sickness is not unto death, but for
the glory of God, that the Son of God might be glorified thereby.

Now Jesus loved Martha, and her sister, and Lazarus.

When he had heard therefore that he was sick, he abode two days still in
the same place where he was.

Then after that saith he to his disciples, Let us go into Judaea again.
(11:1–7)

223. Hanukkah stone lamp from the Talmudic period with eight spouts (Einhorn Collection, Tel Aviv).

The "feast of dedication" refers to the festival of Hanukkah, celebrated about December. According to a well-founded tradition it was instituted by Judah Maccabee and his followers, to commemorate the rededication of the altar in the Temple which had been defiled during the Maccabean wars. The Second Book of Maccabees relates that the eight-day dedication ceremony was performed in the manner of Solomon's dedication of the First Temple in 1 Kings 8. Josephus calls it the Festival of Lights and says that the right to serve God came to the people unexpectedly, like a sudden light.

Then when Jesus came, he found that he had lain in the grave four days already.

Now Bethany was nigh unto Jerusalem, about fifteen furlongs off:

And many of the Jews came to Martha and Mary, to comfort them concerning their brother.

Then Martha, as soon as she heard that Jesus was coming, went and met him: but Mary sat still in the house.

Then said Martha unto Jesus, Lord, if thou hadst been here, my brother had not died.

But I know, that even now, whatsoever thou wilt ask of God, God will give it thee.

Jesus saith unto her, Thy brother shall rise again.

Martha saith unto him, I know that he shall rise again in the resurrection at the last day.

Jesus said unto her, I am the resurrection, and the life: he that believeth in me, though he were dead, yet shall he live:

And whosoever liveth and believeth in me shall never die. Believest thou this?

She saith unto him, Yea, Lord: I believe that thou art the Christ, the Son of God, which should come into the world.

(11:17–27)

When Jesus therefore saw her weeping, and the Jews also weeping which came with her, he groaned in the spirit, and was troubled,

And said, Where have ye laid him? They said unto him, Lord, come and see.

Jesus wept.

Then said the Jews, Behold how he loved him!

And some of them said, Could not this man, which opened the eyes of the blind, have caused that even this man should not have died?

Jesus therefore again groaning in himself cometh to the grave. It was a cave, and a stone lay upon it.

Jesus said, Take ye away the stone. Martha, the sister of him that was dead, saith unto him, Lord, by this time he stinketh: for he hath been dead four days.

Jesus saith unto her, Said I not unto thee, that, if thou wouldest believe, thou shouldest see the glory of God?

Then they took away the stone from the place where the dead was laid. And Jesus lifted up his eyes, and said, Father, I thank thee that thou hast heard me.

And I knew that thou hearest me always: but because of the people which stand by I said it, that they may believe that thou hast sent me.

And when he thus had spoken, he cried with a loud voice, Lazarus, come forth.

And he that was dead came forth, bound hand and foot with grave-clothes: and his face was bound about with a napkin. Jesus saith unto them, Loose him, and let him go.

Then many of the Jews which came to Mary, and had seen the things which Jesus did, believed on him.

(11:33–45)

224. Steps leading to Lazarus' tomb in Bethany, carved out of the rock in the hillside. The grotto on the site of the tomb was made into a shrine in the 4th century.

225. A view of Bethany with the silver dome of the Church of Lazarus in the center.

226. The Church of Lazarus at Bethany.

227. The events in Bethany depicted on the lintel of the portals of the Church of the Holy Sepulcher by Crusader artists.
They are carved on a fine marble plaque. In one scene Jesus stands. He is wearing a toga over a tunic, his right hand is raised in blessing, his left hand holds the edge of the toga, with an open book resting upon the arm. His blessing is directed towards two women, Martha, who kisses his feet, and Mary, who raises her hands in worship. The women wear veils, wrapped around and draped.
The second scene is the resurrection of Lazarus: Jesus holds an open book in his left hand and blesses with his right hand. Martha raises both hands in thanksgiving. On the side, two figures roll away the stone at the entrance to the tomb. Lazarus, revived, stands by the tomb. He is surrounded by women raising their hands, others putting their hands to their faces.

228. Model of the house of Caiaphas, reconstructed on the basis of excavations conducted in the courtyard of the Armenian Monastery of St. Savior, just outside Zion Gate. The Pilgrim of Bordeaux, who visited the Holy Land in A.D. 333, mentions that the house of the high priest Caiaphas had stood in this place.

Joseph Caiaphas was the son-in-law of Annas (John 18:13). He was of the Sadducee party which cooperated with the Roman authorities. Here Caiaphas unwittingly prophesied that Jesus was to die for the nation of the Jews. Later, when Jesus was brought before the Sanhedrin, it was Caiaphas who put the crucial question to Jesus.

Then gathered the chief priests and the Pharisees a council, and said, What do we? for this man doeth many miracles.

If we let him thus alone, all men will believe on him: and the Romans shall come and take away both our place and nation.

And one of them, named Caiaphas, being the high priest that same year, said unto them, Ye know nothing at all,

Nor consider that it is expedient for us, that one man should die for the people, and that the whole nation perish not.

And this spake he not of himself: but being high priest that year, he prophesied that Jesus should die for that nation;

And not for that nation only, but that also he should gather together in one the children of God that were scattered abroad.

Then from that day forth they took counsel together for to put him to death.

(11:47–53)

229. Large ceramic basin, with "foot-support" in the middle, probably used for foot washing, 2nd century B.C. (Israel Department of Antiquities, Jerusalem).

In the Middle East, where the climate is generally warm, and where people wore open sandals and traveled on foot on dusty roads, washing a guest's feet was a gesture of profound respect. Generally, the host would provide vessels and water for visitors to wash their own feet.

There are many examples of this custom in the Old Testament, as, for instance, in the story of David and Abigail (I Judges, 25:41).

Now before the feast of the passover, when Jesus knew that his hour was come that he should depart out of this world unto the Father, having loved his own which were in the world, he loved them unto the end.

And supper being ended, the devil having now put into the heart of Judas Iscariot, Simon's son, to betray him;

Jesus knowing that the Father had given all things into his hands, and that he was come from God, and went to God;

He riseth from supper, and laid aside his garments; and took a towel, and girded himself.

After that he poureth water into a bason, and began to wash the disciples' feet, and to wipe them with the towel wherewith he was girded.

Then cometh he to Simon Peter: and Peter saith unto him, Lord, dost thou wash my feet?

Jesus answered and said unto him, What I do thou knowest not now; but thou shalt know hereafter.

Peter saith unto him, Thou shalt never wash my feet. Jesus answered him, If I wash thee not, thou hast no part with me.

Simon Peter saith unto him, Lord, not my feet only, but also my hands and my head.

Jesus saith to him, He that is washed needeth not save to wash his feet, but is clean every whit: and ye are clean, but not all.

For he knew who should betray him; therefore said he, Ye are not all clean.

So after he had washed their feet, and had taken his garments, and was set down again, he said unto them, Know ye what I have done to you?

Ye call me Master and Lord: and ye say well; for so I am.

If I then, your Lord and Master, have washed your feet; ye also ought to wash one another's feet.

For I have given you an example, that ye should do as I have done to you.

Verily, verily, I say unto you, The servant is not greater than his lord; neither he that is sent greater than he that sent him.

If ye know these things, happy are ye if ye do them.

230. Part of one of the carved marble plaques that were above the portals of the Holy Sepulcher, depicting the Last Supper. Jesus sits at a curved table covered with a cloth, flanked by his disciples. Judas Iscariot is before the table. The disciple whose head is held by Jesus – and who is not named in the New Testament – is traditionally thought to be John.

I speak not of you all: I know whom I have chosen: but that the scripture may be fulfilled, He that eateth bread with me hath lifted up his heel against me.

Now I tell you before it come, that, when it is come to pass, ye may believe that I am he.

Verily, verily, I say unto you, He that receiveth whomsoever I send receiveth me; and he that receiveth me receiveth him that sent me.

When Jesus had thus said, he was troubled in spirit, and testified, and said, Verily, verily, I say unto you, that one of you shall betray me.

Then the disciples looked one on another, doubting of whom he spake.

Now there was leaning on Jesus' bosom one of his disciples, whom Jesus loved. (13:1–23)

I am the true vine, and my Father is the husbandman.

231. Vine, "husbandmen," and basket of fruit on a Byzantine mosaic floor from Beth-shean.
The vine symbolizes Christ and the believers. Christ is the true vine, whose branches are the believers, abiding in fruitful union with Him. God, the Father, is the husbandman, the cultivator, the source of life, substance, soil, water, air and sunshine to the vine. These verses give a marvellous picture of the vine and the branches as a living organism, to glorify the Father by expressing the riches of the divine life.

Every branch in me that beareth not fruit he taketh away: and every branch that beareth fruit, he purgeth it, that it may bring forth more fruit.

Now ye are clean through the word which I have spoken unto you.

Abide in me, and I in you. As the branch cannot bear fruit of itself, except it abide in the vine; no more can ye, except ye abide in me.

I am the vine, ye are the branches: He that abideth in me, and I in him, the same bringeth forth much fruit: for without me ye can do nothing.

If a man abide not in me, he is cast forth as a branch, and is withered; and men gather them, and cast them into the fire, and they are burned.

If ye abide in me, and my words abide in you, ye shall ask what ye will, and it shall be done unto you. Herein is my Father glorified, that ye bear much fruit; so shall ye be my disciples.

As the Father hath loved me, so have I loved you: continue ye in my love.

If ye keep my commandments, ye shall abide in my love; even as I have kept my Father's commandments, and abide in his love.

These things have I spoken unto you, that my joy might remain in you, and that your joy might be full. This is my commandment, That ye love one another, as I have loved you. Greater love hath no man than this, that a man lay down his life for his friends.

Ye are my friends, if ye do whatsoever I command you.

Henceforth I call you not servants; for the servant knoweth not what his lord doeth: but I have called you friends; for all things that I have heard of my Father I have made known unto you.

Ye have not chosen me, but I have chosen you, and ordained you, that ye should go and bring forth fruit, and that your fruit should remain: that whatsoever ye shall ask of the Father in my name, he may give it you.

(15:1–16)

When Jesus had spoken these words, he went forth with his disciples over the brook Cedron, where was a garden, into the which he entered, and his disciples. And Judas also, which betrayed him, knew the place: for Jesus ofttimes resorted thither with his disciples.

Judas then, having received a band of men and officers from the chief priests and Pharisees, cometh thither with lanterns and torches and weapons.

Jesus therefore, knowing all things that should come upon him, went forth, and said unto them, Whom seek ye?

They answered him, Jesus of Nazareth. Jesus saith unto them, I am he. And Judas also, which betrayed him, stood with them.

As soon then as he had said unto them, I am he, they went backward, and fell to the ground. Then asked he them again, Whom seek ye? And they said, Jesus of Nazareth.

Jesus answered, I have told you that I am he: if therefore ye seek me, let these go their way: That the saying might be fulfilled, which he spake, Of them which thou gavest me have I lost none.

(18:1–9)

232. The Grotto of the Betrayal, on the Mount of Olives.
From this spot, it is said, Jesus went out to meet his captors.

Then the band and the captain and officers of the Jews took Jesus, and bound him,

And led him away to Annas first; for he was father in law to Caiaphas, which was the high priest that same year.

Now Caiaphas was he, which gave counsel to the Jews, that it was expedient that one man should die for the people.

And Simon Peter followed Jesus, and so did another disciple: that disciple was known unto the high priest, and went in with Jesus into the palace of the high priest.

But Peter stood at the door without. Then went out that other disciple, which was known unto the high priest, and spake unto her that kept the door, and brought in Peter.

Then saith the damsel that kept the door unto Peter, Art not thou also one of this man's disciples? He saith, I am not.

And the servants and officers stood there, who had made a fire of coals; for it was cold: and they warmed themselves: and Peter stood with them, and warmed himself.

The high priest then asked Jesus of his disciples, and of his doctrine.

Jesus answered him, I spake openly to the world; I ever taught in the synagogue, and in the temple, whither the Jews always resort; and in secret have I said nothing.

Why askest thou me? ask them which heard me, what I have said unto them: behold, they know what I said.

And when he had thus spoken, one of the officers which stood by struck Jesus with the palm of his hand, saying, Answerest thou the high priest so?

Jesus answered him, If I have spoken evil, bear witness of the evil: but if well, why smitest thou me? Now Annas had sent him bound unto Caiaphas the high priest.   (18:12–24)

233. Under the Church of Gallicantu is a vast burial place with many chambers. Tradition places the palace of Caiaphas here, and the chamber shown is believed to have been the prison of the high priest's palace.

Pilate saith unto him, What is truth? And when he had said this he went out again unto the Jews, and saith unto them, I find in him no fault at all.

But ye have a custom, that I should release unto you one at the passover: will ye therefore that I release unto you the King of the Jews?

Then cried they all again, saying, Not this man, but Barabbas. Now Barabbas was a robber.

(18:38–40)

234. Among the many caves along the Way of the Cross in the Old City, the Greek Orthodox community in Jerusalem points out this cave as the prison of Christ, or perhaps of Barabbas.

235. The Chapel of the Flagellation, close to St. Stephen's Gate, recalls Jesus' scourging on Pilate's orders. The ceiling of the chapel is decorated with a mosaic in the form of a crown of thorns.

236. A branch of thorns from the tree known as the Christ-thorn *(Zizyphus spina Christi)*, which grows in almost every part of the Holy Land. Some of these Christ-thorn trees are hundreds of years old and of considerable size. They are traditionally associated with the crown of thorns that the Roman soldiers mockingly set on Jesus' head.

Then Pilate therefore took Jesus, and scourged him.

And the soldiers platted a crown of thorns, and put it on his head, and they put on him a purple robe,

And said, Hail, King of the Jews! and they smote him with their hands.

(19:1–3)

When Pilate therefore heard that saying, he brought Jesus forth, and sat down in the judgment seat in a place that is called the Pavement, but in the Hebrew, Gabbatha.

And it was the preparation of the passover, and about the sixth hour: and he saith unto the Jews, Behold your King!

But they cried out, Away with him, away with him, crucify him. Pilate saith unto them, Shall I crucify your King? The chief priests answered, We have no king but Caesar.

Then delivered he him therefore unto them to be crucified. And they took Jesus, and led him away.

And he bearing his cross went forth into a place called the place of a skull, which is called in the Hebrew Golgotha:

Where they crucified him, and two other with him, on either side one, and Jesus in the midst.

(19:13–18)

237. A street in the Old City of Jerusalem, part of the Via Dolorosa, the path followed by Jesus when he left the Praetorium after his trial and on his way to the place of crucifixion on Golgotha.

It was only in the 14th century that the Via Dolorosa acquired its spiritual significance. It was at this time that the Franciscan friars held their first afternoon procession along the Via Dolorosa, carrying heavy crosses on their backs. The custom has survived to this day, and many pilgrims join the weekly procession. The exact route of the Way of the Cross is still disputed by scholars, as are the sites of the Stations along it. Only some of these are mentioned in the New Testament, others were adopted by popular tradition. Churches and shrines mark nine Stations on the Via Dolorosa, each one commemorating one of the dramatic incidents which occurred on Jesus' last journey. There are fourteen Stations altogether, and the last five are inside the Church of the Holy Sepulcher.

238. Facade of the Holy Sepulcher in one of the alleys of the Old City of Jerusalem.
The Church of the Holy Sepulcher was built on the traditional site of Jesus' crucifixion and burial. The church encloses both, since as John says: "the tomb was close at hand."
The church stands inside the northwest quarter of the wall of the Old City of Jerusalem. During the first two centuries A.D. the early Christians were persecuted and unable to make pilgrimages or to build conspicuous shrines. In 135 the emperor Hadrian destroyed Jerusalem and built in its place a pagan city which he named Aelia Capitolina. Over the place where the tomb of Jesus is now shown was built a shrine to Venus and a statue of Jupiter, with the aim of discouraging Christians from visiting the spot. Ironically, this served to mark the site permanently. Thus it remained until 326, when Emperor Constantine officially recognized the church. The Emperor's mother Helena visited the Holy Land, seeking traces of the life and death of Jesus. She established the place of his birth at Bethlehem and that of his crucifixion and resurrection in Jerusalem. On these sites splendid churches were built, relics of which are embodied in the Church of the Nativity and the Church of the Holy Sepulcher – which later was called Anastasis (Resurrection).
The grandiose monument that Constantine built over the Holy Sepulcher and the Calvary was inaugurated in 335. It was burned by the Persians in the 7th century, restored on a more modest scale, and destroyed again by the caliph al-Hakim in c. 1009. It was restored by the Byzantine emperor Constantine Monomachus some forty years later. In the 12th century the Crusaders carried out a general reconstruction of the church.
Since then, war, fires, earthquakes and natural deterioration caused the edifice to be restored and remodeled several times. The present church dates mainly from the early 19th century.

237

And after this Joseph of Arimathaea, being a disciple of Jesus, but secretly for fear of the Jews, besought Pilate that he might take away the body of Jesus: and Pilate gave him leave. He came therefore, and took the body of Jesus.

And there came also Nicodemus, which at the first came to Jesus by night, and brought a mixture of myrrh and aloes, about an hundred pound weight.

Then took they the body of Jesus, and wound it in linen clothes with the spices, as the manner of the Jews is to bury.

Now in the place where he was crucified there was a garden; and in the garden a new sepulchre, wherein was never man yet laid.

There laid they Jesus therefore because of the Jews' preparation day; for the sepulchre was nigh at hand. (19:38–42)

239. Aloes *(Aloe succotrina)* in the courtyard of a Jerusalem garden.
Since these verses deal with Jesus' burial, it is possible that the aloes referred to here were bitter aloes, used by the Egyptians in embalming.

240. The upper part of the Golgotha chapel.

238

239

240

241

241. Calvary, where the crucifixion took place, is reached by a staircase, as it lies several feet above the level of the floor of the Church of the Holy Sepulcher. It was not part of the church in Constantine's time, but was incorporated into the monument built by the Crusaders.

The sanctuary is divided into two chapels: the one to the right belongs to the Latins, and here are venerated the sites known as the 10th and 11th Stations of the Way of the Cross: Jesus is stripped of his garments and nailed to the cross.

The altar to the left, belonging to the Greek Orthodox Church, marks the place where the cross stood. The exact spot is marked by a silver disc with an opening in the center, between the columns which support the table of the altar. On either side of the altar black marble discs mark the place of the crosses of the two thieves who were crucified with Jesus, as told by Luke (23:32): "And they were two other malefactors, led with him to be put to death." To the right of the altar is shown the crack caused by the earthquake at the time of Jesus' death, when "the earth did quake, and the rocks rent" (Matthew 27:51).

Between the two chapels is an altar dedicated to "Our Lady of Dolors." The statue of the Virgin recalls the prophecy of Simeon: "Yea, a sword shall pierce through thy own soul also" (Luke 2:35). It was here that Mary received in her arms the lifeless body of Jesus taken down from the cross.

Under the altar can be seen the rock of Calvary enclosed by a bronze railing.

242. The Chapel of the Angel in the Church of the Holy Sepulcher: The tomb where Jesus was laid to rest consisted of two rooms connected by a very low door. The inner chamber was the burial place proper. The bigger front chamber was the place for the mourners to gather. It is now called the Chapel of the Angel. The low door leads to the burial chamber.

243. The burial chamber believed to be the tomb of Jesus. It contains the ledge upon which Jesus was laid to rest.

242

And the other disciples came in a little ship; (for they were not far from land, but as it were two hundred cubits,) dragging the net with fishes.

As soon then as they were come to land, they saw a fire of coals there, and fish laid thereon, and bread.

Jesus saith unto them, Bring of the fish which ye have now caught.

Simon Peter went up, and drew the net to land full of great fishes, an hundred and fifty and three: and for all there were so many, yet was not the net broken.

Jesus saith unto them, Come and dine. And none of the disciples durst ask him, Who art thou? knowing that it was the Lord.

Jesus then cometh, and taketh bread, and giveth them, and fish likewise.

This is now the third time that Jesus shewed himself to his disciples, after that he was risen from the dead.

So when they had dined, Jesus saith to Simon Peter, Simon, son of Jonas, lovest thou me more than these? He saith unto him, Yea, Lord; thou knowest that I love thee. He saith unto him, Feed my lambs.

He saith to him again the second time, Simon, son of Jonas, lovest thou me? He saith unto him, Yea, Lord; thou knowest that I love thee. He saith unto him, Feed my sheep.

He saith unto him the third time, Simon, son of Jonas, lovest thou me? Peter was grieved because he said unto him the third time, Lovest thou me?

247. On the shore of the Sea of Galilee, near Tabgha, where the river falls into the Sea of Galilee, stands the Church of the Primacy, marking the site where, it is believed, Jesus, risen from the dead, appeared to his disciples and prepared a meal for them on the rocks. The rock protruding inside the church is called *Mensa Christi* (Christ's Table). Here also Peter was appointed to the leadership (primacy) of all other disciples of Christ.
The church was built in 1933 by the Franciscan order. At the farthest end from the altar the base of the walls of a late 4th-century building is visible. The eastern end of the edifice is cut in the rock. The text in John: "there was some bread there, and a charcoal fire," explains why the site was known as the Place of Coals.

247

And he said unto him, Lord, thou knowest all things; thou knowest that I love thee. Jesus saith unto him, Feed my sheep.

Verily, verily, I say unto thee, When thou wast young, thou girdedst thyself, and walkedst whither thou wouldest: but when thou shalt be old, thou shalt stretch forth thy hands, and another shall gird thee, and carry thee whither thou wouldest not.

This spake he, signifying by what death he should glorify God. And when he had spoken this, he saith unto him, Follow me.

Then Peter, turning about, seeth the disciple whom Jesus loved following; which also leaned on his breast at supper, and said, Lord, which is he that betrayeth thee?

Peter seeing him saith to Jesus, Lord, and what shall this man do?

Jesus saith unto him, If I will that he tarry till I come, what is that to thee? follow thou me.

Then went this saying abroad among the brethren, that that disciple should not die: yet Jesus said not unto him, He shall not die; but, If I will that he tarry till I come, what is that to thee?

This is the disciple which testifieth of these things, and wrote these things: and we know that his testimony is true.

And there are also many other things which Jesus did, the which, if they should be written every one, I suppose that even the world itself could not contain the books that should be written. Amen.   (21:1–25)

248. *Mensa Christi:* the Table of Christ inside the Church of the Primacy.

249

250

251

The former treatise have I made, O Theophilus, of all that Jesus began both to do and teach,

Until the day in which he was taken up, after that he through the Holy Ghost had given commandments unto the apostles whom he had chosen:

To whom also he shewed himself alive after his passion by many infallible proofs, being seen of them forty days, and speaking of the things pertaining to the kingdom of God: And, being assembled together with them, commanded them that they should not depart from Jerusalem, but wait for the promise of the Father which, saith he, ye have heard of me. For John truly baptized with water; but ye shall be baptized with the Holy Ghost not many days hence.

When they therefore were come together, they asked of him, saying, Lord, wilt thou at this time restore again the kingdom to Israel?

And he said unto them, It is not for you to know the times or the seasons, which the Father hath put in his own power.

But ye shall receive power, after that the Holy Ghost is come upon you: and ye shall be witnesses unto me both in Jerusalem, and in all Judaea, and in Samaria, and unto the uttermost part of the earth.

And when he had spoken these things, while they beheld, he was taken up; and a cloud received him out of their sight.

And while they looked stedfastly toward heaven as he went up, behold, two men stood by them in white apparel;

Which also said, Ye men of Galilee, why stand ye gazing up into heaven? this same Jesus, which is taken up from you into heaven, shall so come in like manner as ye have seen him go into heaven.

Then returned they unto Jerusalem from the mount called Olivet, which is from Jerusalem a sabbath day's journey.

And when they were come in, they went up into an upper room, where abode both Peter, and James, and John, and Andrew, Philip, and Thomas, Bartholomew, and Matthew, James the son of Alphaeus, and Simon Zelotes, and Judas the brother of James.

These all continued with one accord in prayer and supplication, with the women, and Mary the mother of Jesus, and with his brethren.

And in those days Peter stood up in the midst of the disciples, and said, (the number of names together were about an hundred and twenty,)

Men and brethren, this scripture must needs have been fulfilled, which the Holy Ghost by the mouth of David spake before concerning Judas, which was guide to them that took Jesus.

For he was numbered with us, and had obtained part of this ministry.

Now this man purchased a field with the reward of iniquity; and falling headlong, he burst asunder in the midst, and all his bowels gushed out.

And it was known unto all the dwellers at Jerusalem; insomuch as that field is called in their proper tongue, Aceldama, that is to say, The field of blood. (1:1–19)

And when the day of Pentecost was fully come, they were all with one accord in one place.

And suddenly there came a sound from heaven as of a rushing mighty wind, and it filled all the house where they were sitting.

And there appeared unto them cloven tongues like as of fire, and it sat upon each of them.

And they were all filled with the Holy Ghost, and began to speak with other tongues, as the Spirit gave them utterance.

And there were dwelling at Jerusalem Jews, devout men, out of every nation under heaven. Now when this was noised abroad, the multitude came together, and were confounded, because that every man heard them speak in his own language. (2:1–6)

And they were all amazed, and were in doubt, saying one to another, What meaneth this? Others mocking said, These men are full of new wine.

But Peter, standing up with the eleven, lifted up his voice, and said unto them, Ye men of Judaea, and all ye that dwell at Jerusalem, be this known unto you, and hearken to my words:

For these are not drunken, as ye suppose, seeing it is but the third hour of the day. But this is that which was spoken by the prophet Joel;

And it shall come to pass in the last days, saith God, I will pour out of my Spirit upon all flesh: and your sons and your daughters shall prophesy, and your young men shall see visions, and your old men shall dream dreams:

249. The Church of the Ascension. The cupola over the shrine is a Moslem one, for at one time the church served as a mosque. The base is reminiscent of Crusader architecture. The courtyard surrounding the shrine was built in 1835 on the remains of the 12th-century church which was destroyed by the Moslems. Beneath the dome lies the stone bearing a footprint, which according to tradition was left by Jesus as he rose from the earth.

250. The Judas tree is the common name given to a small tree which is recognized from afar by the pinkish glow of its flowers. According to Christian tradition Judas Iscariot hanged himself on such a tree.

251. The "Aceldama" (Akeldama in Aramaic means field of blood) is in the Valley of Hinnom.
This was the field that the Temple authorities purchased with the money Judas Iscariot received for his betrayal of Jesus. This "blood money" could not be used for the Temple, so a field was bought to serve as a burial place for strangers (Matthew 27:3–10). This is also believed to be the place where Judas committed suicide by hanging himself on a tree at the edge of an escarpment that did not resist the weight of his body.

252. Enamel plaque, representing the cloven tongues "like as of fire" "sitting" on the disciples; Pentecost, Verdun Altar, 1180 (Klosterneuburg Abbey).
In the Old Testament, Pentecost is called the Feast of Weeks (Exodus 34:22, Deuteronomy 16:10), or the Feast of Harvest (Exodus 23:16), or of Firstfruits (Numbers 28:26). It marked the end of the barley harvest and the beginning of the wheat harvest and was one of the three annual pilgrimages to Jerusalem. According to Deuteronomy 16:10, it was celebrated seven weeks after the sickle was put to the standing grain, and according to Leviticus 23:15ff., seven weeks after the Sabbath that followed after the Passover. After the destruction of the Temple in A.D.70 the festival was also held to mark the giving of the Law at Sinai, fifty days after the Exodus.
In the Book of the Acts of the Apostles, Pentecost is the day on which the outpouring of the Holy Spirit occurred, thus bringing the church into being fifty days after the Resurrection.

And on my servants and on my handmaidens I will pour out in those days of my Spirit; and they shall prophesy:

And I will shew wonders in heaven above, and signs in the earth beneath; blood, and fire, and vapour of smoke:

The sun shall be turned into darkness, and the moon into blood, before that great and notable day of the Lord come:

And it shall come to pass, that whosoever shall call on the name of the Lord shall be saved. (2:12–21)

And the word of God increased; and the number of the disciples multiplied in Jerusalem greatly; and a great company of the priests were obedient to the faith.

253. St. Stephen's Gate, or Lions' Gate, as it is also called, is one of the gates in the wall surrounding the Old City of Jerusalem. It faces the Kidron Valley. Two pairs of lions are carved on the lintel of the gate. St. Stephen, the first Christian martyr, is said to have been stoned to death close by.

The lions over the gate which date from the 18th century have given rise to various legends which have no connection with St. Stephen. One of these tells that the 8th-century Caliph Suleiman oppressed the city and imposed heavy taxes upon it. One night he dreamt that four lions were tearing him to pieces. The caliph woke up terrified. None of his wise men could interpret this fearsome dream. Then came an old man who said: "Don't you know that Jerusalem is sacred to Allah for all time? There dwelt His glory and there reigned David and Solomon and their descendants after them. Lions guarded their thrones as long as they held sway. And now, as you planned evil against the Holy City, Allah sent lions to destroy you." The caliph decided to atone for his evil intents. He went to Jerusalem and ordered a new wall to be built around the city for the defense of its inhabitants, with a great gate at the spot where the work had begun. The lions were to mark forever Allah's changing of the king's intentions regarding the Holy City. In actuality, lions were the royal emblem of Caliph Suleiman, known as The Magnificent.

And Stephen, full of faith and power, did great wonders and miracles among the people.

Then there arose certain of the synagogue, which is called the synagogue of the Libertines, and Cyrenians, and Alexandrians, and of them of Cilicia and of Asia, disputing with Stephen.

And they were not able to resist the wisdom and the spirit by which he spake.

Then they suborned men, which said, We have heard him speak blasphemous words against Moses, and against God.

And they stirred up the people, and the elders, and the scribes, and came upon him, and caught him, and brought him to the council.

And set up false witnesses, which said, This man ceaseth not to speak blasphemous words against this holy place, and the law:

For we have heard him say, that this Jesus of Nazareth shall destroy

254. The stoning of St. Stephen, depicted on a Limoges-enamel of the 12th century (Trésor de l'Eglise Gimel-les-Cascades, France). The martyrdom of Stephen is symbolic of the struggle of the early Church. As multitudes

this place, and shall change the customs which Moses delivered us.

And all sat in the council, looking stedfastly on him, saw his face as it had been the face of an angel.   (6:7–15)

Ye stiffnecked and uncircumcised in heart and ears, ye do always resist the Holy Ghost: as your fathers did, so do ye.

Which of the prophets have not your fathers persecuted? and they have slain them which shewed before of the coming of the Just One; of whom ye have been now the betrayers and murderers:

Who have received the law by the disposition of angels, and have not kept it.

When they heard these things, they were cut to the heart, and they

were converted there were disputes and cross-currents among them. This led to the appointment of seven deacons (Acts 6), to act as spiritual leaders. Stephen was one of these. He was "full of faith and power." Among the several synagogues in the city of Jerusalem for different sects of Jews, the synagogue of the Libertines, Cyrenians and "them of Cilicia" – probably including Saul of Tarsus among them – opposed Stephen. Nevertheless, "they were not able to resist the wisdom and the spirit by which he spake." False witnesses were brought to testify that he had spoken blasphemous words against Moses, and against God, and that he had stated that Jesus of Nazareth would destroy

254

gnashed on him with their teeth.

But he, being full of the Holy Ghost, looked up and stedfastly into heaven, and saw the glory of God, and Jesus standing on the right hand of God,

And said, Behold, I see the heavens opened, and the Son of man standing on the right hand of God.

Then they cried out with a loud voice, and stopped their ears, and ran upon him with one accord,

And cast him out of the city, and stoned him: and the witnesses laid down their clothes at a young man's feet, whose name was Saul.

And they stoned Stephen, calling upon God, and saying, Lord Jesus, receive my spirit.

And he kneeled down, and cried with a loud voice, Lord, lay not this sin to their charge. And when he had said this, he fell asleep.   (7:51–60)

this place and change the customs delivered to them by Moses.

Stephen's speech recapitulated some highlights in the ancient history of the Jews, especially with reference to Joseph and Moses. He charged his accusers with resisting the Holy Spirit, with disobeying the Law and being "the betrayers and murderers of the Just One." But his infuriated audience took him out of the city and stoned him.

However, the effect of Stephen's martyrdom was the wider spread of the gospel, which his persecutors were seeking to hinder. "And at that time there was a great persecution against the church which was at Jerusalem and they were all scattered abroad throughout the regions of Judea and Samaria, except the apostles" (Acts 8:1). "They that were scattered abroad went everywhere preaching the word" (verse 4).

255. Remains of the Roman forum in Sebaste, or Samaria.
Samaria had been the capital of the northern kingdom of Israel, and its name was sometimes applied to the entire region.
In 27 B.C. Herod the Great began to develop Samaria and renamed it Sebaste (a Greek form for the Latin name Augustus), in honor of the first Roman emperor.
On his way to and from Jerusalem, Jesus passed through the district situated between Judea and the Galilee.

256. Group of paralytics waiting to be healed; mosaic from the 14th-century church of Kariye, Istanbul, Turkey.
The Samaritan sorcerer Simon became a believer when he saw the miracles performed by Philip the evangelist. The story of Simon illustrates the possibility that faith in a higher power is not necessarily a genuine religious faith, and that a true change of heart must accompany it.
Considering the highly unfavorable circumstances of the Apostolic age, the rapid spread of the early church is surprising. The English historian Gibbon attributed it to five main causes: the doctrine of the immortality of the soul – which was more definite than the ambiguous ideas on this subject of the ancient

Then Philip went down to the city of Samaria, and preached Christ unto them.

And the people with one accord gave heed unto those things which Philip spake, hearing and seeing the miracles which he did.

For unclean spirits, crying with loud voice, came out of many that were possessed with them: and many taken with palsies, and that were lame, were healed.

And there was great joy in that city.

But there was a certain man, called Simon, which beforetime in the same city used sorcery, and bewitched the people of Samaria, giving out that himself was some great one:

To whom they all gave heed, from the least to the greatest, saying, This man is the great power of God.

And to him they had regard, because that of long time he had bewitched them with sorceries.

But when they believed Philip preaching the things concerning the kingdom of God, and the name of Jesus Christ, they were baptized, both men and women.

Then Simon himself believed also: and when he was baptized, he continued with Philip, and wondered, beholding the miracles and signs which were done.

(8:5–13)

philosophers; the pure and austere morality of the first Christians; the unity and discipline of the Church, and the miraculous powers attributed to it.

257. Manned chariot and horses on a relief from the Mourners' Sarcophagus, Sidon, 50 B.C.

The call of Philip to go to Gaza to preach the Gospel to one man was unexpected. Philip was at the height of his great success as a preacher in Samaria, where he had won respect and affection. The new believers would naturally look to him for further light and instruction. Nevertheless, the angel of the Lord says to Philip: "Arise, and go toward the south . . . unto Gaza which is desert." Philip's unquestioning and immediate obedience to the Spirit is exemplary. Once the Ethiopian eunuch believed and was baptized, Philip was again "caught away" by the Spirit and was suddenly found at Azotus (verses 38–40).

Philip the evangelist was one of the seven (Acts 6:5; 21:8) leaders of the Hellenistic, Greek-speaking congregation in the early church in Jerusalem. He was an effective missionary in Samaria (Acts 8:5ff.), and on the coast of Palestine from Ashdod to Caesarea (Acts 8:40) where he took up residence. Paul stayed with Philip when he visited Caesarea on his last journey to Jerusalem. With his conversion of the Ethiopian eunuch, Philip became the first to cross the frontiers of Jewish Christianity. Acts 21:9 relates that Philip "had four daughters, virgins, which did prophesy."

And they, when they had testified and preached the word of the Lord, returned to Jerusalem, and preached the gospel in many villages of the Samaritans.

And the angel of the Lord spake unto Philip, saying, Arise, and go toward the south unto the way that goeth down from Jerusalem unto Gaza, which is desert.

And he arose and went: and, behold, a man of Ethiopia, an eunuch of great authority under Candace queen of the Ethiopians, who had the charge of all her treasure, and had come to Jerusalem to worship,

Was returning, and sitting in his chariot read Esaias the prophet.

Then the Spirit said unto Philip, Go near, and join thyself to this chariot.

And Philip ran thither to him, and heard him read the prophet Esaias, and said, Understandest thou what thou readest?

And he said, How can I, except some man should guide me? And he desired Philip that he would come up and sit with him.

The place of the scripture which he read was this, He was led as a sheep to the slaughter; and like a lamb dumb before his shearer, so opened he not his mouth:

In his humiliation his judgment was taken away: and who shall declare his generation? for his life is taken from the earth.

And the eunuch answered Philip, and said, I pray thee, of whom speaketh the prophet this? of himself, or of some other man?

Then Philip opened his mouth, and began at the same scripture, and preached unto him Jesus.

And as they went on their way, they came unto a certain water: and the eunuch said, See, here is water; what doth hinder me to be baptized?

And Philip said, If though believest with all thine heart, thou mayest. And he anwered and said, I believe that Jesus Christ is the Son of God.

And he commanded the chariot to stand still: and they went down both into the water, both Philip and the eunuch; and he baptized him.

And when they were come up out of the water, the Spirit of the Lord caught away Philip, that the eunuch saw him no more: and he went on his way rejoicing. But Philip was found at Azotus: and passing through he preached in all the cities, till he came to Caesarea.   (8:25–40)

And Saul, yet breathing out threatenings and slaughter against the disciples of the Lord, went unto the high priest,

And desired of him letters to Damascus to the synagogues, that if he found any of this way, whether they were men or women, he might bring them bound unto Jerusalem.

And as he journeyed, he came near Damascus: and suddenly there shined round about him a light from heaven: And he fell to the earth, and heard a voice saying unto him, Saul, Saul, why persecutest thou me?

And he said, Who art thou, Lord? And the Lord said, I am Jesus whom thou persecutest: it is hard for thee to kick against the pricks.

And he trembling and astonished said, Lord, what wilt thou have me to do? And the Lord said unto him, Arise, and go into the city, and it shall be told thee what thou must do.

And the men which journeyed with him stood speechless, hearing a voice, but seeing no man. And Saul arose from the earth; and when his eyes were opened, he saw no man: but they led him by the hand, and brought him into Damascus.   (9:1–8)

258. Gamla in the Golan, east of the Sea of Galilee, takes its name from the Hebrew word *gamal*, camel, perhaps because the hill is shaped rather like a camel's hump. Excavations in the area have uncovered one of the earliest synagogues in the Holy Land. Paul passed this way en route to Damascus.
Damascus was the ancient capital of the Aramean kingdom mentioned in the Old Testament, and later one of the Assyrian provinces. It was conquered by Alexander the Great and was rebuilt in the Hellenistic period. In 64 B.C. Pompey made the city part of the Roman province of Syria. At that time there was a large Jewish community there. Following the martyrdom of Stephen, many Christians fled from Jerusalem and settled in Damascus. Paul intended to arrest those "Nazarenes" and bring them back to Jerusalem to face trial for heresy.

258

But the Lord said unto him, Go thy way: for he is a chosen vessel unto me, to bear my name before the Gentiles, and kings, and the children of Israel:

For I will shew him how great things he must suffer for my name's sake.

And Ananias went his way, and entered into the house; and putting his hands on him said, Brother Saul, the Lord, even Jesus, that appeared unto thee in the way as thou camest, hath sent me, that thou mightest receive thy sight, and be filled with the Holy Ghost.

And immediately there fell from his eyes as it had been scales: and he received sight forthwith, and arose, and was baptized.

And when he had received meat, he was strengthened. Then was Saul certain days with the disciples which were at Damascus.

And straightway he preached Christ in the synagogues, that he is the Son of God.

But all that heard him were amazed, and said; Is not this he that destroyed them which called on this name in Jerusalem, and came hither for that intent, that he might bring them bound unto the chief priests?

But Saul increased the more in strength, and confounded the Jews which dwelt at Damascus, proving that this is very Christ.

And after that many days were fulfilled, the Jews took counsel to kill him:

But their laying await was known of Saul. And they watched the gates day and night to kill him.

The the disciples took him by night, and let him down by the wall in a basket.
(9:15–25)

259. Saul (Paul) fleeing Damascus; enamel plaque of the 11th century (Victoria and Albert Museum, London).

Saul's opponents being unable to match him in debate, resorted to the last argument of a desperate cause – assassination. Saul became acquainted with the conspiracy and took the necessary precautions. But the political circumstances in Damascus at the time made escape difficult. The governor of Damascus alerted the garrison to apprehend him, and the disciples had to let him down in a basket from a window in an unguarded part of the wall (II Corinthians 11:32–33).

Thus the Apostle Paul experiences the first of his perils: "In journeying often, in perils of waters, in perils of robbers, in perils of mine own countrymen, in perils by the heathen, in perils in the city, in perils in the wilderness, in perils in the sea, in perils among false brethren" (II Corinthians 11:26), learning what great things he was to suffer for the name of Christ (Acts 9:16).

260

Now there was at Joppa a certain disciple named Tabitha, which by interpretation is called Dorcas: this woman was full of good works and almsdeeds which she did.

And it came to pass in those days, that she was sick, and died: whom when they had washed, they laid her in an upper chamber.

And forasmuch as Lydda was nigh to Joppa, and the disciples had heard that Peter was there, they sent unto him two men, desiring him that he would not delay to come to them.

Then Peter arose and went with them. When he was come, they brought him into the upper chamber: and all the widows stood by him weeping, and shewing the coats and garments which Dorcas made, while she was with them.

But Peter put them all forth, and kneeled down, and prayed; and turning him to the body said, Tabitha, arise. And she opened her eyes: and when she saw Peter, she sat up.

And he gave her his hand, and lifted her up, and when he had called the saints and widows, presented her alive.

And it was known throughout all Joppa; and many believed in the Lord.

And it came to pass, that he tarried many days in Joppa with one Simon a tanner.

(9:36–43)

261

260. Capital of a column showing St. Peter healing Tabitha.
This is one of several column capitals from the time of the Crusaders, found at Nazareth.

261. In a narrow street in the old city of Jaffa, this is pointed out as the house of Simon the Tanner.

262. A view of Jaffa from the sea.
Jaffa, or Joppa, is popularly believed to be the oldest port of the world. The harbor facilities of this port were developed at the time of King Solomon. It was to Joppa that the Tyrians

On the morrow, as they went on their journey, and drew nigh unto the city, Peter went up upon the housetop to pray about the sixth hour:

And he became very hungry, and would have eaten: but while they made ready, he fell into a trance,

And saw heaven opened, and a certain vessel descending unto him, as it had been a great sheet knit at the four corners, and let down to the earth:

Wherein were all manners of fourfooted beasts of the earth, and wild beasts, and creeping things, and fowls of the air.

And there came a voice to him, Rise, Peter; kill, and eat.

But Peter said, Not so, Lord; for I have never eaten any thing that is

common or unclean.

And the voice spake unto him again the second time, What God hath cleansed, that call not thou common.

This was done thrice: and the vessel was received up again into heaven.

Now while Peter doubted in himself what this vision which he had seen should mean, behold, the men which were sent from Cornelius had made inquiry for Simon's house, and stood before the gate,

And called, and asked whether Simon, which was surnamed Peter, were lodged there.

shipped cedars from the forests of Lebanon for the construction of the Temple (II Chronicles 2:16).

263. A bird's eye view of the Roman remains of Caesarea.
An important seaport, it was built in the latter part of the first century B.C. by Herod the Great, who received the site as a gift from Caesar Augustus.

264. Roman aqueduct near Caesarea.

(10:9–18)

265

265. A coin minted at Caesarea.
The first coins with the name Caesarea on them appeared in the middle of the first century A.D. In time, however, the mint at Caesarea became increasingly productive. One of the coins minted there depicts the ceremony that the Roman rulers performed when a city was established as a Roman colony; to commemorate this important occasion, the emperor, or his representative, plowed a furrow in the earth. Caesarea was a true Roman colony, and this gave it a privileged position. Only a few cities in the Roman Empire had the title Colonia – colony.

266. The baptism of Cornelius by Peter at Caesarea, depicted on 4th century sarcophagus (Musée Lapidaire Chrétien, Arles).
Caesarea was the main headquarters for the Roman military forces, and its population was mixed, being mostly Greek and Jewish.
From Caesarea, Paul was sent by the disciples to his home town, Tarsus. It was at Caesarea that Peter witnessed the baptism of the first uncircumcised believers in Christ.
It was to Caesarea that Herod Agrippa I withdrew after his unsuccessful imprisonment of Peter. He died there ("because he gave not God the glory").
Paul went through Caesarea on his return to the Holy Land, when "he sailed from Ephesus. And when he had landed at Caesarea, and gone up, and saluted the church, he went down to Antioch" (Acts 18:21–23). Later Paul was taken to Caesarea as a prisoner to be tried by the Roman governor, because he was a Roman citizen (Acts. 23:23–24). But Paul appealed to Caesar and was sent to Rome for trial.

And the morrow after they entered into Caesarea. And Cornelius waited for them, and had called together his kinsmen and near friends.

And as Peter was coming in, Cornelius met him, and fell down at his feet, and worshipped him.

But Peter took him up, saying, Stand up; I myself also am a man.

And as he talked with him, he went in, and found many that were come together.

And he said unto them, Ye know how that it is an unlawful thing for a man that is a Jew to keep company, or come unto one of another nation; but God hath shewed me that I should not call any man common or unclean.

Therefore came I unto you without gainsaying, as soon as I was sent for: I ask therefore for what intent ye have sent for me?

And Cornelius said, Four days ago I was fasting until this hour; and at the ninth hour I prayed in my house, and, behold, a man stood before me in bright clothing,

And said, Cornelius, thy prayer is heard, and thine alms are had in remembrance in the sight of God.

Send therefore to Joppa, and call hither Simon, whose surname is Peter; he is lodged in the house of one Simon a tanner by the sea side: who, when he cometh, shall speak unto thee. (10:24–32)

While Peter yet spake these words, the Holy Ghost fell on all them which heard the word.

And they of the circumcision which believed were astonished, as many as came with Peter, because that on the Gentiles also was poured out the gift of the Holy Ghost.

For they heard them speak with tongues, and magnify God. Then answered Peter,

Can any man forbid water, that these should not be baptized, which have received the Holy Ghost as well as we?

And he commanded them to be baptized in the name of the Lord. Then prayed they him to tarry certain days. (10:44–48)

Now they which were scattered abroad upon the persecution that arose about Stephen travelled as far as Phenice, and Cyprus, and Antioch, preaching the word to none but unto the Jews only.

And some of them were men of Cyprus and Cyrene, which, when they were come to Antioch, spake unto the Grecians, preaching the Lord Jesus.

And the hand of the Lord was with them: and a great number believed, and turned unto the Lord.

Then tidings of these things came unto the ears of the church which was in Jerusalem: and they sent forth Barnabas, that he should go as far as Antioch.

Who, when he came, and had seen the grace of God, was glad, and exhorted them all, that with purpose of heart they would cleave unto the Lord.

For he was a good man, and full of the Holy Ghost and of faith: and much people was added unto the Lord.

Then departed Barnabas to Tarsus, for to seek Saul:

And when he had found him, he brought him unto Antioch. And it came to pass, that a whole year they assembled themselves with the church, and taught much people. And the disciples were called Christians first in Antioch.

(11:19–26)

Now about that time Herod the king stretched forth his hands to vex certain of the church.

And he killed James the brother of John with the sword.

And because he saw it pleased the Jews, he proceeded further to take Peter also. (Then were the days of unleavened bread.)

And when he had apprehended him, he put him in prison, and delivered him to four quaternions of soldiers to keep him; intending after Easter to bring him forth to the people.

Peter therefore was kept in prison: but prayer was made without ceasing of the church unto God for him.

(12:1–5)

267. The harbor wall of Seleucia, the port of Antioch (Antakya).
The city was founded at the end of the 4th century B.C. by Seleucus I Nicator together with the coastal town of Seleucia, which served as its port. He named it after his father, the Macedonian general Antiochus. Settlers of all nations had been given equal rights of citizenship. In 64 B.C. Syria became a Roman province, and more temples, theaters, baths and aqueducts were added to Antioch.
It was called "Antioch on the Orontes," and was considered for a long time the third city of the Roman empire in size and importance. There was a large Jewish community there since its foundation.
During the Roman period the Jewish population had been augmented by many converts to Judaism. There were also "Nazarenes," who now for the first time adopted the name "Christians," namely, followers of *Christos* – in Greek, the "Anointed One," or Messiah. They settled in Antioch to avoid the persecutions to which they were subjected in Jerusalem.

268. A statue of Tyche, goddess of Antioch, with the river Orontes at her feet, seated on a rock representing Mt. Silpius on which the city was built.

269. The so-called Grotto of St. James, in the Kidron Valley in Jerusalem. The tomb shown here has been identified as the tomb of the priestly family of Beni Hezir. Christian tradition holds that James concealed himself here at the time of Jesus' arrest.

270. Portal of the cathedral of Santiago de Compostela in Spain.
"Santiago" is the Spanish for St. James, whose shrine this is. In the 9th century a tomb discovered in the vicinity was said to have been supernaturally revealed to be that of the apostle James. According to legend, his body had been transported from Jerusalem to Spain. During the Middle Ages the town grew around the shrine that was built over the tomb and became an important place of pilgrimage. The cathedral was consecrated in 1128.

271. Remains of an ancient synagogue at Paphos on the west coast of Cyprus.
Cyprus, the "Kittim" of the Old Testament (Genesis 10:4) was renowned for its timber and its copper (the word "copper" derives from the name of the island, *Kypros* in Greek). In 58 B.C. the island was annexed to the Roman province of Cilicia. There were many contacts between Judea and the Jews of Cyprus, whose presence on the island is said to date back to the 2nd century B.C. According to Josephus, Herod the Great received a portion of the revenues of the copper mines there.

272. Remains of a frieze of a Greek temple at Antioch in Pisidia (Yalvac, Turkey).
This town, too, was founded by Seleucus Nicator and named after his father. It was situated on the border of Phrygia and Pisidia. It became a free city under Roman rule in 189 B.C. and Augustus later conferred upon it the status of Roman colony. It was on the trade route between Cilicia and Ephesus. Though a

And when they were at Salamis, they preached the word of God in the synagogues of the Jews: and they had also John to their minister.

And when they had gone through the isle unto Paphos, they found a certain sorcerer, a false prophet, a Jew, whose name was Barjesus:

Which was with the deputy of the country, Sergius Paulus, a prudent man; who called for Barnabas and Saul, and desired to hear the word of God.

But Elymas the sorcerer (for so is his name by interpretation) withstood them, seeking to turn away the deputy from the faith.

Then Saul, (who also is called Paul,) filled with the Holy Ghost, set his eyes on him,

And said, O full of all subtilty and all mischief, thou child of the devil, thou enemy of all righteousness, wilt thou not cease to pervert the right ways of the Lord?

And now, behold, the hand of the Lord is upon thee, and thou shalt be blind, not seeing the sun for a season. And immediately there fell on him a mist and a darkness; and he went about seeking some to lead him by the hand.

Then the deputy, when he saw what was done, believed, being astonished at the doctrine of the Lord.

Now when Paul and his company loosed from Paphos, they came to Perga in Pamphylia: and John departing from them returned to Jerusalem.

But when they departed from Perga, they came to Antioch in Pisidia, and went into the synogogue on the sabbath day, and sat down.

And after the reading of the law and the prophets the rulers of the synagogue sent unto them, saying, Ye men and brethren, if ye have any word of exhortation for the people, say on.

The Paul stood up, and beckoning with his hand said, Men of Israel, and ye that fear God, give audience.

(13:5–16)

*Therefore loosing from Troas, we came with a straight course to Samo-
thracia, and the next day to Neapolis;*

*And from thence to Philippi, which is the chief city of that part of
Macedonia, and a colony: and we were in that city abiding certain days.*

*And on the sabbath we went out of the city by a river side, where prayer
was wont to be made; and we sat down, and spake unto the women which
resorted thither.*

*And a certain woman named Lydia, a seller of purple, of the city of
Thyatira, which worshipped God, heard us: whose heart the Lord opened,
that she attended unto the things which were spoken of Paul.*

(16:11–14)

*And it came to pass, as we went to prayer, a certain damsel possessed
with a spirit of divination met us, which brought her masters much gain by
soothsaying:*

The same followed Paul and us, and cried, saying, These men are the

completely Hellenistic city, it had a large Jewish community.

273. The king of Athens, Aegus, consulting
the priestess of Apollo at Delphi, depicted on
a Greek painted vase.
Pythia, the priestess, was believed to be the
medium through which the god answered
those who consulted him. The priestess of the
oracle would sit on a tripod and, in a state of
ecstasy, caused by an exhalation from the
earth or by chewing laurel leaves, she would
utter her replies. A few of these priestesses
were corrupt, and gave advantageous answers to consultants.
All forms of divination were condemned by
the Bible: "There shall not be found among
you any one that maketh his son or his daughter to pass through the fire, or that useth divination, or an observer of times, or an

servants of the most high God, which shew unto us the way of salvation.

And this did she many days. But Paul, being grieved, turned and said to the spirit, I command thee in the name of Jesus Christ to come out of her. And he came out the same hour.

And when her masters saw that the hope of their gains was gone, they caught Paul and Silas, and drew them into the marketplace unto the rulers.

(16:16–19)

Now when they had passed though Amphipolis and Appolonia, they came to Thessalonica, where was a synagogue of the Jews:

And Paul, as his manner was, went in unto them, and three sabbath days reasoned with them out of the scriptures,

Opening and alleging, that Christ must needs have suffered, and risen again from the dead; and that this Jesus, whom I preach unto you, is Christ.

And some of them believed, and consorted with Paul and Silas; and of the devout Greeks a great multitude, and of the chief women not a few.

But the Jews which believed not, moved with envy, took unto them certain lewd fellows of the baser sort, and gathered a company, and set all the city on an uproar, and assaulted the house of Jason, and sought to bring them out to the people.

(17:1–5)

275

enchanter, or a witch, or a charmer, or a consulter with familiar spirits, or a wizard, or a necromancer. For all that do these things are an abomination unto the Lord: and because of these abominations the Lord thy God doth drive them out from before thee" (Deuteronomy 18:10–12).

274. The marshy coast near Kavalla, thought to be Neapolis. It served as a seaport for Philippi, Greece, at the northern end of the Aegean Sea.

275. Detail on the remains of Galerius' triumphal arch at Salonika, formerly called Thessalonica.
This was the principal seaport of Macedonia at the time Paul visited it. Jews from Alexandria settled there in 140 B.C. and the community increased in the Hellenistic period. The Romans granted autonomy to the community, which concentrated near the port. Paul preached in the synagogue there and established a Christian congregation. Its first bishop, Gaius, was one of Paul's companions (Acts 19:29).

276. Remains of the Parthenon, the temple of Athena, on the Acropolis at Athens.

277. Paul disputing with Jews and Gentiles; enamel plaque, 11th century (Victoria and Albert Museum, London).

Paul, coming to Athens, center of philosophy, to which people came from all over the world, was not impressed with its reputation as a cultural center, but rather, "his spirit stirred in him, when he saw the city wholly given to idolatry" (verse 17). The philosophical Athenians took great pride in their intellectual achievements. But Paul was unimpressed by the forms of earthly beauty, and by words of human wisdom, which in his view were valueless (I Corinthians 1), and even worse than valueless, since he felt that they made vice into a god and falsehood attractive.

In his speech at Athens, Paul first points out the Athenians' carefulness in religion ("ye are too superstitious"), thus agreeing with the judgement of his contemporary, Josephus. Greek religion was polytheistic, and Greek culture was esthetically-oriented and relished the exercise of the intellect.

Only the Stoics and the Epicureans are mentioned as coming in contact with Paul. These were in fact the most influential schools of thought in his day, being concerned with questions of morality. Stoicism especially approached Christian belief to some extent, with its condemnation of worship of images and the use of temples, though it justified the popular belief in many gods. They aspired to magnanimous self-denial, an austere apathy, untouched by human passion and unmoved by change of circumstance.

The Epicureans were atheists. Their philosophy was one of materialism in the strictest sense of the word. They derided popular mythology, but offered no positive faith in anything better.

As Paul saw it, their view of life was, "If the dead rise not, let us eat and drink: for tomorrow we die" (I Corinthians 15:32).

Paul found in his audience at Athens philosophers who were always eager for fresh subjects of intellectual discussion. The response of these listeners ranged from contemptuous derision to excited curiosity and a desire to hear more.

Now while Paul waited for them at Athens, his spirit was stirred in him, when he saw the city wholly given to idolatry.

Therefore disputed he in the synagogue with the Jews, and with the devout persons, and in the market daily with them that met with him.

Then certain philosophers of the Epicureans, and of the Stoicks, encountered him.

And some said, What will this babbler say? other some, He seemeth to be a setter forth of strange gods: because he preached unto them Jesus, and the resurrection.

And they took him, and brought him unto Areopagus, saying, May we know what this new doctrine, whereof thou speakest, is?

For thou bringest certain strange things to our ears: we would know therefore what these things mean.

(For all the Athenians and strangers which were there spent their time in nothing else, but either to tell, or to hear some new thing.)

Then Paul stood in the midst of Mars' hill, and said, Ye men of Athens, I perceive that in all things ye are too superstitious.

For as I passed by, and beheld your devotions, I found an altar with this inscription, to the unknown God. Whom therefore ye ignorantly worship, him declare I unto you.

God that made the world and all things therein, seeing that he is Lord of heaven and earth, dwelleth not in temples made with hands;

Neither is worshipped with men's hands, as though he needed any thing, seeing he giveth to all life, and breath, and all things;

And hath made of one blood all nations of men for to dwell on all the face of the earth, and hath determined the times before appointed, and the bounds of their habitation;

278

279

That they should seek the Lord, if haply they might feel after him, and find him, though he be not far from every one of us:

For in him we live, and move, and have our being; as certain also of your own poets have said, For we are also his offspring.

Forasmuch then as we are the offspring of God, we ought not to think that the Godhead is like unto gold, or silver, or stone, graven by art and man's device.

(17:16–29)

278. The Roman emperor Claudius (41 B.C.–A.D. 54).
In c. 50, Claudius ordered the expulsion of the Jews from Rome, following disturbances caused by the Judeo-Christians.

279. Street leading from the center of Corinth to the port of Lechaum on the Corinthian Gulf.
Situated on the isthmus between the Peloponnese and central Greece, between the Aegean and Ionian Seas, Corinth was one of the oldest and most prominent cities of ancient Greece. Its importance resulted in large degree from its location. The city had two harbors, one on the Corinthian Gulf and the other on the Saronic Gulf. In ancient times ships were dragged across the isthmus by a system of rails. Merchandise from large vessels was unloaded at one harbor and transported overland to the other.
On the Acrocorinth, 1890 feet high, the citadel (acropolis) of the ancient town was built. The city was on the lower slopes. On top of the Acrocorinth stood the temple of Aphrodite where a thousand women served the goddess as temple prostitutes. This gave Corinth a bad reputation and its name became a symbol of wanton luxury and licentiousness.
Corinth had temples to many other gods and

After these things Paul departed from Athens, and came to Corinth;

And found a certain Jew named Aquila, born in Pontus, lately come from Italy, with his wife Priscilla; (because that Claudius had commanded all Jews to depart from Rome:) and came unto them.

And because he was of the same craft, he abode with them, and wrought: for by their occupation they were tentmakers.

And he reasoned in the synagogue every sabbath, and persuaded the Jews and the Greeks.

And when Silas and Timotheus were come from Macedonia, Paul was pressed in the spirit, and testified to the Jews that Jesus was Christ.

And when they opposed themselves, and blasphemed, he shook his raiment, and said unto them, Your blood be upon your own heads; I am clean: from henceforth I will go unto the Gentiles.

And he departed thence, and entered into a certain man's house, named Justus, one that worshipped God, whose house joined hard to the synagogue.

And Crispus, the chief ruler of the synagogue believed on the Lord with all his house; and many of the Corinthians hearing believed, and were baptized.

Then spake the Lord to Paul in the night by a vision, Be not afraid, but speak, and hold not thy peace:

For I am with thee, and no man shall set on thee to hurt thee: for I have much people in this city. And he continued there a year and six months, teaching the word of God among them.

And when Gallio was the deputy of Achaia, the Jews made insurrection with one accord against Paul, and brought him to the judgment seat,

Saying, This fellow persuadeth men to worship God contrary to the law.

And when Paul was now about to open his mouth, Gallio said unto the Jews, If it were a matter of wrong or wicked lewdness, O ye Jews, reason would that I should bear with you:

But if it be a question of words and names, and of your law, look ye to it; for I will be no judge of such matters.

And he drave them from the judgment seat.

Then all the Greeks took Sosthenes, the chief ruler of the synagogue, and beat him before the judgment seat. And Gallio cared for none of those things.

And Paul after this tarried there yet a good while, and then took his leave of the brethren, and sailed thence into Syria, and with him Priscilla and Aquila; having shorn his head in Cenchrea: for he had a vow.

And he came to Ephesus, and left them there: but he himself entered into the synagogue, and reasoned with the Jews.

When they desired him to tarry longer time with them, he consented not;

But bade them farewell, saying, I must by all means keep this feast that cometh in Jerusalem: but I will return again unto you, if God will. And he sailed from Ephesus.

And when he had landed at Caesarea, and gone up, and saluted the church, he went down to Antioch.   (18:1–22)

goddesses, including one dedicted to Asklepias (Aesculapius), the god of healing. Archaeologists have found numerous offerings in the form of sick limbs at the site of the temple.

280. Remains of the *agora* (market-place) at Corinth. It was lined with colonnades; rows of shops and public buildings opened onto the market-place. Near the center of the agora was the Rostrum, believed to be the "judgement seat", where Jews opposed to Paul's preaching brought him for a hearing before the proconsul Gallio.

281. A cloth and cushion merchant showing his wares to customers, depicted on a Roman relief.

282

And it came to pass, that while Apollos was at Corinth, Paul having passed through the upper coasts came to Ephesus: and finding certain disciples, He said unto them, Have ye received the Holy Ghost since ye believed? And they said unto him, We have not so much as heard whether there be any Holy Ghost.

And he said unto them, Unto what then were ye baptized? And they said, Unto John's baptism. Then said Paul, John verily baptized with the baptism of repentance, saying unto the people, that they should come after him, that is, on Christ Jesus.

When they heard this, they were baptized in the name of the Lord Jesus.

And when Paul had laid his hands upon them, the Holy Ghost came on them; and they spake with tongues, and prophesised.

And all the men were about twelve.

And he went into the synagogue, and spake boldly for the space of three months, disputing and persuading the things concerning the kingdom of God. But when divers were hardened, and believed not, but spake evil of that way before the multitude, he departed from them, and separated the disciples, disputing daily in the school of one Tyrannus.

And this continued by the space of two years; so that all they which dwelt in Asia heard the word of the Lord Jesus, both Jews and Greeks. And God wrought special miracles by the hands of Paul. (19:1–11)

And the same time there arose no small stir about that way.

For a certain man named Demetrius, a silversmith, which made silver shrines for Diana, brought no small gain unto the craftsmen;

Whom he called together with the workmen of like occupation, and said, Sirs, ye know that by this craft we have our wealth.

Moreover ye see and hear, that not alone at Ephesus, but almost throughout all Asia, this Paul hath persuaded and turned away much people, saying that they be no gods, which are made with hands:

So that not only this our craft is in danger to be set at nought; but also that the temple of the great goddess Diana should be despised, and her magnificence should be destroyed, whom all Asia and the world worshippeth.

And when they heard these sayings, they were full of wrath, and cried out, saying, Great is Diana of the Ephesians.

And the whole city was filled with confusion: and having caught Gaius and Aristarchus, men of Macedonia, Paul's companions in travel, they rushed with one accord into the theatre. And when Paul would have entered in unto the people, the disciples suffered him not.

And certain of the chief of Asia, which were his friends, sent unto him, desiring him that he would not adventure himself into the theatre.

Some therefore cried one thing, and some another: for the assembly was confused: and the more part knew not wherefore they were come together.

And they drew Alexander out of the multitude, the Jews putting him forward. And Alexander beckoned with the hand, and would have made his defence unto the people.

But when they knew that he was a Jew, all with one voice about the space of two hours cried out, Great is Diana of the Ephesians. (19:23–34)

282. Image of the Diana of Ephesus.

283. Ephesus: the triumphal road followed by Antony and Cleopatra entering the city.

284. Remains of the theater rebuilt by Nero (54–68) at Ephesus. This stadium was the site of athletic games and probably also gladiatorial combats. Its facade was decorated with pillars, niches and statues. The marble seats for 25,000 spectators were arranged in a semi-circle of 66 rows. The acoustics of the theater were excellent: a word spoken in a low voice on the stage could be heard in the top seats. A colonnaded road ran from the theater to the harbor.
Ephesus, on the west coast of Asia Minor, almost facing the island of Samos, spread over the slopes and the foot of several hills. In ancient times it was a wealthy and important religious and commercial center, on the main route from Rome to the East.

285. Part of the agora at Ephesus.

286. The most outstanding edifice of the city was the temple of Artemis (or Diana), which was said to have been one of the seven wonders of the world. Only a lonely column remains of the temple.
The cult of Artemis, the divine virgin huntress, spread all over the Greek world and in some places she was a city goddess. In Asia Minor her most important cult was at Ephesus. The goddess was said to be the daughter of Zeus and Leto and sister of Apollo.
There was a fairly large Jewish community at Ephesus in the first century. This community was at first fiercely opposed to Paul's mission, as were the non-Jews who worshipped Artemis: "For a certain man named Demetrius, a silversmith, which made silver shrines for Diana, brought no small gain unto the craftsmen," "So that not only this our craft is in danger to be set at nought; but also that the temple of the great goddess Diana should be despised, and her magnificence should be destroyed, whom all Asia, and the world worshippeth."
Paul visited Ephesus twice and laid the foundations of a church in spite of opposition; it was to become one of the most important ones in Asia Minor.

And we sailed away from Philippi after the days of unleavened bread, and came unto them to Troas in five days; where we abode seven days.

And upon the first day of the week, when the disciples came together to break bread, Paul preached unto them, ready to depart on the morrow; and continued his speech until midnight.

And there were many lights in the upper chamber, where they were gathered together.

And there sat in a window a certain young man named Eutychus, being fallen into a deep sleep: and as Paul was long preaching, he sunk down with sleep, and fell down from the third loft, and was taken up dead.

And Paul went down, and fell on him, and embracing him said, Trouble not yourselves; for his life is in him.

When he therefore was come up again, and had broken bread, and eaten, and talked a long while, even till break of day, so he departed.

And they brought the young man alive, and were not a little comforted. And we went before to ship, and sailed unto Assos, there intending to take in Paul: for so had he appointed, minding himself to go afoot. And when he met with us at Assos, we took him in, and came to Mitylene.

287. Greco-Roman remains at Troas, a seaport on the northwestern coast of Asia Minor (in Turkey today). It was a short distance from the traditional site of ancient Troy. The city of Troas was first built by Antigonus, one of Alexander the Great's generals. It came under Roman control in 133 B.C.

288. Remains of the temple of Hera (Juno), goddess of marriage and childbirth, at Samos, which competed in splendor with the temple of Artemis at Ephesus.
Samos is an island in the Aegean Sea near the west coast of Asia Minor. Its main city and port was also named Samos.

289. The ancient harbor at Miletus, on the west coast of Asia Minor (now Turkey). The city is now in ruins. It was a prosperous commercial center, famous for its woolen goods.

290

290. View of Lindus, the most important port of the island of Rhodes, whose capital city was also called Rhodes.
Because of its strategic location and good harbors, Rhodes was a prosperous trading island. In the Hellenistic period Rhodes became a center of culture.

And we sailed thence, and came the next day over against Chios; and the next day we arrived at Samos, and tarried at Trogyllium; and the next day we came to Miletus.

For Paul had determined to sail by Ephesus, because he would not spend the time in Asia: for he hasted, if it were possible for him, to be at Jerusalem the day of Pentecost.

And from Miletus he sent to Ephesus, and called the elders of the church. (20:6–17)

And it came to pass, that after we were gotten from them, and had launched, we came with a straight course unto Coos, and the day following unto Rhodes, and from thence unto Patara. (21:1)

291. A staircase leading up to the Temple Mount, dating from Second Temple times, on the southern side of the Temple Mount in Jerusalem.

Paul entered Jerusalem on the eve of the Feast of Pentecost and went to the Temple with four Judeo-Christians who, according to Jewish custom, desired to make the vows of a Nazirite, as prescribed in Numbers 6. Paul may have hoped to conciliate those who were hostile to him because they believed him to be hostile to Judaism, and he probably succeeded, insofar as the local church in Jerusalem was concerned. But among the crowds who had come from all over to celebrate the Feast of Weeks were "Jews which were of Asia," possibly including some who had argued in the synagogue at Ephesus. A crowd rushed to the scene, aggravated to hear that Paul had brought Greeks into the inner Temple, which was forbidden to Gentiles. Paul was dragged out of the Temple and the Levites shut the gates behind him. The apostle's life was saved by the approach of a squad of Roman soldiers, whereupon "they left off beating of Paul." The commander of the garrison, himself Claudius Lysias, rushed down into the Temple court to see what was going on, and saw that the center of the tumult was Paul. Lysias at first mistook him for the Egyptian false prophet mentioned by Josephus, who had threatened to overtake the Roman garrison in Jerusalem, and demanded to know who he was (verses 33–34). Paul was led up to the steps of the Temple court in order to get him away from the crowd. Paul then, with great presence of mind, boldly asked permission to address the crowd, and surprisingly enough, Lysias granted it, no doubt in deference to Paul's manner of addressing him in Greek and his demand to be treated respectfully as a citizen of Tarsus.

Then Paul took the men, and the next day purifying himself with them entered into the temple, to signify the accomplishment of the days of purification, until that an offering should be offered for every one of them.

And when the seven days were almost ended, the Jews which were of Asia, when they saw him in the temple, stirred up all the people, and laid hands on him,

Crying out, Men of Israel, help: This is the man, that teacheth all men every where against the people, and the law, and this place: and further brought Greeks also into the temple, and hath polluted this holy place.

(For they had seen before with him in the city Trophimus an Ephesian, whom they supposed that Paul had brought into the temple.)

And all the city was moved, and the people ran together: and they took Paul, and drew him out of the temple: and forthwith the doors were shut. (21:26–30)

But Paul said, I am a man which am a Jew of Tarsus, a city in Cilicia, a citizen of no mean city: and, I beseech thee, suffer me to speak unto the people.

And when he had given him licence, Paul stood on the stairs, and beckoned with the hand unto the people. And when there was made a great silence, he spake unto them in the Hebrew tongue, saying, (21:39–40)

Men, brethren, and fathers, hear ye my defence which I make now unto you.

(And when they heard that he spake in the Hebrew tongue to them, they kept the more silence: and he saith,)

I am verily a man which am a Jew, born in Tarsus, a city in Cilicia, yet brought up in this city at the feet of Gamaliel, and taught according to the perfect manner of the law of the fathers, and was zealous toward God, as ye all are this day.

And I persecuted this way unto the death, binding and delivering into prisons both men and women.

292. The Roman city gate at Tarsus, known as the Cleopatra Gate.

Tarsus, the birthplace of Paul, was the principal city and capital of the Roman province of Cilicia. The city was surrounded by fertile coastal land where flax was cultivated, which provided for flourishing industries, such as the weaving of linens and tentmaking. Its geographical location also contributed to its wealth, as its harbor was a link in an important trade route.

Tarsus was also a famous seat of learning. A number of historical personages visited Tarsus, including Julius Caesar, Mark Antony and Cleopatra, as well as several Roman emperors. Cicero was the city's governor from 51 to 50 B.C. For good reasons, therefore, Paul could boast that his native city was "no obscure city."

The New Testament gives a fair amount of information on the life of Paul. His original name was Saul, and he was born in the first years of this era and died c. 65. A Jew by birth and a native of Tarsus in Cilicia, he was a Roman citizen. According to Jerome, his family originated from Giscala (Gush-Halav) in Galilee. He adhered to the Pharisee form of Judaism and he studied in Jerusalem, where he was a pupil of Gamaliel the Elder.

He was a tentmaker by profession, and probably learned the trade from his father. Paul was versed in Greek and in Hebrew (Acts 21:37–40). At the time of his travels he was not married (I Corinthians 7). He had a nephew in Jerusalem (Acts 23:7).

He was at first a fanatical enemy of the Christians, and was sent to Damascus to arrest any Christians that he found and bring them to Jerusalem to stand trial. On the way he had a vision of Jesus, and he became a believer and was baptized at Damascus. He made three missionary journeys, converting Gentiles to Christianity and founding churches. Paul was not the first to preach Christ to the Gentiles, but he was the most active. The first followers of Jesus were Jews, and they formed a sect within Jewry, and some had reservations about preaching to Gentiles. Paul, furthermore, strongly opposed the observance of all Jewish practices in Christian communities made up of Gentiles. He was therefore often persecuted by both Gentiles and Jews.

As also the high priest doth bear me witness, and all the estate of the elders: from whom also I received letters unto the brethren, and went to Damascus, to bring them which were there bound unto Jerusalem, for to be punished.

And it came to pass, that, as I made my journey, and was come nigh unto Damascus about noon, suddenly there shone from heaven a great light round about me.

And I fell unto the ground, and heard a voice saying unto me, Saul, Saul, why persecutest thou me?

And I answered, Who art thou, Lord? And he said unto me, I am Jesus of Nazareth, whom thou persecutest.

And they that were with me saw indeed the light, and were afraid; but they heard not the voice of him that spake to me.

And I said, What shall I do, Lord? And the Lord said unto me, Arise, and go into Damascus; and there it shall be told thee of all things which are appointed for thee to do.

(22:1–10)

293. Entrance to the tomb of Rabbi Gamaliel at Beth Shearim.

Gamaliel, known as Gamaliel the Elder, was president of the Sanhedrin, the ancient Jewish rabbinical court. Gamaliel was a Pharisee and the most famous rabbinic teacher of the day, and played an important part in the religious life of his time. The sages expressed their regard for Gamaliel by saying "When Rabban Gamaliel died, the glory of the Torah (Law) ceased, and purity and saintliness."

294. An aerial view of the fortress erected by the Turks in the 17th century on the ruins of the Crusader castle of Antipatris. Herod the Great founded the city of Antipatris on the road from Jerusalem to Caesarea and named it after his father Antipater. This was also the site of ancient Aphek of the Old Testament (I Samuel 4:1).

Then the soldiers, as it was commanded them, took Paul, and brought him by night to Antipatris.

(23:31)

And after certain days, when Felix came with his wife Drusilla, which was a Jewess, he sent for Paul, and heard him concerning the faith in Christ.

And as he reasoned of righteousness, temperance, and judgment to come, Felix trembled, and answered, Go thy way for this time; when I have a convenient season, I will call for thee.

He hoped also that money should have been given him of Paul, that he might loose him: wherefore he sent for him the oftener, and communed with him.

But after two years Porcius Festus came into Felix' room: and Felix, willing to shew the Jews a pleasure, left Paul bound.

(24:24–27)

295. Coin of Felix, the Roman procurator of Judea, from 52 to 60. Felix was the brother of an influential freedman in imperial Rome, and was appointed to the procuratorship by the emperor Claudius. He married Drusilla, daughter of Agrippa I. His governorship of Judea was marked by unrest. He sought closer relations with the Jewish aristocracy, and faced constant friction and strained relations with the Jewish masses. He was recalled to Rome and was succeeded by Festus Porcius.

296

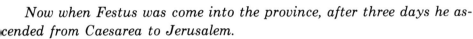

Now when Festus was come into the province, after three days he ascended from Caesarea to Jerusalem.

Then the high priest and the chief of the Jews informed him against Paul, and besought him,

And desired favour against him, that he would send for him to Jerusalem, laying wait in the way to kill him.

But Festus answered, that Paul should be kept at Caesarea, and that he himself would depart shortly thither.

Let them therefore, said he, which among you are able, go down with me, and accuse this man, if there be any wickedness in him.

And when he had tarried among them more than ten days, he went down unto Caesarea; and the next day sitting on the judgment seat commanded Paul to be brought.

And when he was come, the Jews which came down from Jerusalem stood round about, and laid many and grievous complaints against Paul, which they could not prove.

While he answered for himself, Neither against the law of the Jews, neither against the temple, nor yet against Caesar, have I offended any thing at all.

But Festus, willing to do the Jews a pleasure, answered Paul, and said, Wilt thou go up to Jerusalem, and there be judged of these things before me?

Then said Paul, I stand at Casear's judgment seat, where I ought to be judged: to the Jews have I done no wrong, as thou very well knowest.

For if I be an offender, or have committed any thing worthy of death, I refuse not to die: but if there be none of these things whereof these accuse me, no man may deliver me unto them. I appeal unto Caesar.

Then Festus, when he had conferred with the council, answered, Hast thou appealed unto Caesar? unto Caesar shalt thou go.

(25:1–12)

296. Capital embellished with a *menorah*, found among the remains of an ancient synagogue at Caesarea.

297. Nero, the Roman emperor to whom Paul referred at his trial in Caesarea before Festus. As a Roman citizen Paul exercised his right to be judged by the highest court of the empire in Rome.

297

298. The harbor of Caesarea with columns from the ruins of the ancient port city.

And because the haven was not commodious to winter in, the more part advised to depart thence also, if by any means they might attain to Phenice, and there to winter; which is an haven of Crete, and lieth toward the south west and north west. (27:12)

And we being exceedingly tossed with a tempest, the next day they lightened the ship; And the third day we cast out with our own hands the tackling of the ship.

And when neither sun nor stars in many days appeared, and no small tempest lay on us, all hope that we should be saved was then taken away.

But after long abstinence Paul stood forth in the midst of them, and said, Sirs, ye should have hearkened unto me, and not loosed from Crete, and to have gained this harm and loss.

And now I exhort you to be of good cheer: for there shall be no loss of any man's life among you, but of the ship. For there stood by me this night the angel of God, whose I am, and whom I serve,

Saying, Fear not, Paul; thou must be brought before Caesar: and, lo, God hath given thee all them that sail with thee.

Wherefore, sirs, be of good cheer: for I believe God, that it shall be even as it was told me. (27:18–25)

And falling into a place where two seas met, they ran the ship aground; and the fore-part stuck fast, and remained unmoveable, but the hinder part was broken with the violence of the waves.

And the soldiers' counsel was to kill the prisoners, lest any of them should swim out and escape.

But the centurion, willing to save Paul, kept them from their purpose; and commanded that they which could swim should first cast themselves first into the sea, and get to land:

And the rest, some on boards, and some on broken pieces of the ship. And so it came to pass, that they escaped all safe to land. (27:41–44)

299. The ancient harbor of Knossos in Crete.

300. A sailing ship in stormy weather, depicted on a 3rd-century Roman sarcophagus.

300

301

And when they were escaped, then they knew that the island was called Melita.

And the barbarous people shewed us no little kindness: for they kindled a fire, and received us every one, because of the present rain, and because of the cold.

And when Paul had gathered a bundle of sticks, and laid them on the fire, there came a viper out of the heat, and fastened on his hand.

And when the barbarians saw the venomous beast hang on his hand, they said among themselves, No doubt this man is a murderer, whom, though he hath escaped the sea, yet vengeance suffereth not to live.

And he shook off the beast into the fire, and felt no harm.

Howbeit they looked when he should have swollen, or fallen down dead suddenly: but after they had looked a great while, and saw no harm come to him, they changed their minds, and said that he was a god.

(28:1–6)

302

301. The miracle of Paul and the serpent at Malta, depicted on a fresco of the 11th century at Canterbury Cathedral, England.
Melita, where Paul was shipwrecked, has been identified as Malta, the largest of a group of five islands south of Sicily.
It was settled by Phoenicians about 1000 B.C. The Carthaginians, themselves of Phoenician origin, colonized Malta in the 8th or 7th century B.C. In 218 B.C. the Romans established a garrison there, but allowed the inhabitants to control their own affairs. The "barbarous" character of the people means that they did not speak Greek, nor had they adopted Hellenistic culture.

And from thence we fetched a compass, and came to Rhegium: and after one day the south wind blew, and we came the next day to Puteoli:

Where we found brethren, and were desired to tarry with them seven days: and so we went toward Rome.

And from thence, when the brethren heard of us, they came to meet us as far as Appii forum, and The three taverns: whom when Paul saw, he thanked God, and took courage.

And when we came to Rome, the centurion delivered the prisoners to the captain of the guard: but Paul was suffered to dwell by himself with a soldier that kept him.

(28:13–16)

302. View of the Appian Way.
From Puteoli Paul and his party travelled to Rome by the Appian Way. The market place of Appius, also called "Appii Forum," was a station on the Via Appia, running from Puteoli to Rome.

303. Remains of a temple (1st century B.C.) in the ancient port of Pozzuoli, a few miles from Naples. It was the harbor of ancient Rome, and may have been the town of Puteoli mentioned in the New Testament.

304. "Three Taverns," south of Rome. This has been identified as the place where the Christians of Rome came to meet Paul.

305. Old houses in Rome today.
In Rome Paul was able to live in a rented house for two years, establish contact with the Jewish community and receive visitors, thus continuing his apostolic ministry.

And Paul dwelt two whole years in his own hired house, and received all that came in unto him,

Preaching the kingdom of God, and teaching those things which concern the Lord Jesus Christ, with all confidence, no man forbidding him.

(28:30–31)

306. Glass roundel decorated with Jewish ritual objects from the catacombs in Rome (Israel Museum, Jerusalem).
Several burial galleries in the catacombs were used by Jews and early Christians in the 1st century. Some of the inscriptions date from the period between the 1st and 4th centuries. Some are in Greek and some in Latin.

307. Ancient street in Rome.
Paul addresses his epistle to the church in Rome. At this time he has not yet been to Rome, the center of the Roman Empire. The church may have already been established by Roman Jews and proselytes who had heard Peter preach in Jerusalem (Acts 2:10). Jews had been living in Rome since the second century B.C. After the Romans invaded Judea in 63 B.C., Jewish prisoners were brought as slaves to Rome, merchants came on business and the Jewish community was also augmented by proselytes (i.e., pagans who converted to Judaism but were not all circumcised). There were several synagogues founded by freedmen.

308. Jewish ritual circumcision implements (Israel Museum, Jerusalem).
The custom of circumcision goes back to prehistoric times, and is one of the oldest operations performed by man. An ancient Egyptian custom, it was prescribed by Mosaic Law, to be performed on the eighth day of life (Leviticus, 12:2–3). It is also mandatory for adult men converting to Judaism.
Circumcision is also used figuratively in the Bible, the word "uncircumcised" being equal to "unclean." "Circumcise therefore the foreskin of your hearts and be no more stiffnecked. For the Lord your God is God of Gods, a mighty, and a terrible, which regardeth not persons nor taketh reward: He doth execute the judgement of the fatherless and widow, and loveth the stranger, in giving him food and raiment. Love ye therefore the stranger: for ye were strangers in the land of Egypt." (Deuteronomy 10:16–19.)

Paul, a servant of Jesus Christ, called to be an apostle, separated unto the gospel of God,

(Which he had promised afore by his prophets in the holy scriptures,)

Concerning his Son Jesus Christ our Lord, which was made of the seed of David according to the flesh;

And declared to be the Son of God with power, according to the spirit of holiness, by the resurrection from the dead:

By whom we have received grace and apostleship, for obedience to the faith among all nations, for his name:

Among whom are ye also the called of Jesus Christ:

To all that be in Rome, beloved of God, called to be saints: Grace to you and peace from God our Father, and the Lord Jesus Christ.

First, I thank my God through Jesus Christ for you all, that your faith is spoken of throughout the whole world.

For God is my witness, whom I serve with my spirit in the gospel of his Son, that without ceasing I make mention of you always in my prayers;

Making request, if by any means now at length I might have a prosperous journey by the will of God to come unto you.

For I long to see you, that I may impart unto you some spiritual gift, to the end ye may be established; That is, that I may be comforted together with you by the mutual faith both of you and me.

Now I would not have you ignorant, brethren, that oftentimes I purposed to come unto you, (but was let hitherto,) that I might have some fruit among you also, even as among other Gentiles.

I am debtor both to the Greeks, and to the Barbarians; both to the wise, and to the unwise. So, as much as in me is, I am ready to preach the gospel to you that are at Rome also.

For I am not ashamed of the gospel of Christ: for it is the power of God unto salvation to every one that believeth; to the Jew first, and also to the Greek.
(1:1–16)

Cometh this blessedness then upon the circumcision only, or upon the uncircumcision also? for we say that faith was reckoned to Abraham for righteousness.

306

How was it then reckoned? when he was in circumcision, or in uncircumcision? Not in circumcision, but in uncircumcision.

And he received the sign of circumcision, a seal of the righteousness of the faith which he had yet being uncircumcised: that he might be the father of all them that believe, though they be not circumcised; that righteousness might be imputed unto them also:

And the father of circumcision to them who are not of the circumcision only, but who also walk in the steps of that faith of our father Abraham, which he had being yet uncircumcised.   (4:9–12)

Wherefore, as by one man sin entered into the world, and death by sin; and so death passed upon all men, for that all have sinned: For until the law sin was in the world: but sin is not imputed when there is no law.

Nevertheless death reigned from Adam to Moses, even over them that had not sinned after the similitude of Adam's transgression, who is the figure of him that was to come.

But not as the offence, so also is the free gift. For if through the offence of one many be dead, much more the grace of God, and the gift by grace, which is by one man, Jesus Christ, hath abounded unto many.

And not as it was by one that sinned, so is the gift: for the judgment was by one to condemnation, but the free gift is of many offences unto justification.

For if by one man's offence death reigned by one; much more they which receive abundance of grace and of the gift of righteousness shall reign in life by one, Jesus Christ.

Therefore as by the offence of one judgment came upon all men to condemnation; even so by the righteousness of one the free gift came upon all men unto justification of life.

For as by one man's disobedience many were made sinners, so by the obedience of one shall many be made righteous.

Moreover the law entered, that the offence might abound. But where sin abounded, grace did much more abound:

That as sin hath reigned unto death, even so might grace reign through righteousness unto eternal life by Jesus Christ our Lord.   (5:12-21)

For if the firstfruit be holy, the lump is also holy: and if the root be holy, so are the branches.

And if some of the branches be broken off, and thou, being a wild olive tree, wert graffed in among them, and with them partakest of the root and fatness of the olive tree;

Boast not against the branches. But if thou boast, thou bearest not the root, but the root thee.

Thou wilt say then, The branches were broken off, that I might be graffed in.

Well; because of unbelief they were broken off, and thou standest by faith. Be not highminded, but fear: For if God spared not the natural branches, take heed lest he also spare not thee.

Behold therefore the goodness and severity of God: on them which fell, severity; but toward thee, goodness, if thou continue in his goodness: otherwise thou also shalt be cut off.

308

309

309. Adam; detail from a relief on a 4th-century sarcophagus (Grotto Vaticane, Rome). Adam signifies here "the figure of him that was to come," that is, Christ – as Paul sees it, the head of mankind, and thus as a type of Christ, the head of the new corporate man, the church (Ephesians 2:15–16).

This idea of the first, fallen Adam and the second, the redeeming Adam is also found in I Corinthians 15:45: "The first man Adam was made a living soul, the last Adam was made a quickening [life-giving] spirit." Paul thus represents the whole world as two men, Adam and Christ, and one is "in Adam" by birth and "in Christ" by believing in him. Those who are in Adam, according to Paul, are "earthy" and "natural," whereas those who are in Christ, the beginning of the new creation, are "heavenly" and "spiritual" (I Corinthians 15:46–47).

And they also, if they abide not still in unbelief, shall be graffed in: for God is able to graff them in again.

For if thou wert cut out of the olive tree which is wild by nature, and wert graffed contrary to nature into a good olive tree: how much more shall these, which be the natural branches, be graffed into their own olive tree?

For I would not, brethren, that ye should be ignorant of this mystery, lest ye should be wise in your own conceits; that blindness in part is happened to Israel, until the fulness of the Gentiles be come in.

And so all Israel shall be saved: as it is written, There shall come out of Sion the Deliverer, and shall turn away ungodliness from Jacob.

(11:16-26)

I beseech you therefore, brethren, by the mercies of God, that ye present your bodies a living sacrifice, holy, acceptable unto God, which is your reasonable service.

And be not conformed to this world: but be ye transformed by the renewing of your mind, that ye may prove what is that good, and acceptable, and perfect, will of God.

For I say, through the grace given unto me, to every man that is among you, not to think of himself more highly than he ought to think; but to think soberly, according as God hath dealt to every man the measure of faith.

For as we have many members in one body, and all members have not the same office: So we, being many, are one body in Christ, and every one members one of another.

Having then gifts differing according to the grace that is given to us, whether prophecy, let us prophesy according to the proportion of faith;

310. Root of an ancient olive tree. Paul likens the salvation of the nations (Gentiles) to branches which were grafted in place of those broken off (referring to the "stumbling" or unbelief of the Jews), to the root and fatness of the olive tree. Yet he reminds the nations that "thou bearest not the root, but the root thee." The "root and fatness" is all the promises given to the fathers in the Old Testament. The nations, the wild olive tree, should then not boast over the branches or be high-minded, but continue in God's goodness in fear.

Or ministry, let us wait on our ministering: or he that teacheth, on teaching;

Or he that exhorteth, on exhortation: he that giveth, let him do it with simplicity; he that ruleth, with diligence; he that sheweth mercy, with cheerfulness.

Let love be without dissimulation. Abhor that which is evil; cleave to that which is good.

Be kindly affectioned one to another with brotherly love; in honour preferring one another;

Not slothful in business; fervent in spirit; serving the Lord;

Rejoicing in hope; patient in tribulation; continuing instant in prayer;

Distributing to the necessity of saints; given to hospitality.

Bless them which persecute you: bless, and curse not.

Rejoice with them that do rejoice, and weep with them that weep.

Be of the same mind one toward another. Mind not high things, but condescend to men of low estate. Be not wise in your own conceits.

Recompense to no man evil for evil. Provide things honest in the sight of all men.

If it be possible, as much as lieth in you, live peaceably with all men.

Dearly beloved, avenge not yourselves, but rather give place unto wrath: for it is written, Vengeance is mine; I will repay, saith the Lord.

Therefore if thine enemy hunger, feed him; if he thirst, give him drink: for in so doing thou shalt heap coals of fire on his head.

Be not overcome of evil, but overcome evil with good.

(12:1-21)

311. Woman and her four daughters gambling; encaustic on marble from Herculanum, 1st century (Museo Nazionale, Naples). Gambling is one of the oldest and most widespread human activities. Innumerable traces of gambling are to be found in what was the Roman Empire. Though Paul does not refer explicitly to gambling here, it was certainly one of the manifestations of wordliness to be avoided. It is one of the world's enticements that the "brethren" should not conform to, but rather "be ye transformed by the renewing of your mind" (verse 2).

312. Column from a Roman temple at Corinth.

313. Portrait of Chilon, one of the seven sages from Ephoros in Sparta; Roman fresco c. A.D. 200–220 from Ephesus.

The seven sages of Greece were historical figures of the 7th/6th century B.C. Famous for their wisdom in philosophy and statesmanship, they represent the epitome of practical wisdom. They are mentioned by Plato. The numerous references to them by ancient writers are mainly in connection with three topics: a wisdom contest, and the prize given to the wisest; a banquet-symposium where they displayed their wisdom in a formal setting; and quotations of their maxims, including "Know thyself" and "Nothing in excess", which were carved on the temple of Apollo at Delphi.

Paul asks:"where is the wise, where is the scribe?" The exponents of Judaism were above all fierce defenders of monotheism, and believed that their religion provided the ideal and norm for daily life and piety. During the period of the Second Temple, a new institution arose in Jewish life: the scribes, interpreters of the Law to the observant community. The scribes were regarded as the authors of the Oral Law, or *Halakhah*, the continuation, interpretation and supplement to the Law of Moses. This was needed to meet the changing conditions of life. The scribal class, with its continual involvement in ques-

Paul, called to be an apostle of Jesus Christ through the will of God, and Sosthenes our brother,

Unto the church of God which is at Corinth, to them that are sanctified in Christ Jesus, called to be saints, with all that in every place call upon the name of Jesus Christ our Lord, both theirs and ours:

Grace be unto you, and peace, from God our Father, and from the Lord Jesus Christ.

I thank my God always on your behalf, for the grace of God which is given you by Jesus Christ;

That in every thing ye are enriched by him, in all utterance, and in all knowledge;

Even as the testimony of Christ was confirmed in you:

So that ye come behind in no gift; waiting for the coming of our Lord Jesus Christ:

Who shall also confirm you unto the end, that ye may be blameless in the day of our Lord Jesus Christ.

God is faithful, by whom ye were called unto the fellowship of his Son Jesus Christ our Lord.

Now I beseech you, brethren, by the name of our Lord Jesus Christ, that ye all speak the same thing, and that there be no divisions among you; but that ye be perfectly joined together in the same mind and in the same judgment.

(1:1–10)

312

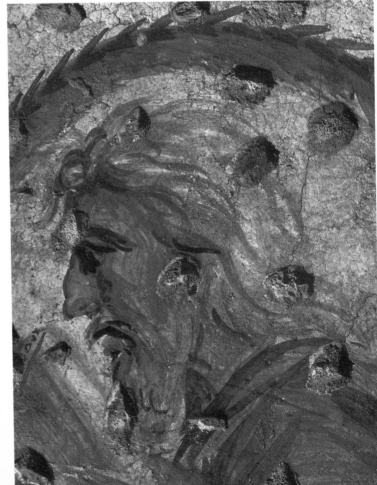

Where is the wise? where is the scribe? where is the disputer of this world? hath not God made foolish the wisdom of this world?

For after that in the wisdom of God the world by wisdom knew not God, it pleased God by the foolishness of preaching to save them that believe.

For the Jews require a sign, and the Greeks seek after wisdom:

But we preach Christ crucified, unto the Jews a stumblingblock, and unto the Greeks foolishness;

But unto them which are called, both Jews and Greeks, Christ the power of God, and the wisdom of God.

Because the foolishness of God is wiser than men; and the weakness of God is stronger than men.

For ye see your calling, brethren, how that not many wise men after the flesh, not many mighty, mot many noble, are called:

But God hath chosen the foolish things of the world to confound the wise; and God hath chosen the weak things of the world to confound the things which are mighty;

And base things of the world, and things which are despised, hath God chosen, yea, and things which are not, to bring to nought things that are:

That no flesh should glory in his presence.

But of him are ye in Christ Jesus, who of God is made unto us wisdom, and righteousness, and sanctification, and redemption:

That, according as it is written, He that glorieth, let him glory in the Lord.
                                                                  (1:20–31)

tions of religion, law, custom, ritual and justice, came to acquire a specific theology and gave rise to a number of religious movements.

314. Group of aristocratic women in elegant Byzantine dress, depicted on a mosaic from the Kariye Church, Istanbul.
Paul points out that God calls upon people of his own choosing, without regard to their social standing. Thus, few "noble" or well-born persons have been called. Rather, God has chosen the "base things" – that is the low-born and the despised, so "that no flesh should glory in his presence" (verse 29).

315

316

Who then is Paul, and who is Apollos, but ministers by whom ye believed, even as the Lord gave to every man?

I have planted, Apollos watered; but God gave the increase.

So then neither is he that planteth any thing, neither he that watereth, but God that giveth the increase.

Now he that planteth and he that watereth are one: and every man shall receive his own reward according to his own labour.

For we are labourers together with God: ye are God's husbandry, ye are God's building.

(3:5–9)

Know ye not that the unrighteous shall not inherit the kingdom of God? Be not deceived: neither fornicators, nor idolaters, nor adulterers, nor effeminate, nor abusers of themselves with mankind,

Nor thieves, nor covetous, nor drunkards, nor revilers, nor extortioners, shall inherit the kingdom of God.

And such were some of you: but ye are washed, but ye are sanctified, but ye are justified in the name of the Lord Jesus and by the Spirit of our God.

(6:9–11)

317

315. Byzantine mosaic from Beth-Shean, showing the months of the year and the agricultural activities with each season. Paul's metaphor is that the believers are God's farm. The Corinthian believers overestimated the planter and the waterer, but neglected the One who causes to grow.

316. A youth with a feminine hairstyle; part of a relief from Herculanum, 1st century, B.C. (Museo Nazionale, Naples).

317. Oedipus sacrificing to the Delphic oracle in front of a statue of Apollo; detail from a 3rd-century sarcophagus (Lateran Museum, Rome).

Now as touching things offered unto idols, we know that we all have knowledge. Knowledge puffeth up, but charity edifieth.

And if any man think that he knoweth any thing, he knoweth nothing yet as he ought to know. But if any man love God, the same is known of him.

As concerning therefore the eating of those things that are offered in sacrifice unto idols, we know that an idol is nothing in the world, and that there is none other God but one.

For though there be that are called gods, whether in heaven or in earth, (as there be gods many, and lords many,)

But to us there is but one God, the Father, of whom are all things, and we in him; and one Lord Jesus Christ, by whom are all things; and we by him.

Howbeit there is not in every man that knowledge: for some with conscience of the idol unto this hour eat it as a thing offered unto an idol; and their conscience being weak is defiled.

But meat commendeth us not to God: for neither, if we eat, are we the better; neither, if we eat not, are we the worse. But take heed lest by any means this liberty of yours become a stumblingblock to them that are weak.

For if any man see thee which hast knowledge sit at meat in the idol's temple, shall not the conscience of him which is weak be emboldened to eat those things which are offered to idols; And through thy knowledge shall the weak brother perish, for whom Christ died?

But when ye sin so against the brethren, and wound their weak conscience, ye sin against Christ.

Wherefore, if meat make my brother to offend, I will eat no flesh while the world standeth, lest I make my brother to offend. (8:1–13)

318. Sacrificial scene; bronze, 2nd century (Magyar Nemzeti Muzeum, Budapest).
In the pagan world meat was commonly offered to the gods. Part of the meat was burned on the altar, part went to the officiating priest, and the remainder to the worshippers. Sometimes the remainder was sold in the market, and the question of its acceptability troubled the early Christians. Paul returns to this issue in I Corinthians 10:25–29.
Sacrifices in the Temple of Jerusalem in honor of the emperor were instituted originally by Augustus and were offered twice daily. They consisted of two lambs and a bull. Josephus relates that one of the causes of the great war with Rome was that Eleazar, the son of Ananias the high priest – "a very rash

319

Know ye not that they which run in a race run all, but one receiveth the prize? So run, that ye may obtain.

And every man that striveth for the mastery is temperate in all things. Now they do it to obtain a corruptible crown; but we an incorruptible.

I therefore so run, not as uncertainly; so fight I, not as one that beateth the air:

But I keep under my body, and bring it into subjection: lest that by any means, when I have preached to others, I myself should be a castaway. (9:24–27)

Moreover, brethren, I would not that ye should be ignorant, how that all our fathers were under the cloud, and all passed through the sea; And were all baptized unto Moses in the cloud and in the sea; And did all eat the same spiritual meat;

young man" – persuaded the officiating priests not to accept gifts or sacrifices from foreigners, which included the sacrifices offered for Rome and the emperor.

319. Runner with gymnast's shoes and wash-basin; Attic red-figured cup, 3rd century B.C. (Louvre, Paris).
The judges crowned the winners with wreaths of wild olive leaves. Athletic games were held in all Greek cities, and in all the cities in the Orient that had adopted Greek culture. The great games were held mainly at Olympia, Delphi, Argos and Corinth, and drew large crowds, and the prize-winners were greatly honored.
Paul appeals to the Corinthian Christians to exercise self-control to attain the prize, just as

the athletes of the famous games had to practice great self-discipline in order to win.

320. A little boy playing with a goose; marble sculpture, Roman copy of a Greek original, 2nd century A.D., found at Ephesus (Kunsthistorisches Museum, Vienna).
These verses show the excelling of love over all other gifts, here described as "childish things."

321. Wall painting from the synagogue in Dura-Europos showing a well which Moses touches with his rod.
According to the Jewish tradition illustrated in this painting, this well followed the Israelites on their wanderings in the wilderness. This notion of a water supply which accompanied the twelve tribes in the wilderness from station to station, is expressed by the twelve streams which flow out from the central well, struck by Moses, to twelve tents, in each of which stands a short figure.

And did all drink the same spiritual drink: for they drank of that spiritual Rock that followed them: and that Rock was Christ.

But with many of them God was not well pleased: for they were overthrown in the wilderness.

Now these things were our examples, to the intent we should not lust after evil things, as they also lusted. Neither be ye idolaters, as were some of them; as it is written, The people sat down to eat and drink, and rose up to play.

Neither let us commit fornication, as some of them committed, and fell in one day three and twenty thousand. Neither let us tempt Christ, as some of them also tempted, and were destroyed of serpents. Neither murmur ye, as some of them also murmured, and were destroyed of the destroyer.

Now all these things happened unto them for ensamples: and they are written for admonition, upon whom the ends of the world are come.

Wherefore let him that thinketh he standeth take heed lest he fall.

(10:1–12)

320

This passage employs the Old Testament account of the wandering in the wilderness as an illustration of the believer's experience, and derives from it a warning against idolatry, fornication, tempting the Lord or murmuring. Verse 1 begins with the parting of the Red Sea, continues with the manna and finally the smitten rock.

Charity never faileth: but whether there be prophecies, they shall fail; whether there be tongues, they shall cease; whether there be knowledge, it shall vanish away. For we know in part, and we prophesy in part. But when that which is perfect is come, then that which is in part shall be done away.

When I was a child, I spake as a child, I understood as a child, I thought as a child: but when I became a man, I put away childish things.

For now we see through a glass, darkly; but then face to face: now I know in part; but then shall I know even as also I am known. (13:8–12)

But if the ministration of death, written and engraven in stones, was glorious, so that the children of Israel could not stedfastly behold the face of Moses for the glory of his countenance; which glory was to be done away:

How shall not the ministration of the spirit be rather glorious?

For if the ministration of condemnation be glory, much more doth the ministration of righteousness exceed in glory.

For even that which was made glorious had no glory in this respect, by reason of the glory that excelleth. For if that which is done away was glorious, much more that which remaineth is glorious.

Seeing then that we have such hope, we use great plainness of speech:

And not as Moses, which put a vail over his face, that the children of Israel could not stedfastly look to the end of that which is abolished:

But their minds were blinded: for until this day remaineth the same vail untaken away in the reading of the old testament; which vail is done away in Christ. But even unto this day, when Moses is read, the vail is upon their heart. Nevertheless when it shall turn to the Lord, the vail shall be taken away.   (3:7–16)

322

322. Moses with horns: detail of the famous statue by Michelangelo.
The "horns" derive from an ancient interpretation of the Hebrew root KRN, which can mean horn but in this instance meant ray (of light). This old interpretation appears in the Latin translation of the Old Testament. Moses' face shone when he came down from Mount Sinai after receiving the Tablets of the Law (Exodus 34:29–35), and this is the "glory of his countenance" which Paul refers to in his discussion of the merits of the new covenant, as opposed to the old covenant of the Law.

323. Pottery for every-day use, 1st century A.D., found in Israel (Israel Museum, Jerusalem).
Paul uses five expressive metaphors in the Second Book of Corinthians to illustrate the character and ministry of the New Testament believers: captives in a triumphant procession for the celebration of Christ's victory (2:14); incense-bearers to spread the fragrance of Christ (2:14–16); letters written with Christ as the content (3:1–3); mirrors beholding and reflecting the glory of Christ, to be transformed into his image (3:18), and, as here, earthen vessels to contain the excellent treasure – Christ.

But we have this treasure in earthen vessels, that the excellency of the power may be of God, and not of us. We are troubled on every side, yet not distressed; we are perplexed, but not in despair; Persecuted, but not forsaken; cast down, but not destroyed;

Always bearing about in the body the dying of the Lord Jesus, that the life also of Jesus might be made manifest in our body.

For we which live are alway delivered unto death for Jesus' sake, that the life also of Jesus might be made manifest in our mortal flesh.

So then death worketh in us, but life in you.   (4:7–12)

324

324. Pillar of the Flagellation of St. Paul, at New Paphos, Cyprus.

In biblical law, flogging or whipping was the standard punishment for most offenses (Deuteronomy 25:2: "And it shall be, if the wicked man be worthy to be beaten, that the judge shall cause him to lie down, and to be beaten before his face, according to his fault, by a certain number"). The judges determined the number of strokes according to the gravity of the offense, but they were not to exceed forty: "Forty stripes he may give him, and not exceed: lest, if he should exceed, and beat him above these with many stripes, then thy brother should seem vile unto thee," (Deuteronomy 25:3). This was meant to be a corrective disciplinary measure, not a vindictive or a humiliating one.

The person administering the beating had to count one stroke less than the number prescribed, in order not to exceed it by mistake. Paul himself had Christians flogged in the synagogue before his conversion (Acts 22:19). Paul was beaten and threatened to be stoned to death by the Jews on several occasions: at Philippi (Acts 16:22) and in Jerusalem (Acts 21:32).

The Romans also beat prisoners, but Roman citizens were exempted (Acts 22:25–26). The Romans used rods or the scourge. The outer garments were stripped off and the victim was stretched out, his hands tied to a post with thongs. The most terrible instrument for scourging was called the *flagellum*, consisting of thongs weighted with pieces of bone or metal.

325. Greek and Trojan warriors in single combat; relief from Trysa, Turkey (Kunsthistorisches Museum, Vienna, Austria).

Being human, the Apostles are still in flesh and thus walk in the flesh, but they do not conduct themselves at the behest of the flesh,

We then, as workers together with him, beseech you also that ye receive not the grace of God in vain.

(For he saith, I have heard thee in a time accepted, and in the day of salvation have I succoured thee: behold, now is the accepted time; behold, now is the day of salvation.)

Giving no offence in any thing, that the ministry be not blamed:

But in all things approving ourselves as the ministers of God, in much patience, in afflictions, in necessities, in distresses, In stripes, in imprisonments, in tumults, in labours, in watchings, in fastings;

By pureness, by knowledge, by longsuffering, by kindness, by the Holy Ghost, by love unfeigned,

By the word of truth, by the power of God, by the armour of righteousness on the right hand and on the left,

By honour and dishonour, by evil report and good report: as deceivers, and yet true;

As unknown, and yet well known; as dying, and, behold, we live; as chastened, and not killed;

As sorrowful, yet alway rejoicing; as poor, yet making many rich; as

having nothing, and yet possessing all things. (6:1–10)

Now I Paul myself beseech you by the meekness and gentleness of Christ, who in presence am base among you, but being absent am bold toward you:

But I beseech you, that I may not be bold when I am present with that confidence, wherewith I think to be bold against some, which think of us as if we walked according to the flesh.

For though we walk in the flesh, we do not war after the flesh:

(For the weapons of our warfare are not carnal, but mighty through God to the pulling down of strong holds;)

Casting down imaginations, and every high thing that exalteth itself against the knowledge of God, and bringing into captivity every thought to the obedience of Christ; And having in a readiness to revenge all disobedience, when your obedience is fulfilled.

Do ye look on things after the outward appearance? If any man trust to himself that he is Christ's, let him of himself think this again, that, as he is Christ's, even so are we Christ's.

For though I should boast somewhat more of our authority, which the Lord hath given us for edification, and not for your destruction, I should not be ashamed:

That I may not seem as if I would terrify you by letters.   (10:1–9)

Would to God ye could bear with me a little in my folly: and indeed bear with me.

For I am jealous over you with godly jealousy: for I have espoused you to one husband, that I may present you as a chaste virgin to Christ.

But I fear, lest by any means, as the serpent beguiled Eve through his

especially in their spiritual mission – they walk after the spirit (Romans 8:4). Since their spiritual struggle is not against the flesh, but against spiritual forces (Ephesians 6:12: "against principalities, against powers, against the rulers of the darkness of this world, against spiritual wickedness in high places"), their weapons should not be fleshly but spiritual, "mighty through God to the pulling down of strong holds." According to verse 5, these strongholds are actually the "imaginations, and every high thing that exalteth itself against the knowledge of God" (verse 5).

326. The seduction of Eve by the serpent, relief from the chapel of Tyrol Castle, Meran, Italy, 15th century A.D.

subtilty, so your minds should be corrupted from the simplicity that is in Christ.   (11:1–3)

For we are glad, when we are weak, and ye are strong: and this also we wish, even your perfection.

Therefore I write these things being absent, lest being present I should use sharpness, according to the power which the Lord hath given me to edification, and not to destruction.

Finally, brethren, farewell. Be perfect, be of good comfort, be of one mind, live in peace; and the God of love and peace shall be with you.

Greet one another with an holy kiss. All the saints salute you.

The grace of the Lord Jesus Christ, and the love of God, and the communion of the Holy Ghost, be with you all. Amen.   (13:9–14)

327. Aramaic text of Paul's Epistle to the Galatians, with commentary in Greek; from a 7th-century manuscript now at St. Mark's monastery in Jerusalem.
Galatia was a Roman province in central Asia Minor. It was bounded by the Roman provinces of Cappadocia, Bithynia and Pontius, Asia and Pamphylia. The city of Ancyra (now Ankara) was in the north-central region.
In the 3rd century B.C., hordes of people variously known as Celts, or Galli, (whom the Greeks called *Galati*, hence the name of this region), settled there, and engaged in plundering raids, until they were finally subdued by the Romans.
The older inhabitants remained on the land but had to pay tribute to the Gallic overlords. The Galli formed a small military aristocracy, living in fortified villages. For centuries they retained their own language and customs, and it was not until the second century A.D. that Galatia became fully Hellenized.
Paul and Peter (I Peter) both wrote letters to the churches in the province of Galatia. Paul and Barnabas had visited cities in Galatia: Antioch in Pisidia (Acts 13:14), and Iconium (Acts 13:50–51), but the Jews "expelled them out of their coasts".

328. Detail from a bas-relief of the 4th century, showing the busts of the Apostles Peter and Paul facing each other (Museo Archeologico Aquileia, Italy).

Paul, an apostle, (not of men, neither by man, but by Jesus Christ, and God the Father, who raised him from the dead;)

And all the brethren which are with me, unto the churches of Galatia:

Grace be to you and peace from God the Father, and from our Lord Jesus Christ.

Who gave himself for our sins, that he might deliver us from this present evil world, according to the will of God and our Father:

To whom be glory for ever and ever. Amen.

I marvel that ye are so soon removed from him that called you into the grace of Christ unto another gospel:

Which is not another; but there be some that trouble you, and would pervert the gospel of Christ.

But though we, or an angel from heaven, preach any other gospel unto you than that which we have preached unto you, let him be accursed.

(1:1–8)

But when Peter was come to Antioch, I withstood him to the face, because he was to be blamed.

For before that certain came from James, he did eat with the Gentiles: but when they were come, he withdrew and separated himself, fearing them which were of the circumcision.

And the other Jews dissembled likewise with him; insomuch that Barnabas also was carried away with their dissimulation.

But when I saw that they walked not uprightly according to the truth of the gospel, I said unto Peter before them all, If thou, being a Jew, livest after the manner of Gentiles, and not as do the Jews, why compellest thou the Gentiles to live as do the Jews?

We who are Jews by nature, and not sinners of the Gentiles,

Knowing that a man is not justified by the works of the law, but by the faith of Jesus Christ, even we have believed in Jesus Christ, that we might be justified by the faith of Christ, and not by the works of the law: for by the works of the law shall no flesh be justified.

(2:11–16)

For as many as are of the works of the law are under the curse: for it is written, Cursed is every one that continueth not in all things which are written in the book of the law to do them.

But that no man is justified by the law in the sight of God it is evident: for, The just shall live by faith. And the law is not of faith: but, The man that doeth them shall live in them.

Christ hath redeemed us from the curse of the law, being made a curse for us: for it is written, Cursed is every one that hangeth on a tree:

That the blessing of Abraham might come on the Gentiles through Jesus Christ; that we might receive the promise of the Spirit through faith.

(3:10–14)

For if the inheritance be of the law, it is no more of promise: but God gave it to Abraham by promise.

Wherefore then serveth the law? It was added because of transgressions, till the seed should come to whom the promise was made; and it was ordained by angels in the hand of a mediator.

Now a mediator is not a mediator of one, but God is one.

Is the law then against the promises of God? God forbid: for if there had been a law given which could have given life, verily righteousness should have been by the law.

But the scripture hath concluded all under sin, that the promise by faith of Jesus Christ might be given to them that believe.

But before faith came, we were kept under the law, shut up unto the faith which should afterwards be revealed. Wherefore the law was our schoolmaster to bring us unto Christ, that we might be justified by faith.

But after that faith is come, we are no longer under a schoolmaster.

For ye are all the children of God by faith in Christ Jesus.

For as many of you as have been baptized into Christ have put on Christ. There is neither Jew nor Greek, there is neither bond nor free, there is neither male nor female: for ye are all one in Christ Jesus.

And if ye be Christ's, then are ye Abraham's seed, and heirs according to the promise.

(3:18–29)

329. Trees in the Valley of the Cross, from where, according to tradition, wood for the cross of Christ was taken.
Paul quotes Deuteronomy 21:23, making "tree" refer to the cross of Christ. In these verses Paul argues the blessing of faith as opposed to the curse of the Law, making use of the Old Testament, as he does in all his letters.

330. Woman taking her child from a nurse-maid; painting on a Lekythos vase from Eretria.
The word "schoolmaster" here refers to the slave or servant hired by households to accompany a child to and from its teacher. This metaphor is employed by Paul to illustrate the function of the Law.

330

331.

331. Remains of Hadrian's temple at Ephesus.

332. Inscription in Greek forbidding Gentiles to enter the Temple: "Let no one of the Gentiles enter inside the barrier and the fence around the sanctuary. And if he transgresses he shall himself bear the blame for his ensuing death."
There were special regulations governing admission to every part of the Temple's precincts. The Holy of Holies could be entered only by the High Priest. Male Israelites could enter the Inner Court, in which the "house" and altar stood. Women were permitted to go only as far as the Women's Court. Gentiles could enter the outer court up to the barrier encircling the Inner Temple. On two occasions Jesus expelled those who had made the "house of his Father" a place of commerce. Paul was once accused of bringing "Greeks" into the Temple (Acts 21:28) and the enraged worshippers tried to kill him.

332.

Paul, an apostle of Jesus Christ by the will of God, to the saints which are at Ephesus, and to the faithful in Christ Jesus:

Grace be to you, and peace, from God our Father, and from the Lord Jesus Christ.

Blessed be the God and Father of our Lord Jesus Christ, who hath blessed us with all spiritual blessings in heavenly places in Christ:

According as he hath chosen us in him before the foundation of the world, that we should be holy and without blame before him in love:

Having predestinated us unto the adoption of children by Jesus Christ to himself, according to the good pleasure of his will,

To the praise of the glory of his grace, wherein he hath made us accepted in the beloved.

(1:1–6)

Wherefore remember, that ye being in time past Gentiles in the flesh, who are called Uncircumcision by that which is called the Circumcision in the flesh made by hands;

That at that time ye were without Christ, being aliens from the commonwealth of Israel, and strangers from the covenants of promise, having no hope, and without God in the world:

But now in Christ Jesus ye who sometimes were far off are made nigh by the blood of Christ.

For he is our peace, who hath made both one, and hath broken down the middle wall of partition between us;

Having abolished in his flesh the enmity, even the law of commandments contained in ordinances; for to make in himself of twain one new man, so making peace;

And that he might reconcile both unto God in one body by the cross, having slain the enmity thereby:

And came and preached peace to you which were afar off, and to them that were nigh.

For through him we both have access by one Spirit unto the Father.

Now therefore ye are no more strangers and foreigners, but fellowcitizens with the saints, and of the household of God.

And are built upon the foundation of the apostles and prophets, Jesus Christ himself being the chief corner stone;

In whom all the building fitly framed together groweth unto an holy temple in the Lord:

In whom ye also are builded together for an habitation of God through the Spirit.

(2:11–22)

For this cause I Paul, the prisoner of Jesus Christ for you Gentiles,

If ye have heard of the dispensation of the grace of God which is given me to youward:

How that by revelation he made known unto me the mystery; (as I wrote afore in few words,

Whereby, when ye read, ye may understand my knowledge in the mystery of Christ)

Which in other ages was not made known unto the sons of men, as it is now revealed unto his holy apostles and prophets by the Spirit;

That the Gentiles should be fellowheirs, and of the same body, and partakers of his promise in Christ by the gospel:

Whereof I was made a minister, according to the gift of the grace of God given unto me by the effectual working of his power.

Unto me, who am less than the least of all saints, is this grace given, that I should preach among the Gentiles the unsearchable riches of Christ;

And to make all men see what is the fellowship of the mystery, which from the beginning of the world hath been hid in God, who created all things by Jesus Christ:

To the intent that now unto the principalities and powers in heavenly places might be known by the church the manifold wisdom of God,

According to the eternal purpose which he purposed in Christ Jesus our Lord:

In whom we have boldness and access with confidence by the faith of him.

Wherefore I desire that ye faint not at my tribulations for you, which is your glory.

(3:1–13)

But all things that are reproved are made manifest by the light: for whatsoever doth make manifest is light.

Wherefore he saith, Awake thou that sleepest, and arise from the dead, and Christ shall give thee light.

See then that ye walk circumspectly, not as fools, but as wise,

Redeeming the time, because the days are evil.

Wherefore be ye not unwise, but understanding what the will of the Lord is.

And be not drunk with wine, wherein is excess; but be filled with the Spirit;

Speaking to yourselves in psalms and hymns and spiritual songs, singing and making melody in your heart to the Lord;

Giving thanks always for all things unto God and the Father in the name of our Lord Jesus Christ;

Submitting yourselves one to another in the fear of God.

(5:13–21)

333

Josephus also mentions "the permitted area", beyond which the pagan governor, Neapolitanus, did not venture in his attempt to conciliate the outraged Jews of Jerusalem after the acts of his predecessor, Florus. Gentiles were not allowed to come close to the sanctuary, as they did not observe the Jewish ritual laws of purity. The barrier which marked the limit was a low latticed wall about 5 feet high. At regular intervals, stood carved stone stelae bearing inscriptions in Greek and Latin, prohibiting Gentiles from entering the inner courtyards of the Temple, on pain of death. Two such stelae have been discovered in excavations at the Temple Mount.
In these verses Paul alludes to the "middle wall of partition" as a symbol of separation between Jews and Gentiles.

333. Scene of mystery cult; wall painting from Pompeii, 1st century (Louvre, Paris).
The mystery cults had a wide following in the Hellenistic age. They characteristically kept their rites a secret revealed only to initiates, who were sworn to secrecy. They were generally associated with certain divinities – chiefly the archaic goddesses of Greece and Egypt. They were believed to confer a special protection on their devotees.
Paul, however, presents the mystery as nothing less than the very purpose of God, hidden in times past but now made known by revelation. In his Epistle to the Colossians Paul speaks of Christ as the mystery of God. Here, the mystery of Christ is the church, in line with

the main theme of the Epistle to the Ephesians – Christ and the church.

334. Sleeping goddess; marble sculpture, 3rd–2nd century B.C. (Louvre, Paris).
Paul refers here to Isaiah 60:1: "Arise, shine, for thy light is come, and the glory of the Lord is risen upon thee."

335. Romans drinking at an inn; from a relief on a 3rd-century sarcophagus from Ostia (Monumenti E Gallerie Pontificie, Vatican).
Judging by the many representations of such scenes, drinking wine and even drunkenness were common in the ancient world. Drunkenness is condemned in the Bible. If a son is "stubborn and rebellious," "a glutton, and a drunkard" (Deuteronomy 21:18–20) he may be condemned to death. Proverbs 31:4–7 warns kings against strong drink, and Paul, writing to Timothy concerning the qualifications of a bishop in a local church, mentions, among other things, that he must not be given to wine. Moderate drinking, however, is not necessarily to be condemned if it is "wine that maketh glad the heart of man" (Psalm 104:15).

Wives, submit yourselves unto your own husbands, as unto the Lord.

For the husband is the head of the wife, even as Christ is the head of the church: and he is the saviour of the body.

Therefore as the church is subject unto Christ, so let the wives be to their own husbands in every thing. Husbands, love your wives, even as Christ also loved the church, and gave himself for it; That he might sanctify and cleanse it with the washing of water by word,

That he might present it to himself a glorious church, not having spot, or wrinkle, or any such thing; but that it should be holy and without blemish. So ought men to love their wives as their own bodies. He that loveth his wife loveth himself.

For no man ever yet hated his own flesh; but nourisheth and cherisheth it, even as the Lord the church:

For we are members of his body, of his flesh, and of his bones.

For this cause shall a man leave his father and mother, and shall be joined unto his wife, and they two shall be one flesh.

This is a great mystery: but I speak concerning Christ and the church.

Nevertheless let every one of you in particular so love his wife even as himself; and the wife see that she reverence her husband. (5:22–33)

336. Portrait of a couple in a wall painting from Pompeii (Museo Nazionale, Naples, Italy).
The relationship between husband and wife is shown by Paul as an analogy to Christ and the church. The wife's subjection and the husband's love constitute the proper married life, just as the church is subject to Christ and Christ loves the church.

Put on the whole armour of God, that ye may be able to stand against the wiles of the devil.

For we wrestle not against flesh and blood, but against principalities, against powers, against the rulers of the darkness of this world, against spiritual wickedness in high places.

Wherefore take unto you the whole armour of God, that ye may be able to withstand in the evil day, and having done all, to stand.

Stand therefore, having your loins girt about with truth, and having on the breastplate of righteousness;

And your feet shod with the preparation of the gospel of peace;

Above all, taking the shield of faith, wherewith ye shall be able to quench all the fiery darts of the wicked. And take the helmet of salvation, and the sword of the Spirit, which is the word of God:

Praying always with all prayer and supplication in the Spirit, and watching thereunto with all perseverance and supplication for all saints;·

And for me, that utterance may be given unto me, that I may open my mouth boldly, to make known the mystery of the gospel,

For which I am an ambassador in bonds: that therein I may speak boldly, as I ought to speak.

But that ye also may know my affairs, and how I do, Tychicus, a beloved brother and faithful minister in the Lord, shall make known to you all things: Whom I have sent unto you for the same purpose, that ye might know our affairs, and that he might comfort your hearts.

Peace be to the brethren, and love with faith, from God the Father and the Lord Jesus Christ.

Grace be with all them that love our Lord Jesus Christ in sincerity. Amen.

(6:11–24)

337. Two soldiers at war; relief on a Roman column, 2nd century A.D. (Roemisch – Germanisches Zentralmuseum, Mainz, W. Germany).

338. Tombstone of a Roman legionary, showing his horse, helmet and armor, 1st century A.D. (Museum Carnuntum, Deutsch Altenburg, Austria).

338

339. Arete (efficiency), one of the four allegories of virtue of the philosopher Celsus; 2nd-century Roman copy of 2nd-century B.C. Greek original sculpture (Kunsthistorisches Museum, Vienna).

The concept of *arete* was one of the most distinctive ideas of the Greek Stoic philosophers, implying both success in life and the qualities needed for achieving it. Paul makes several indirect references to Stoic philosophy in the book of Philippians as in 3:16: "Let us walk by the same rule" (Greek *Stoicheo*, from which the work Stoic is derived), and especially in 4:11 – "to be content," that is, self-sufficient and satisfied. The Stoic school of philosophy believed that *arete* was something that could be taught. In verses 5–9 Paul presents the excellence of Christian life, charging the believers to "think on," or rather "take account of these things" (verse 8).

Paul and Timotheus, the servants of Jesus Christ, to all the saints in Christ Jesus which are at Philippi, with the bishops and deacons:

Grace be unto you, and peace, from God our Father, and from the Lord Jesus Christ.

I thank my God upon every remembrance of you, Always in every prayer of mine for you all making request with joy,

For your fellowship in the gospel from the first day until now.

Being confident of this very thing, that he which hath begun a good work in you will perform it until the day of Jesus Christ:

Even as it is meet for me to think this of you all, because I have you in my heart; inasmuch as both in my bonds, and in the defence and confirmation of the gospel, ye all are partakers of my grace.

(1:1–7)

Let this mind be in you, which was also in Christ Jesus:

Who, being in the form of God, thought it not robbery to be equal with God:

But made himself of no reputation, and took upon him the form of a servant, and was made in the likeness of men:

And being found in fashion as a man, he humbled himself, and became obedient unto death, even the death of the cross.

Wherefore God also hath highly exalted him, and given him a name which is above every name:

That at the name of Jesus every knee should bow, of things in heaven, and things in earth, and things under the earth;

And that every tongue should confess that Jesus Christ is Lord, to the glory of God the Father.

(2:5–11)

339

341

For we are the circumcision, which worship God in the spirit, and rejoice in Christ Jesus, and have no confidence in the flesh.

Though I might also have confidence in the flesh. If any other man thinketh that he hath whereof he might trust in the flesh, I more:

Circumcised the eighth day, of the stock of Israel, of the tribe of Benjamin, an Hebrew of the Hebrews; as touching the law, a Pharisee;

Concerning zeal, persecuting the church; touching the righteousness which is in the law, blameless.

But what things were gain to me, those I counted loss for Christ.

Yea doubtless, and I count all things but loss for the excellency of the knowledge of Christ Jesus my Lord: for whom I have suffered the loss of all things, and do count them but dung, that I may win Christ,

And be found in him, not having mine own righteousness, which is of the law, but that which is through the faith of Christ, the righteousness which is of God by faith:

That I may know him, and the power of his resurrection, and the fellowship of his sufferings, being made comfortable unto his death;

If by any means I might attain unto the resurrection of the dead.

Not as though I had already attained, either were already perfect: but I follow after, if that I may apprehend that for which also I am apprehended of Christ Jesus.

Brethren, I count not myself to have apprehended: but this one thing I do, forgetting those things which are behind, and reaching forth unto those things which are before,

I press toward the mark for the prize of the high calling of God in Christ Jesus.

(3:3–14)

Finally, brethren, whatsoever things are true, whatsoever things are honest, whatsoever things are just, whatsoever things are pure, whatsoever things are lovely, whatsoever things are of good report; if there be any virtue, and if there be any praise, think on these things.

Those things, which ye have both learned, and received, and heard, and seen in me, do: and the God of peace shall be with you. (4:8–9)

340. Hebrew inscription on a sarcophagus, c. A.D. 100.
The inscription reads "Yeshua," i.e., Jesus in Hebrew, a fairly common name at the time of Christ. Jesus is the Greek form of the name Joshua or Jeshua. It means "Jehovah is salvation."

341. Paul seeing the light on the road to Damascus; enamel plaque, 11th century (Musée des Beaux-Arts, Lyon).
Paul refers here to his own conversion, in order to encourage the believers to pursue and gain Christ, to serve God in spirit and count all things a loss on account of Christ. Paul counted as loss on account of Christ not only the things of his former religion, but also all things, which, he now feels, are as worthless as dung. There is only one purpose for which one must strive zealously, he says, and that is "the high calling of God in Jesus Christ."

342. Head of an athlete; 3rd-century B.C. sculpture (Israel Department of Antiquities).
The fillet worn on the head probably indicates that he has been victorious in some contest.

343. Remains of Roman baths near Hierapolis, not far from the site of ancient Colossae.

344. An omphalos, "navel," of the world; Delphi, Greece, 5th century B.C.
In the Greco-Roman world, various cults were associated with the omphalos, which represented a mythological-philosophical conception of the "hub" of the universe. Paul reacts to the influence of Gnosticism – a mystic movement which drew its beliefs from Judaism, Stoicism, Platonism, Zoroastrianism and Christianity – in the early church, by showing Christ as the pre-eminent and all-inclusive one, the centrality and universality of God. He is the portion of the saints, the believers (verses 9–14), the image of God and the first-born in both creation and in resurrection. "By him all things consist," or "all things subsist together in him," meaning that all things cohere around the hub.

Paul, an apostle of Jesus Christ by the will of God, and Timotheus our brother,

To the saints and faithful brethren in Christ which are at Colosse: Grace be unto you, and peace, from God our Father and the Lord Jesus Christ

We give thanks to God and the Father of our Lord Jesus Christ, praying always for you, Since we heard of your faith in Christ Jesus, and of the love which ye have to all the saints,

For the hope which is laid up for you in heaven, whereof ye heard before in the word of the truth of the gospel;

Which is come unto you, as it is in all the world; and bringeth forth fruit as it doth also in you, since the day ye heard of it, and knew the grace of God in truth. (1:1–6

Giving thanks unto the Father, which had made us meet to be partakers of the inheritance of the saints in light:

Who hath delivered us from the power of darkness, and hath translated us into the kingdom of his dear Son:

In whom we have redemption through his blood, even the forgiveness of sins:

Who is the image of the invisible God, the firstborn of every creature

For by him were all things created, that are in heaven, and that are in earth, visible and invisible, whether they be thrones, or dominions, or principalities, or powers: all things were created by him, and for him:

And he is before all things, and by him all things consist.

And he is the head of the body, the church: who is the beginning, the firstborn from the dead; that in all things he might have the preeminence

For it pleased the Father that in him should all fulness dwell;

And, having made peace through the blood of his cross, by him to reconcile all things unto himself; by him, I say, whether they be things in earth, or things in heaven.

And you, that were sometime alienated and enemies in your mind by wicked works, yet now hath he reconciled In the body of his flesh through death, to present you holy and unblameable and unreproveable in his sight

If ye continue in the faith grounded and settled, and be not moved away from the hope of the gospel, which ye have heard, and which was preached to every creature which is under heaven; whereof I Paul am made a minister

Who now rejoice in my sufferings for you, and fill up that which is behind of the afflictions of Christ in my flesh for his body's sake, which is the church:

Whereof I am made a minister, according to the dispensation of God which is given to me for you, to fulfil the word of God;

Even the mystery which hath been hid from ages and from generations but now is made manifest to his saints:

To whom God would make known what is the riches of the glory of this mystery among the Gentiles; which is Christ in you, the hope of glory:

Whom we preach, warning every man, and teaching every man in all wisdom; that we may present every man perfect in Christ Jesus:

Whereunto I also labour, striving according to his working, which worketh in me mightily. (1:12–29

346

345. Paul holding a book; plaque from an ivory book cover, Syria, 7th century (Musée de Cluny, Paris).
Paul writes that he was made a minister "to fulfill the word of God," implying that he completed the word of God, the divine revelation, with his ministry concerning the unveiled mystery of Christ and the church. Paul mentions the "mystery" also in Ephesians 3:3–5, 9: "How that by revelation he made known unto me the mystery . . . whereby, when ye read, ye may understand my knowledge in the mystery of Christ . . . and to make all men see what is the fellowship of the mystery," Romans 16:25–26, and later in the book of Colossians, 2:2. In Ephesians 5:22 Paul writes: "This is a great mystery: but I speak concerning Christ and the church."

346. Bust of a philosopher, found in Samaria, 1st century (Israel Department of Antiquities, Jerusalem).
The "philosophy" referred to here is probably Gnosticism, a school which flourished in the early centuries of the Christian Era. By *gnosis*, knowledge, or revelation, the souls could be redeemed and returned to their original place of abode in heaven.
Gnostics also believed in life after death for devotees who performed their rites faithfully. Further light on the Gnostic faith has been shed by the recent discovery of the Nag Hammadi gnostic papyri in Egypt.
Both Judaism and Christianity viewed Gnosticism as a heresy which had to be fought against.

Beware lest any man spoil you through philosophy and vain deceit, after the tradition of men, after the rudiments of the world, and not after Christ.

For in him dwelleth all the fulness of the Godhead bodily.

And ye are complete in him, which is the head of all principality and power: In whom also ye are circumcised with the circumcision made without hands, in putting off the body of the sins of the flesh by the circumcision of Christ:

Buried with him in baptism, wherein also ye are risen with him through the faith of the operation of God, who hath raised him from the dead.

(2:8–12)

347. Angel, depicted on a medallion; gilt copper and enamel, Limoges, 13th century (Municipal Museum, Lomoges).
Another early heresy which appeared in the early churches was that the saints were unworthy to worship God directly, but must approach him through the mediation of angels. Paul says this amounts to their being defrauded of their reward, or prize, which is Christ, who is the sole mediator, in whom believers worship God directly.

348. Mineral springs at Hierapolis, in the Roman province of Asia, a few miles from Colossae and from Laodicea. Paul directed the Colossians to share his epistle with the church of Laodicea (Colossians 4:16).
Paul never visited Hierapolis or Colossae, but there were churches there thanks to the labors of Epaphras.

349. Two barbarian prisoners led before Emperor Marcus Aurelius; detail from a stone plaque from a monument honoring the emperor, 2nd century A.D.
The Greeks, and later the Romans, called everyone who did not speak their languages a barbarian. To Paul, all men are alike, and all divisions are false.

350. Scythian horseman; detail of Scythian felt cloth from the frozen burial chambers in the Altai Mountains, 300 B.C. (Hermitage, Leningrad).
The Scythians were a wild race which wandered between the Danube and the Don rivers, and spread from the Caucasus to the Caspian Sea.

351. Remains of a Roman aqueduct at Laodicea.

347

348

Let no man beguile you of your reward in a voluntary humility and worshipping of angels, intruding into those things which he hath not seen, vainly puffed up by his fleshly mind, And not holding the Head, from which all the body by joints and bands having nourishment ministered, and knit together, increaseth with the increase of God. (2:18–19)

Mortify therefore your members which are upon the earth; fornication, uncleanness, inordinate affection, evil concupiscence, and covetousness, which is idolatry: For which things' sake the wrath of God cometh on the children of disobedience:

In the which ye also walked some time, when ye lived in them.

But now ye also put off all these: anger, wrath, malice, blasphemy, filthy communication out of your mouth. Lie not one to another, seeing that ye have put off the old man with his deeds; And have put on the new man, which is renewed in knowledge after the image of him that created him:

Where there is neither Greek nor Jew, circumcision nor uncircumcision, Barbarian, Scythian, bond nor free: but Christ is all, and in all. (3:5–11)

Epaphras, who is one of you, a servant of Christ, saluteth you, always labouring fervently for you in prayers, that ye may stand perfect and complete in all the will of God. For I bear him record, that he hath a great zeal for you, and them that are in Laodicea, and them in Hierapolis. (4:12–13)

352. Nurse holding a child against her bosom; terracotta figurine from Boeotia, last quarter of the 4th century, B.C. (Louvre). The apostles' fostering the young church at Thessalonika is likened to that of a nursing mother cherishing her children.

353. Burial niches in the catacombs of Pope Callistus (218–223) on the Via Appia in Rome. "Asleep," in these verses, refers to the death of believers, which is likened to sleep.

The catacombs, or underground tombs of Rome, are of importance in early church history, and their discovery was as moving as that of the cities of Pompeii and Herculanum. Since most of the early Christians of Rome were of eastern and Jewish descent, they followed the oriental custom of hewing their tombs in the bedrock, usually in long tunnel-like galleries.

Most of the catacombs were constructed during the first three centuries, and a few may even be traced to the Apostolic age. After Constantine, Christians could bury their dead above ground without fear. Some catacombs were begun by individuals or families, and others belonged to churches. The Christians wrote fitting epitaphs and consoling thoughts on the tombs, and painted on them their favorite symbols. They were not regular places of worship, though at times they did serve as a refuge from persecutions. The devotional use of the catacombs began only later, when they ceased to be used for burial. The catacombs began to draw pious pilgrims and little chapels were built in memory of the martyrs.

352

Paul and Silvanus, and Timotheus, unto the church of Thessalonians which is in God the Father and in the Lord Jesus Christ: Grace be unto you, and peace, from God our Father, and the Lord Jesus Christ.

We give thanks to God always for you all, making mention of you in our prayers;

Remembering without ceasing your work of faith, and labour of love, and patience of hope in our Lord Jesus Christ, in the sight of God and our Father;

Knowing, brethren beloved, your election of God.

For our gospel came not unto you in word only, but also in power, and in the Holy Ghost, and in much assurance: as ye know what manner of men we were among you for your sake.

And ye became followers of us, and of the Lord, having received the word in much affliction, with joy of the Holy Ghost:

So that ye were ensamples to all that believe in Macedonia and Achaia.

(1:1–7)

For neither at any time used we flattering words, as ye know, nor a cloke of covetousness; God is witness:

Nor of men sought we glory, neither of you, nor yet of others, when we might have been burdensome, as the apostles of Christ.

But we were gentle among you, even as a nurse cherisheth her children:

So being affectionately desirous of you, we were willing to have imparted unto you, not the gospel of God only, but also our own souls, because ye were dear unto us.

For ye remember, brethren, our labour and travail: for labouring night and day, because we would not be chargeable unto any of you, we preached unto you the gospel of God.

Ye are witnesses, and God also, how holily and justly and unblameably we behaved ourselves among you that believe:

As ye know how we exhorted and comforted and charged every one of you, as a father doth his children,

That ye would walk worthy of God, who hath called you unto his kingdom and glory.

(2:5–12)

But I would not have you to be ignorant, brethren, concerning them which are asleep, that ye sorrow not, even as others which have no hope.

For if we believe that Jesus died and rose again, even so them also which sleep in Jesus will God bring with him.

For this we say unto you by the word of the Lord, that we which are alive and remain unto the coming of the Lord shall not prevent them which are asleep.

For the Lord himself shall descend from heaven with a shout, with the voice of the archangel, and with the trump of God: and the dead in Christ shall rise first:

Then we which are alive and remain shall be caught up together with them in the clouds, to meet the Lord in the air: and so shall we ever be with the Lord.

Wherefore comfort one another with these words.

(4:13–18)

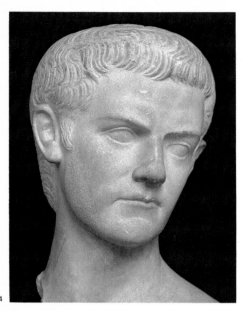

Now we beseech you, brethren, by the coming of our Lord Jesus Christ, and by our gathering together unto him,

That ye be not soon shaken in mind, or be troubled, neither by spirit, nor by word, nor by letter as from us, as that the day of Christ is at hand.

Let no man deceive you by any means: for that day shall not come, except there come a falling away first, and that man of sin be revealed, the son of perdition;

Who opposeth and exalteth himself above all that is called God, or that is worshipped; so that he as God sitteth in the temple of God, shewing himself that he is God.

(2:1–4)

Now we command you, brethren, in the name of our Lord Jesus Christ, that ye withdraw yourselves from every brother that walketh disorderly, and not after the tradition which he received of us.

For yourselves know how ye ought to follow us: for we behaved not ourselves disorderly among you;

Neither did we eat any man's bread for nought; but wrought with labour and travail night and day, that we might not be chargeable to any of you:

Not because we have not power, but to make ourselves an ensample unto you to follow us.

For even when we were with you, this we commanded you, that if any would not work, neither should he eat.

For we hear that there are some which walk among you disorderly, working not at all, but are busybodies.

Now them that are such we command and exhort by our Lord Jesus Christ, that with quietness they work, and eat their own bread.

(3:6–12)

354. Bust of Emperor Caligula (A.D. 37–41); marble sculpture, 1st century (Museo Nazionale, Naples).

The infamous Caligula became emperor of Rome in A.D. 37, after the death of Tiberius. He ruled moderately at first but after a severe illness, seven months after becoming emperor, his personality seemed to change. He squandered the huge treasury left by Tiberius, and had innumerable citizens executed. His ambition to conquer Germany and Britain came to nothing. He demanded divine honors, and it was only due to the intervention of Petronius, the governor of Syria, that Caligula's order to place his image in the Temple in Jerusalem was not carried out.

In A.D. 41, a successful conspiracy put an end to his life.

355. Shoemaker, Gallo-Roman tombstone (Musée Rollin, Autun, France).

Neither give heed to fables and endless genealogies, which minister questions, rather than godly edifying which is in faith: so do.

Now the end of the commandment is charity out of a pure heart, and of a good conscience, and of faith unfeigned:

From which some having swerved have turned aside unto vain jangling;

Desiring to be teachers of the law; understanding neither what they say, now whereof they affirm.

But we know that the law is good, if a man use it lawfully;

Knowing this, that the law is not made for a righteous man, but for the lawless and disobedient, for the ungodly and for sinners, for unholy and profane, for murderers of fathers and murderers of mothers, for manslayers,

For whoremongers, for them that defile themselves with mankind, for menstealers, for liars, for perjured persons, and if there be any other thing that is contrary to sound doctrine; According to the glorious gospel of the blessed God, which was committed to my trust.

(1:4–11)

356. Lintel from the academy of Rabbi Eleazar Ha-Kappar, found in a synagogue in the village of Dabbura in the Golan.
The Hebrew inscription reads: "This is the academy of the Rabbi Eleazar Ha-Kappar." The lintel was apparently part of the main entrance to the School of Eleazar Ha-Kappar. Its workmanship and script are reminiscent of the 3rd-century A.D. remains found in other synagogues in the Galilee, at Capernaum, Chorazin and other places. Rabbi Eleazar Ha-Kappar was a famous Talmudic sage who flourished at the end of the second century and early third century A.D.

357. Detail from a Roman sarcophagus, showing two ships sailing against the waves; marble, 2nd-3rd century A.D. (Ny-Carlsberg-Glyptothek, Copenhagen, Denmark).
The word shipwreck implies that the Christian life and the church life are like a ship sailing on a stormy sea, needing to be safeguarded by faith and a good conscience.

358

358. Young Achaeans engaged in athletic contest; marble relief, 6th-century B.C. (National Archaeological Museum, Athens, Greece).

359. Initial of a Gothic missal representing two monks showing a book to each other, possibly disputing the interpretation of some passage or using the scripture to uphold a certain interpretation; 14th century A.D. (Library of Abbey of Admont, Styria, Austria). Paul points out here that the "wholesome" or "healthy" words of the Lord are the source of the teaching according to godliness. Paul mentions the differing teachings which issue from people's pride and self-conceit. "Doting" or "sick" is in contrast to "wholesome" of verse 3.

360. Man's hand holding a purse; detail of a limestone, Gallo-Roman statue, 1st century A.D., from a sanctuary near the source of the Seine, France (Musée Archéologique, Dijon, France).

This charge I commit unto thee, son Timothy, according to the prophecies which went before on thee, that thou by them mightest war a good warfare:

Holding faith, and a good conscience; which some having put away concerning faith have made shipwreck;

Of whom is Hymenaeus and Alexander; whom I have delivered unto Satan, that they may learn not to blasphemy. (1:18–20)

If thou but the brethen in remembrance of these things, thou shalt be a good minister of Jesus Christ, nourished upon the words of faith and of good doctrine, whereunto thou hast attained.

But refuse profane and old wives, fables, and exercise thyself rather unto godliness.

For bodily exercise profiteth little: but godliness is profitable unto all things, having promise of the life that now is, and of that which is to come.

This is a faithful saying and worthy of all acceptation.

For therefore we both labour and suffer reproach, because we trust in the living God, who is the Saviour of all men, specially of those that believe.

These things command and teach.

Let no man despise thy youth; but be thou an example of the believers, in word, in conversation, in charity, in spirit, in faith, in purity. (4:6–12)

If any man teach otherwise and consent not to wholesome words, even the words of our Lord Jesus Christ, and to the doctrine which is according to godliness;

He is proud, knowing nothing, but doting about questions and strifes of words, whereof cometh envy, strife, railings, evil surmisings,

Perverse disputings of men of corrupt minds, and destitute of the truth, supposing that gain is godliness: from such withdraw thyself.

But godliness with contentment is great gain.

For we brought nothing into this world, and it is certain we can carry nothing out.

And having food and raiment let us be therewith content.

But they that will be rich fall into temptation and a snare, and into

359

many foolish and hurtful lusts, which drown men in destruction and perdition.

For the love of money is the root of all evil: which while some coveted after, they have erred from the faith, and pierced themselves through with many sorrows.

But thou, O man of God, flee these things; and follow after righteousness, godliness, faith, love, patience, meekness.

Fight the good fight of faith, lay hold in eternal life, whereunto thou art also called, and hast professed a good profession before many witnesses.

(6:3–12)

Thou therefore, my son, be strong in the grace that is in Christ Jesus.

And the things that thou hast heard of me among many witnesses, the same commit thou to faithful men, who shall be able to teach others also.

Thou therefore endure hardness, as a good soldier of Jesus Christ.

No man that warreth entangleth himself with the affairs of this life; that he may please him who hath chosen him to be a soldier. (2:1–4)

But shun profane and vain babblings; for they will increase unto more ungodliness.

And their word will eat as doth a canker: of whom is Hymenaeus and Philetus;

Who concerning the truth have erred, saying that the resurrection is past already; and overthrow the faith of some.

Nevertheless the foundation of God standeth sure, having this seal, The Lord knoweth them that are his. And, Let every one that nameth the name of Christ depart from inquity.

But in a great house there are not only vessels of gold and of silver, but also of wood and of earth; and some to honour, and some to dishonour.

If a man therefore purge himself from these, he shall be a vessl unto honour, sanctified, and meet for the master's use, and prepared unto every good work.

Flee also youthful lusts: but follow righteousness, faith, charity, peace, with them that call on the Lord out of a pure heart. (2:16–22)

361. Fragment of a frieze with persons in military dress, 2nd century A.D. (Museo di Antichita, Turino, Italy).

362. Atrium with triclinium (open air dining room) of a villa known as the house of the Neptune from Herculanum, Italy, A.D. 79.
The house of God defined in 1 Timothy 3:15-16 is the Church. The "great house" here actually refers to the deteriorated church in its mixed character, as illustrated by the abnormally big tree in Matthew 13:31-32.
In such a great house there are not only precious vessels, but also base ones. Vessels of honor are the divine nature (gold) and the redeemed and regenerated human nature (silver). Vessels of dishonor are the fallen human nature, represented as wood and earth. Hymenaeus, Philetus and other false believers are of these.

363. A page from the famous Aleppo Codex, the oldest complete manuscript of the Old Testament known to exist, dating from the 10th century.

It was kept jealously in the synagogue in Aleppo, Syria, whose caretakers allowed only a select few individuals to examine it at first hand. In 1948, when the hostilities of Israel's War of Independence broke out, a pogrom was perpetrated against the Jews of Aleppo, in the course of which the synagogue was burned. The fabulous manuscript was thought to be lost but was later discovered in a metal box, having survived the flames. Unfortunately, however, almost the whole first five books of Moses were melted away, as were the concluding books of Chronicles. The manuscript was obtained and brought to Israel by the late president of Israel, Ben-Zvi, and is the basis of the Hebrew University's new critical edition of the biblical text.

Timothy had from childhood a good foundation in the Old Testament. He was thus fully equipped to minister the word of God. Paul stresses the need for a high regard of Holy Scripture as the embodiment or "breathing-out" (inspiration) of God as the Spirit.

But continue thou in the things which thou hast learned and hast been assured of, knowing of whom thou hast learned them;

And that from a child thou hast known the holy scriptures, which are able to make thee wise unto salvation through faith which is in Christ Jesus.

All scripture is given by inspiration of God, and is profitable for doctrine, for reproof, for correction, for instruction in righteousness:

That the man of God may be perfect, throughly furnished unto all good works.

(3:14–17)

For I am now ready to be offered, and the time of my departure is at hand.

364.

364. St. Paul-Outside-the-Walls, built on the site of the traditional tomb of St. Paul.

Many believe that Paul's approaching death is suggested in these words which he wrote to Timothy while imprisoned at Rome. The letter was written c. A.D. 64. At this time a great fire had ravaged Rome. Nero was believed to be responsible for it, and in order to protect himself the emperor placed the blame upon the Christians; it is likely that Paul suffered martyrdom.

The church was founded in 386 on the site of a church erected by Constantine at the site of a 1st-century cemetery within which was St. Paul's grave. This was the most beautiful basilica of Rome until a fire ravaged it in 1828. The basilica was restored on the same plan as the previous one.

365. St. Paul-Outside-the-Walls, interior.

366

366. Jewish gold-glass roundel decorated with gold from the 3rd or 4th century A.D. from the catacombs of Rome. The upper half shows an open cabinet with scrolls neatly arranged in individual compartments, no doubt Torah scrolls and other holy writings. Such was the practice in Greco-Roman times for storing the precious hand-copied book-scrolls.

I have fought a good fight, I have finished my course, I have kept the faith:

Henceforth there is laid up for me a crown of righteousness, which the Lord, the righteous judge, shall give me at that day: and not to me only, but unto all them also that love his appearing.

(4:6–8)

The cloke that I left at Troas with Carpus, when thou comest, bring with thee, and the books, but especially the parchments.

(4:13)

Erastus abode at Corinth: but Trophimus have I left at Miletum sick.
(4:20)

367. Miletus: remains of a Roman theater. Only ruins remain of the once prosperous commercial center on the west coast of Asia. Paul had visited the city (Acts 20:14-17) and had asked the older men of Ephesus to visit him there. It seems that he went there a second time. His travelling companion Trophimus fell ill and Paul was obliged to leave him behind.

368. View of remains of a palace at Knossos, Crete, the fourth largest island in the Mediterranean Sea.

Many scholars have identified the biblical Caphtor, the original home of the Philistines, mentioned in Deuteronomy 2:23, with Crete. The island came under the domination of Greece in the first millennium B.C. The earliest evidence of the presence of Jews in Crete dates back to 142 B.C., and there is no doubt that there were Jewish settlements on the island after its conquest by the Romans in 68 B.C. There were Cretan Jews living in Jerusalem, as mentioned in Acts 2:5; 2:11: "And there were dwelling at Jerusalem, Jews, devout men, out of every nation under heaven . . . Cretes and Arabians . . . ."

The apostle Paul on his way to Rome for trial had passed by Crete aboard a vessel from Alexandria. Because of strong winds the ship "sailed under Crete" over against Salmone (on the northeastern coast of the island), and came to Fair Heavens, a small bay on the southern coast. It seems that Paul went to Crete again and there left Titus to set the new church in order.

Paul, a servant of God, and an apostle of Jesus Christ, according to the faith of God's elect, and the acknowledging of the truth which is after godliness;

In hope of eternal life, which God, that cannot lie, promised before the world began;

But hath in due times manifested his word through preaching, which is committed unto me according to the commandment of God our Saviour;

To Titus, mine own son after the common faith: Grace, mercy, and peace, from God the Father and the Lord Jesus Christ our Saviour.

For this cause left I thee in Crete, that thou shouldest set in order the things that are wanting, and ordain elders in every city, as I had appointed thee. (1:1–5)

For there are many unruly and vain talkers and deceivers, specially they of the circumcision:

Whose mouths must be stopped, who subvert whole houses, teaching things which they ought not, for filty lucre's sake.

One of themselves, even a prophet of their own, said, The Cretians are alway liars, evil beasts, slow bellies.

This witness is true. Wherefore rebuke them sharply, that they may be sound in the faith; Not giving heed to Jewish fables, and commandments of men, that turn from the truth.

Unto the pure all things are pure: but unto them that are defiled and unbelieving is nothing pure; but even their mind and conscience is defiled.

They profess that they know God; but in works they deny him, being abominable, and disobedient, and unto every good work reprobate. (1:10–16)

Put them in mind to be subject to principalities and powers, to obey magistrates, to be ready to every good work.

To speak evil of no man, to be no brawlers, but gentle, shewing all meekness unto all men.

For we ourselves also were sometimes foolish, disobedient, deceived, serving divers lusts and pleasures, living in malice and envy, hateful, and hating one another.

But after that the kindness and love of God our Saviour toward man appeared, Not by works of righteousness which we have done, but according to his mercy he saved us, by the washing of regeneration, and renewing of the Holy Ghost. (3:1–5)

371

369. Wall painting of Cretan acrobat or bull-fighter(?), from Knossos (Heraklion Museum, Crete).

Paul is probably referring here to the poet Epimenides (flourished 6th century B.C.), a native of Crete who styled his fellow Cretans as "always liars, evil beasts, slow bellies (i.e., lazy gluttons)." Such diatribes were popular among the ancient poets.

370. Marble chair of an official, end of 1st century B.C., from the theater at Ephesus (Kunsthistorisches Museum, Vienna, Austria).

371. Slaves being freed, depicted on a Roman relief of the 1st century (Musée Mariemont, Bruxelles).

Slavery was accepted and widespread throughout the ancient world. However, just as a free man could become a slave so could a slave regain his freedom. The Old Testament (Exodus 21:2-6) prescribes that a Hebrew slave or bondsman is not to be held in bondage over seven years. Roman law also provided for the freeing of a slave. Skilled slaves who managed to save money could purchase their freedom from their masters. In some cases it was the nature of the personal relations or the desire of the masters for ostentation that led them to free their slaves.

The relief shown here depicts two slaves being freed. One of them, already a free man, shakes the hand of his former owner; the other is kneeling to be touched by the magistrate's rod as a sign of his release. Both are wearing the high cap worn by freemen.

Paul intercedes on behalf of Onesimus, Philemon's runaway slave, whom he had converted. Paul wishes Philemon to take back Onesimus "not as a servant, but above a servant, a brother beloved, specially to me, but how much more unto thee, both in the flesh and in the Lord."

I beseech thee for my son Onesimus, whom I have begotten in my bonds:

Which in time past was to thee unprofitable, but now profitable to thee and to me:

Whom I have sent again: thou therefore receive him, that is, mine own bowels:

Whom I would have retained with me, that in thy stead he might have ministered unto me in the bonds of the gospel:

But without thy mind would I do nothing; that thy benefit should not be as it were of necessity, but willingly.

For perhaps he therefore departed for a season, that thou shouldest receive him for ever;

Not now as a servant, but above a servant, a brother beloved, specially to me, but how much more unto thee, both in the flesh, and in the Lord?

If thou count me therefore a partner, receive him as myself.

If he hath wronged thee, or oweth thee ought, put that on mine account;

I Paul have written it with mine own hand, I will repay it: albeit I do not say to thee how thou owest unto me even thine own self besides.

(10:19)

372. Atlas carrying the world on his shoulders; marble statue, late Roman period (Museo Nazionale, Naples).
In Greek mythology Atlas was the Titan who led his brothers in war against Zeus and was punished by being forced to carry the world on his shoulders.
The author of the Epistle to the Hebrews presents Christ as "upholding all things by the word of his power." The connection of Christ the Word with the creation is found in several places in the New Testament, and most explicitly in the Epistle to the Hebrews.
God speaks in the Son and the Son upholds all things by his word. This is in line with Psalm

God, who at sundry times and in divers manners spake in time past unto the fathers by the prophets,

Hath in these last days spoken unto us by his Son, whom he hath appointed heir of all things, by whom also he made the worlds;

Who being the brightness of his glory, and the express image of his person, and upholding all things by the word of his power, when he had by himself purged our sins, sat down on the right hand of the Majesty on high;

Being made so much better than the angels, as he hath by inheritance obtained a more excellent name than they.

For unto which of the angels said he at any time, Thou art my Son, this day have I begotten thee? And again, I will be to him a Father, and he shall be to me a Son?

(1:1–5)

Forasmuch then as the children are partakers of flesh and blood, he also himself likewise took part of the same; that through death he might destroy him that had the power of death, that is, the devil;

And deliver them who through fear of death were all their lifetime subject to bondage.

For verily he took not on him the nature of angels; but he took on him the seed of Abraham.

Wherefore in all things it behoved him to be made like unto his brethren, that he might be a merciful and faithful high priest in things pertaining to God, to make reconciliation for the sins of the people.

For in that he himself hath suffered being tempted, he is able to succour them that are tempted.

(2:14–18)

Now when these things were thus ordained, the priests went always into the first tabernacle, accomplishing the service of God.

373.

But into the second went the high priest alone once every year, not without blood, which he offered for himself, and for the errors of the people:

The Holy Ghost this signifying, that the way into the holiest of all was not yet made manifest, while as the first tabernacle was yet standing:

Which was a figure for the time then present, in which were offered both gifts and sacrifices, that could not make him that did the service perfect, as pertaining to the conscience;

Which stood only in meats and drinks, and divers washings, and carnal ordinances, imposed on them until the time of reformation. But Christ being come an high priest of good things to come, by a greater and more perfect tabernacle, not made with hands, that is to say, not of this building;

Neither by the blood of goats and calves, but by his own blood he entered in once into the holy place, having obtained eternal redemption for us.

(9:6–12)

Now faith is the substance of things hoped for, the evidence of things not seen. For by it the elders obtained a good report.

Through faith we understand that the worlds were framed by the word of God, so that things which are seen were not made of things which do appear.

By faith Abel offered unto God a more excellent sacrifice than Cain, by which he obtained witness that he was righteous, God testifying of his gifts: and by it he being dead yet speaketh.

By faith Enoch was translated that he should not see death; and was not found, because God had translated him: for before his translation he had this testimony, that he pleased God.

But without faith it is impossible to please him: for he that cometh to God must believe that he is, and that he is a rewarder of them that diligently seek him.

(11:1–6)

375

33:9 : "For he spake, and it was done, he commanded, and it stood fast."

373. Angel, Byzantine mosaic, 6th century A.D. San Apollinare in Classe, Ravenna, Italy. The first section of the Epistle to the Hebrews, 1:4-10:39, sets forth the superiority of Christ to the angels, to Moses, to Aaron and to the Old Covenant.

In the time of Second Temple it was believed that only the great prophets of earlier times had direct communication with God, while in later times it was held that the mysteries of the end of days, etc., could be discovered only through an intermediary (compare Colossians 2:18). People were thus led to explore the nature and individual character of the angels, which gave an opening to the influence and ideas of pagan magic and demonology. The doctrine of angels was especially prominent in the belief of the Essenes, who according to Josephus carefully guarded a secret list of angels' names. The Qumran scrolls also testify to an organized system of angelology, and angels were thought to be present at the meetings of the sect.

374. Angels of Death taking the souls of dead persons, 14th century fresco (Campo Santo, Pisa, Italy).

Originally death was understood as being a punishment for man's sin (Genesis 3:22 – 23). Soon it was personified and was attributed emissaries and a host of angels (Proverbs 16:14, Hosea 13:14).

In post-biblical times the concept of an Angel of Death emerged, also identified with the demons described in oral tradition, who not only fulfilled God's orders, but also acted on their own initiative in fighting, harming and destroying man. The Angel of Death thus symbolizes the demonic forces responsible for Adam's fall and which continue to fight with his descendants.

375. *Mikveh* (ritual bath) installed in the southeastern section of the casemate wall at Masada, the last bastion of resistance against the Romans, where the Zealots made their dwellings.

Jewish ritual law lays down the specifications for a mikveh: the water must be natural – rain, spring or river water – flowing freely, but not

377

By faith Abraham, when he was tried, offered up Isaac: and he that had received the promises offered up his only begotten son,

Of whom it was said, That in Isaac shall thy seed be called:

Accounting that God was able to raise him up, even from the dead; from whence also he received him in a figure.

By faith Isaac blessed Jacob and Esau concerning things to come.

By faith Jacob, when he was a dying, blessed both the sons of Joseph; and worshipped, leaning upon the top of his staff.

By faith Joseph, when he died, made mention of the departing of the children of Israel; and gave commandment concerning his bones.

(11:17–22)

And what shall I more say? for the time would fail me to tell of Gedeon, and of Barak, and of Samson, and of Jephthae; of David also, and Samuel, and of the prophets:

Who through faith subdued kingdoms, wrought righteousness, obtained promises, stopped the mouths of lions,

Quenched the violence of fire, escaped the edge of the sword, out of weakness were made strong, waxed valiant in fight, turned to flight the armies of the aliens.

Women received their dead raised to life again: and others were tortured, not accepting deliverance; that they might obtain a better resurrection:

And others had trial of cruel mockings and scourgings, yea, moreover of bonds and imprisonments:

They were stoned, they were sawn asunder, were tempted, were slain with the sword: they wandered about in sheepskins and goatskins; being destitute, afflicted, tormented;

(Of whom the world was not worthy:) they wandered in deserts, and in mountains, and in dens and caves of the earth.

And these all, having obtained a good report through faith, received not the promise:

carried to the bath in vessels. The Roman baths at Masada have all the necessary qualifications, with an open plastered conduit leading into one pool (the storage) and this connected to another pool (the immersion bath). The Jewish laws of ritual purity forbade Jews from entering the precincts of the Temple if they had not immersed themselves previously in a *mikveh*. Excavations at the southern end of the Temple Mount have uncovered a number of such ritual baths.

376. Cain and Abel offering their sacrifices to God; stone relief, 13th century, Jacob's Chapel (Treasury of the Cathedral, Pistoia, Italy).

377. Abraham's sacrifice; bas-relief from the upper panel of a 4th century sarcophagus (Grotto Vaticane, Rome, Italy).

378. Wall painting from Dura-Europos; depicting Jacob blessing his sons. On the left Jacob is shown on his deathbed blessing his twelve sons, while on the right he is blessing Ephraim and Manasseh in the presence of Joseph.

379. The three youths in the furnace (Shadrach, Meshach and Abednego), fresco from the 3rd century A.D., catacombs of St. Priscilla, Rome.
The reference in verse 34 to those who by faith "quenched the violence of fire" refers to the story of the fiery furnace in the Book of Daniel.

380. View of Jerusalem.
The "city of the living God, the heavenly Jerusalem," is the "city which hath foundations, whose builder and maker is God" for which Abraham, and all the seekers of a "better country," in faith, looked for (Hebrews 11:10,16). This is also the "Jerusalem which is above" in Galatians 4:26, "the holy city, new Jerusalem" of Revelation 21:2 and 3:12 and the "tabernacle of God" with men in Revelation 21:3. Just as the patriarchs sought and waited for this city, the believers also seek it: "For here have we no continuing city, but we seek one to come" (Hebrews 13:14).

379

God having provided some better thing for us, that they without us
should not be made perfect.   (11:32–40)
　　But ye are come unto mount Sion, and unto the city of the living God,
the heavenly Jerusalem, and to an innumerable company of angels,
　　To the general assembly and church of the firstborn, which are written
in heaven, and to God the Judge of all, and to the spirits of just men made
perfect,
　　And to Jesus the mediator of the new covenant, and to the blood of
sprinkling, that speaketh better things than that of Abel.   (12:22–24)

381. Man pointing to a scroll, engraving of the 14th century (Sala dei Affreschi, Campo Santo, Pisa).
The last chapter of the Epistle to the Hebrews lists the virtues necessary and indicative of a proper church life, including brotherly love, hospitality, marriage held in honor, etc. Verse 9 charges the believers not to be "carried about with divers and strange doctrines," which only cause dissension and even division in the church.

Jesus Christ the same yesterday, and to day, and for ever.

Be not carried about with divers and strange doctrines. For it is a good thing that the heart be established with grace; not with meats, which have not profited them that have been occupied therein. We have an altar, whereof they have no right to eat which serve the tabernacle.

For the bodies of those beasts, whose blood is brought into the sanctuary by the high priest for sin, are burned without the camp.

Wherefore Jesus also, that he might sanctify the people with his own blood, suffered without the gate. Let us go forth therefore unto him without the camp, bearing his reproach.

For here have we no continuing city, but we seek one to come.

By him therefore let us offer the sacrifice of praise to God continually, that is, the fruit of our lips giving thanks to his name.

But to do good and to communicate forget not: for with such sacrifices God is well pleased.

Obey them that have the rule over you, and submit yourselves: for they watch for your souls, as they that must give account, that they may do it with joy, and not with grief: for that is unprofitable for you.

Pray for us: for we trust we have a good conscience, in all things willing to live honestly. But I beseech you the rather to do this, that I may be restored to you the sooner.

Now the God of peace, that brought again from the dead our Lord Jesus, that great shepherd of the sheep, through the blood of the everlasting covenant,

Make you perfect in every good work to do his will, working in you that which is wellpleasing in his sight, through Jesus Christ; to whom be glory for ever and ever. Amen. And I beseech you, brethren, suffer the word of exhortation: for I have written a letter unto you in few words.

Know ye that our brother Timothy is set at liberty; with whom, if he come shortly, I will see you. Salute all them that have the rule over you, and all the saints. They of Italy salute you.

Grace be with you all. Amen.

(13:8–25)

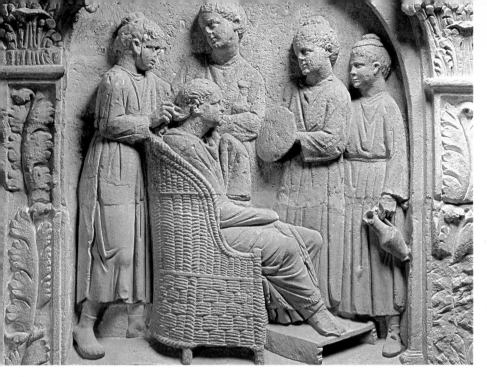

382. Roman lady seated in a wicker chair having her hair dressed by two other women; one holds up a mirror to the seated woman; relief, 1st century B.C. (Rheinisches Landsmuseum, Trier).

But be ye doers of the word, and not hearers only, deceiving your own selves.

For if any be a hearer of the word, and not a doer, he is like unto a man beholding his natural face in a glass:

For he beholdeth himself, and goeth his way, and straightway forgetteth what manner of man he was.

But whoso looketh into the perfect law of liberty, and continueth therein, he being not a forgetful hearer, but a doer of the work, this man shall be blessed in his deed. (1:22–25)

My brethren, be not many masters, knowing that we shall receive the greater condemnation.

For in many things we offend all. If any man offend not in word, the same is a perfect man, and able also to bridle the whole body.

Behold, we put bits in the horses' mouths, that they may obey us; and we turn about their whole body.

Behold also the ships, which though they be great, and are driven of fierce winds, yet are they turned about with a very small helm, whithersoever the governor listeth.

383. Horse's head with bridle, marble, from the archaic Artemis Temple in Ephesus (Museum Selcuk, Turkey).

384

384. Helmsman; fragment of a group in marble from the Cave of Tiberius, mid 1st century B.C. (Museo Nazionale, Naples).

385. Fish and other sea creatures on a marine background; mosaic from Pompeii (Museo Nazionale, Naples).

386. Portrait bust of Agrippina the Younger (Julia), born A.D. 15, mother of Nero.

387. Portrait bust of Julia Domna, wife of Septimus Severus (A.D. 193–211).

388. Portrait bust thought to be that of Julia, only daughter of the emperor Titus (Born in 39 B.C.).
These examples of Roman hair styles show why the fine ladies spent hours at their toilettes.
In Peter's time Roman women had abandoned the fairly simple hair style copied from the Greeks, and adopted elaborate coiffures with innumerable twists and curls.
Peter recommends that women dress modestly and simply, and so did Paul in his epistle to Timothy: "That women adorn themselves in modest apparel, with shamefacedness and sobriety; not with broided hair, or gold, or pearls, or costly array" (I Timothy 2:9).

Even so the tongue is a little member, and boasteth great things. Behold, how great a matter a little fire kindleth!

And the tongue is a fire, a world of iniquity: so is the tongue among our members, that it defileth the whole body, and setteth on fire the course of nature; and it is set on fire of hell.

For every kind of beasts, and of birds, and of serpents, and of things in the sea, is tamed, and hath been tamed of mankind:

But the tongue can no man tame; it is an unruly evil, full of deadly poison.

Therewith bless we God, even the Father; and therewith curse we men, which are made after the similitude of God.

Out of the same mouth proceedeth blessing and cursing. My brethren, these things ought not so to be.

Doth a fountain send forth at the same place sweet water and bitter?

Can the fig tree, my brethren, bear olive berries? either a vine, figs? so can no fountain both yield salt water and fresh.

Who is a wise man and endued with knowledge among you? let him shew out of a good conversation his works with meekness of wisdom.

But if ye have bitter envying and strife in your hearts, glory not, and lie not against the truth.

This wisdom descendeth not from above, but is earthly, sensual, devilish.

For where envying and strife is, there is confusion and every evil work.

But the wisdom that is from above is first pure, then peaceable, gentle, and easy to be entreated, full of mercy and good fruits, without partiality, and without hypocrisy.

And the fruit of righteousness is sown in peace of them that make peace.

(3:1–18)

Likewise, ye wives, be in subjection to your own husbands; that, if any obey not the word, they also may without the word be won by the conversation of the wives;

While they behold your chaste conversation coupled with fear.

Whose adorning let it not be that outward adorning of plaiting the hair, and of wearing of gold, or of putting on of apparel; But let it be the hidden man of the heart, in that which is not corruptible, even the ornament of a meek and quiet spirit, which is in the sight of God of great price.

For after this manner in the old time the holy women also, who trusted in God, adorned themselves, being in subjection unto their own husbands:

Even as Sara obeyed Abraham, calling him lord: whose daughters ye are, as long as ye do well, and are not afraid with any amazement.

(3:1–6)

But and if ye suffer for righteousness' sake, happy are ye: and be not afraid of their terror, neither be troubled;

But sanctify the Lord God in your hearts: and be ready always to give an answer to every man that asketh you a reason of the hope that is in you with meekness and fear:

Having a good conscience; that, whereas they speak evil of you, as of evildoers, they may be ashamed that falsely accuse your good conversation in Christ.

For it is better, if the will of God be so, that ye suffer for well doing, than for evil doing.

For Christ also hath once suffered for sins, the just for the unjust, that he might bring us to God, being put to death in the flesh, but quickened by the Spirit:

By which also he went and preached unto the spirits in prison;

Which sometime were disobedient, when once the longsuffering of God

389. The Building of the Ark, 9th century ivory plaque, Cathedral of San Matteo, Salerno, Italy.
Like Paul, Peter also made use of figurative interpretations of the Old Testament, applying them to real and practical issues in the life of the New Testament believers. Here Noah's ark surviving the flood is presented as a figure of baptism: the water of the flood delivered Noah and his family out of the old manner of life into a new environment. Similarly the water of baptism delivers the believers out of their former vain manner of life into a life of resurrection.

390. A family meal and servants in attendance; detail from a relief on Roman funerary monument of the 3rd century A.D.
The image of a household servant or steward serves Paul to illustrate the functioning of the believers – "as good stewards of the manifold grace of God." The matter of grace is mentioned several times in the First Epistle of Peter. Peter acknowledges that the believers have received the initial grace, but that they need to have this grace multiplied in them, so that eventually they can participate in all grace.

391. St. Peter's Altar in St. Peter's Basilica, Rome.

392 St. Peter's Basilica on Vatican Hill, Rome.
Archaeological reaserch has not proven that this was the site of St. Peter's grave; however, studies have shown that this site has been venerated as the Apostle's grave since the year 160. Constantine erected a basilica over the spot which is now marked by the high altar of the present church.

waited in the days of Noah, while the ark was a preparing, wherein few, that is, eight souls were saved by water.

The like figure whereunto even baptism doth also now save us (not the putting away of the filth of the flesh, but the answer of a good conscience toward God,) by the resurrection of Jesus Christ:

Who is gone into heaven, and is on the right hand of God; angels and authorities and powers being made subject unto him.

(3:14–22)

But the end of all things is at hand: be ye therefore sober, and watch unto prayer.

And above all things have fervent charity among yourselves: for charity shall cover the multitude of sins.

Use hospitality one to another without grudging.

As every man hath received the gift, even so minister the same one to another, as good stewards of the manifold grace of God.

If any man speak, let him speak as the oracles of God; if any man minister, let him do it as of the ability which God giveth: that God in all things may be glorified through Jesus Christ, to whom be praise and dominion for ever and ever. Amen.

(4:7–11)

The elders which are among you I exhort, who am also an elder, and a witness of the sufferings of Christ, and also a partaker of the glory that shall be revealed:

(5:1)

The Lord knoweth how to deliver the godly out of temptations, and to reserve the unjust unto the day of judgment to be punished:

But chiefly them that walk after the flesh in the lust of uncleanness, and despise government. Presumptuous are they, selfwilled, they are not afraid to speak evil of dignities.

Whereas angels, which are greater in power and might, bring not railing accusation against them before the Lord.

But these, as natural brute beasts, made to be taken and destroyed, speak evil of the things that they understand not; and shall utterly perish in their own corruption;

And shall receive the reward of unrighteousness, as they that count it pleasure to riot in the day time. Spots they are and blemishes, sporting themselves with their own deceivings while they feast with you;

Having eyes full of adultery, and that cannot cease from sin; beguiling unstable souls: an heart they have exercised with covetous practices; cursed children:

Which have forsaken the right way, and are gone astray, following the way of Balaam the son of Bosor, who loved the wages of unrighteousness;

But was rebuked for his iniquity: the dumb ass speaking with man's voice forbad the madness of the prophet.

These are wells without water, clouds that are carried with a tempest; to whom the mist of darkness is reserved for ever.

(2:9–17)

393. The "Tempietto" in Rome, built in 1502 by Bramante, at the site where, according to tradition, Peter was crucified.

Peter's death is not mentioned in the New Testament, but it is believed that his martyrdom is suggested by Jesus when he says "...when thou shalt be old thou shalt stretch forth thy hands, and another shall gird thee, and carry thee whither thou wouldest not. This spake he signifying by what death he should glorify God" (John 21:18–19).

When Peter wrote his epistles, he was already an old man.

394. Various beasts in a Byzantine mosaic of the 6th century A.D., San Marco, Venice, Italy. Peter likens the false prophets and teachers "who privily shall bring in damnable heresies, even denying the Lord that bought them" (verse 1) to "natural brute beasts," that is, men living as animals.

399. Woman holding a baby astride her left hip; terracotta figurine from Thebes, 6th century B.C. (Louvre, Paris).
The question of whom John is addressing in this epistle has aroused much discussion among scholars. The two leading opinions are that the address is literally to a Christian woman and her family, or that the reference is to the Church personified, with its constituent members. The former view is preferable, and it may be assumed that the "elect lady" in question, being a member of her local Christian community, would have shared her letter with her fellow believers.

400. Inkwell found at Qumran.
John's epistles, like all the epistles of the New Testament, were probably written on papyrus, like most writings in the early Roman period. The writing was done with a reed dipped in ink, which was composed of lamp-black combined with water and gum, and was very durable.

401. Preparing a meal in a Roman kitchen; detail of one of several reliefs from a sarcophagus of the 3rd century, depicting scenes of everyday life.

The elder unto the elect lady and her children, whom I love in the truth; and not I only, but also all they that have known the truth;

For the truth's sake, which dwelleth in us, and shall be with us for ever.

Grace be with you, mercy, and peace, from God the Father, and from the Lord Jesus Christ, the Son of the Father, in truth and love.

I rejoiced greatly that I found of thy children walking in truth, as we have received a commandment from the Father.

And now I beseech thee, lady, not as though I wrote a new commandment unto thee, but that which we had from the beginning, that we love one another.

And this is love, that we walk after his commandments. This is the commandment, That, as ye have heard from the beginning, ye should walk in it.

For many deceivers are entered into the world, who confess not that Jesus Christ is come in the flesh. This is a deceiver and an anti-christ.

Look to yourselves, that we lose not those things which we have wrought, but that we receive a full reward.

Whosoever transgresseth, and abideth not in the doctrine of Christ, hath not God. He that abideth in the doctrine of Christ, he hath both the Father and the Son.

If there come any unto you, and bring not this doctrine, receive him not into your house, neither bid him God speed: For he that biddeth him God speed is partaker of his evil deeds. (II. 1–11)

Beloved, follow not that which is evil, but that which is good. He that doeth good is of God: but he that doeth evil hath not seen God.

Demetrius hath good report of all men, and of the truth itself: yea, and we also bear record; and ye know that our record is true.

I had many things to write, but I will not with ink and pen write unto thee: But I trust I shall shortly see thee, and we shall speak face to face. Peace be to thee. Our friends salute thee. Greet the friends by name. (III.11–14)

Woe unto them: for they have gone in the way of Cain, and ran greedily after the error of Balaam for reward, and perished in the gainsaying of Core.

These are spots in your feasts of charity, when they feast with you, feeding themselves without fear: clouds they are without water, carried about of winds; trees whose fruit withereth, without fruit, twice dead, plucked up by the roots.

(11,12)

The wealthy Romans were partial to magnificent banquets as described in contemporary literature. In this context, the name of Lucullus, a Roman magnate, has become proverbial in connection with gluttony. (One day when he was dining alone at home, seeing that he was not being served a sumptuous meal as usual, he admonished his steward: "Did you not know that Lucullus was dining at Lucullus' tonight?"

In his epistle to Titus (1:5–12) Paul, like Jude,

warned against gluttony and recommended moderation in eating, as in all other activities (I Timothy 2:2).

Tertullian, an early Christian writer, gives a description of the "feasts of charity" or "love feasts," noting that before eating the participants offered a prayer to God. They would eat and drink with moderation, only enough to satisfy hunger and thirst, and the feast closed with a prayer.

It seems, however, that the original aim of the meal was sometimes forgotten, and Paul reminds them of this in his epistle to the Corinthians, recalling the deep meaning of the Lord's Supper (I Corinthians 11:21–29).

402. "The Breaking of Bread", depicted in a wall painting from the Catacombs of Priscilla in Rome, 2nd/3rd century A.D.
The early Christians celebrated funerary feasts, memorial meals and masses for the dead in the catacombs of Rome.

403. St. John's Grotto at Patmos, where it is said that he had his vision.

404. A view of Patmos, a barren and rocky island in the Aegean Sea, about thirty-five miles west of Asia Minor.
According to ancient tradition, John was exiled by Emperor Domitian to Patmos, which served as a penal colony, and was later released by Domitian's successor, Emperor Nerva (96–98). While on Patmos, John experienced the vision of Revelation, which he wrote down.

The Revelation of Jesus Christ, which God gave unto him, to shew unto his servants things which must shortly come to pass; and he sent and signified it by his angel unto his servant John:

Who bare record of the word of God, and of the testimony of Jesus Christ, and of all things that he saw,

Blessed is he that readeth, and they that hear the words of this prophecy, and keep those things which are written therein: for the time is at hand.

John to the seven churches which are in Asia: Grace be unto you, and peace, from him which is, and which was, and which is to come; and from the seven Spirits which are before his throne;

And from Jesus Christ, who is the faithful witness, and the first begotten of the dead, and the prince of the kings of the earth. Unto him that loved us, and washed us from our sins in his own blood,

And hath made us kings and priests unto God and his Father; to him be glory and dominion for ever and ever. Amen. (1:1–6)

I John, who also am your brother, and companion in tribulation, and in the kingdom and patience of Jesus Christ, was in the isle that is called Patmos, for the word of God, and for the testimony of Jesus Christ.

I was in the Spirit on the Lord's day, and heard behind me a great voice, as of a trumpet,

Saying, I am Alpha and Omega, the first and the last: and, What thou seest, write in a book, and sent it unto the seven churches which are in Asia, unto Ephesus, and unto Smyrna, and unto Pergamos, and unto Thyatira, and unto Sardis, and unto Philadelphia, and unto Laodicea.

And I turned to see the voice that spake with me. And being turned, I saw seven golden candlesticks; And in the midst of the seven candlesticks one like unto the Son of man, clothed with a garment down to the foot, and girt about the paps with a golden girdle. (1:9–13)

And to the angel of the church in Pergamos write; These things saith he which hath the sharp sword with two edges;

I know thy works, and where thou dwellest, even where Satan's seat is: and thou holdest fast my name, and hast not denied my faith, even in those

403

404

405

405. Incised depiction of a seven-branched candelabrum (*menorah*) on two fragments of unpainted plaster dating from the 1st century A.D., discovered in excavations in the Jewish Quarter of the Old City of Jerusalem.
The sketch is the earliest detailed depiction extant of the *menorah* which stood in the Temple, probably drawn by someone who had seen it in the Temple.
The first vision of the Book of Revelation concerns the churches: "the seven candlesticks which thou sawest are the seven churches" (verse 20), which shows their importance in the New Testament economy.

406. The "Red Church" at Pergamum.
Now Bergamo in Turkey, Pergamum was one of the congregations to which John addressed his epistles.
Nothing is known of the early history of the city. It developed during the 2nd century B.C. at the time of the Attalid kings. After the death of the last Attalid king in 133 B.C., the district came under Roman influence as part of the province of Asia.
Relations between Judea and Pergamum during the reign of Herod the Great are mentioned by Josephus.
Pergamum was noted for its temple to Aesculapius. Another aspect of the city was the worship of political rulers. About 29 B.C. the city built a magnificent temple for the worship of Augustus.

days wherein Antipas was my faithful martyr, who was slain among you, where Satan dwelleth.

But I have a few things against thee, because thou hast there them that hold the doctrine of Balaam, who taught Balac to cast a stumblingblock before the children of Israel, to eat things sacrificed unto idols, and to commit fornication.

So hast thou also them that hold the doctrine of the Nicolaitans, which thing I hate.

Repent; or else I will come unto thee quickly, and will fight against them with the sword of my mouth.

He that hath an ear, let him hear what the Spirit saith unto the churches; To him that overcometh will I give to eat of the hidden manna, and will give him a white stone, and in the stone a new name written, which no man knoweth saving he that receiveth it.   (2:12–17)

406

407

408

407. A view from the acropolis of the 4th century A.D. Roman bath-gymnasium complex at Sardis, including the remains of an ancient synagogue. It is thought that there were Jews in Sardis as early as the time of the Persian occupation. Josephus mentions Roman decrees which safeguarded certain rights of the Jews of Sardis.
The synagogue at Sardis is the best preserved ancient synagogue of Asia Minor found so far. It is part of a complex of public buildings built on an artificial terrace, which was probably built following the earthquake which devastated Sardis in A.D. 17. Excavations below the floor of the synagogue show several construction stages within the same building boundaries. Originally it was a part of the pagan gymnasium complex.

408. Ruins of the temple to Artemis at Sardis, the ancient capital of Lydia, in western Asia Minor (now Turkey).
Lydia was part of the Roman province of Asia since 133 B.C. It was a highly developed region due to its fertility and to its rich gold and silver mines. It was in Sardis that the first coins ever struck were minted by Gyges, king of Lydia (c. 650 B.C). The last king of Lydia, the wealthy Croesus (650–546 B.C.), was on good terms with the Greeks and sent rich offerings to Greek temples. Croesus went to war against Cyrus, king of Persia, and was defeated. The conquered country became a Persian satrapy, with Sardis as its capital, and

And unto the angel of the church in Sardis write; These things saith he that hath the seven Spirits of God, and the seven stars; I know thy works, that thou hast a name that thou livest, and art dead.

Be watchful, and strengthen the things which remain, that are ready to die: for I have not found thy works perfect before God.

Remember therefore how thou hast received and heard, and hold fast, and repent. If therefore thou shalt not watch, I will come on thee as a thief, and thou shalt not know what hour I will come upon thee.

Thou hast a few names even in Sardis which have not defiled their garments; and they shall walk with me in white: for they are worthy.

He that overcometh, the same shall be clothed in white raiment; and I will not blot out his name out of the book of life, but I will confess his name before my Father, and before his angels. He that hath an ear, let him hear what the Spirit saith unto the churches.

(3:1–6)

And I beheld when he had opened the sixth seal, and, lo, there was a great earthquake; and the sun became black as sackcloth of hair, and the moon became as blood;

And the stars of heaven fell unto the earth, even as a fig tree casteth her untimely figs, when she is shaken of a mighty wind.

And the heaven departed as a scroll when it is rolled together; and every mountain and island were moved out of their places.

And the kings of the earth, and the great men, and the rich men, and the chief captains, and the mighty men, and every bondman, and every free

409

410

man, hid themselves in the dens and in the rocks of the mountains;

And said to the mountains and rocks, Fall on us, and hide us from the face of him that sitteth on the throne, and from the wrath of the Lamb:

For the great day of his wrath is come; and who shall be able to stand?

(6:12–17)

And another angel came out of the temple which is in heaven, he also having a sharp sickle.

And another angel came out from the altar, which had power over fire; and cried wtih a loud cry to him that had the sharp sickle, saying, Thrust in thy sharp sickle, and gather the clusters of the vine of the earth; for her grapes are fully ripe. And the angel thrust in his sickle into the earth, and gathered the vine of the earth, and cast it into the great winepress of the wrath of God. And the winepress was trodden without the city, and blood came out of the winepress, even unto the horse bridles, by the space of a thousand and six hundred furlongs. (14:17–20)

For they are the spirits of devils, working miracles, which go forth unto the kings of the earth and of the whole world, to gather them to the battle of that great day of God Almighty.

Behold, I come as a thief. Blessed is he that watcheth, and keepeth his garments, lest he walk naked, and they see his shame.

And he gathered them together into a place called in the Hebrew tongue Armageddon.

(16:14–16)

remained such until it was conquered by Alexander the Great (334 B.C.). Later it came under the rule of Pergamum and then Rome. A great earthquake nearly leveled Sardis in A.D. 17, but the city was rebuilt with aid from Rome.

409. Men treading grapes; a Byzantine mosaic floor from Beth-shean.
In the New Testament the Jews are likened to the fig tree (Matthew 24:32), the believers to the wheat (Matthew 13:25,30) and the wicked Gentiles to the grapevine, as here, which is a counterfeit of the true vine comprising Christ and his members (John 15:1–6). The "great winepress of the wrath of God" will be the war at Armageddon (Revelation 16:12–16).

410. Man hiding behind a table; detail of a relief from the wall of the Heroon of Gjoelbaschi-Trysa, Lycia, 4th century B.C. (Kunsthistorisches Museum, Vienna).

412

413

And the merchants of the earth shall weep and mourn over her; for no man buyeth their merchandise any more:

The merchandise of gold, and silver, and precious stones, and of pearls, and fine linen, and purple, and silk, and scarlet, and all thyine wood, and all manner vessels of ivory, and all manner vessels of most precious wood, and of brass, and iron, and marble,

And cinnamon, and odours, and ointments, and frankincense, and wine, and oil, and fine flour, and wheat, and beasts, and sheep, and horses, and chariots, and slaves, and souls of men.

And the fruits that thy soul lusted after are departed from thee, and all things which were dainty and goodly are departed from thee, and thou shalt find them no more at all.

The merchants of these things, which were made rich by her, shall stand afar off for the fear of her torment, weeping and wailing,

And saying, Alas, alas, that great city, that was clothed in fine linen, and purple, and scarlet, and decked with gold, and precious stones, and pearls!

For in one hour so great riches is come to nought. And every shipmaster, and all the company in ships, and sailors, and as many as trade by sea, stood afar off,

And cried when they saw the smoke of her burning, saying, What city is like unto this great city!

And they cast dust on their heads, and cried, weeping and wailing, saying, Alas, alas, that great city, wherein were made rich all that had ships in the sea by reason of her costliness! for in one hour is she made desolate.

Rejoice over her, thou heaven, and ye holy apostles and prophets; for God hath avenged you on her.   (18:11–20)

411. Aerial view of Megiddo and the valley of Megiddo.
The apocalyptic vision of the "valley of Armageddon", the site of the last war before the millennium, probably draws in part on the events associated with Megiddo in the Old Testament. Here Jabin's army under Sisera was destroyed with divine help by Barak (Judges 4:14–16), a victory later celebrated in the song of Deborah (Judges 5:19–22); King Ahaziah of Judah died at Megiddo after being mortally wounded by Jehu (2 Kings 9:27); and King Josiah was killed here in an encounter with Pharoah Necho (2 Kings 23:29–30). Because of its strategic position, many armies through the ages – Saracens, Crusaders, Egyptians, Persians, Druzes, Turks and Arabs – have fought battles in Megiddo.

412. Horse merchant; Gallo-Roman tombstone, 1st century A.D. (Musée Archéologique, Dijon, France).
Chapters 17 and 18 give the vision of the fall of Babylon in its two aspects: religious (chapter 17), and material (chapter 18).

413. Wine merchant in his shop; Gallo-Roman tombstone, 1st century A.D. (Musée Archéologique, Dijon, France).

414

414. Dragon fighting with a pigeon; relief on the right portal of the chapel of Tyrol castle, 15th century A.D., Meran, Italy.

415. Representation of the heavenly Jerusalem; on a fresco from Dura-Europos.
The concept of a heavenly Jerusalem is found in many Jewish sources. It is portrayed here as a typical Hellenistic sanctuary (with winged victories bearing wreaths on its four corners). The artist probably intended to portray Solomon's Temple, but the imaginary quality of the work is evident from the fact that the outer wall is shown as a series of seven walls (seven being a typological number), each a different color. The three gates are thus without a wall and the Temple seems to hover in mid-air.

And I saw an angel come down from heaven, having the key of the bottomless pit and a great chain in his hand.

And he laid hold on the dragon, that old serpent, which is the Devil, and Satan, and bound him a thousand years, (20:1–2)

And I saw a new heaven and a new earth: for the first heaven and the first earth were passed away; and there was no more sea.

And I John saw the holy city, new Jerusalem, coming down from God out of heaven, prepared as a bride adorned for her husband.

And I heard a great voice out of heaven saying, Behold, the tabernacle of God is with men, and he will dwell with them, and they shall be his people, and God himself shall be with them, and be their God.

And God shall wipe away all tears from their eyes; and there shall be no more death, neither sorrow, nor crying, neither shall there be any more pain: for the former things are passed away.

And he that sat upon the throne said, Behold, I make all things new. And he said unto me, Write: for these words are true and faithful.
(21:1–5)

And I saw no temple therein: for the Lord God Almighty and the Lamb are the temple of it.

And the city had no need of the sun, neither of the moon, to shine in it: for the glory of God did lighten it, and the Lamb is the light thereof.

And the nations of them which are saved shall walk in the light of it: and the kings of the earth do bring their glory and honour into it.

And the gates of it shall not be shut at all by day: for there shall be no night there.

And they shall bring the glory and honour of the nations into it.

And there shall in no wise enter into it any thing that defileth, neither whatsoever worketh abomination, or maketh a lie: but they which are written in the Lamb's book of life. (21:22–27)

Blessed are they that do his commandments, that they may have right to the tree of life, and may enter in through the gates into the city.

For without are dogs, and sorcerers, and whoremongers, and murderers, and idolaters, and whosoever loveth and maketh a lie.

I Jesus have sent mine angel to testify unto you these things in the churches. I am the root and the offspring of David, and the bright and morning star.

And the Spirit and the bride say, Come. And let him that heareth say, Come. And let him that is athirst come. And whosoever will, let him take the water of life freely.

For I testify unto every man that heareth the words of the prophecy of this book, If any man shall add unto these things, God shall add unto him the plagues that are written in this book:

And if any man shall take away from the words of the book of this prophecy, God shall take away his part out of the book of life, and out of the holy city, and from the things which are written in this book.

He which testifieth these things saith, Surely I come quickly. Amen. Even so, come, Lord Jesus. The grace of our Lord Jesus Christ be with you all. Amen. (22:14–21)

416. The Golden Gate in Jerusalem, blocked for nearly a thousand years. In its present form, this beautiful structure of two arches dates back to the 8th century.
According to Jewish tradition, the gate will be opened when the Messiah comes. For the Christians it represents the entrance of Jesus into the Temple Mount. Islamic tradition has it that this is the threshold of Heaven and Hell. "New Jerusalem" is a living composition of all God's redeemed throughout the ages. As the "bride," it is Christ's counterpart (John 3:29), and as the "holy city" it is God's habitation. It is the "heavenly Jerusalem" (Hebrews 12:22), prepared for God's people and the one which Abraham, Isaac and Jacob looked and longed for (Hebrews 11:10,16). This is also the Jerusalem above, which is the mother of us all (Galatians 4:26).

417. Oil lamp ornamented with the Tree of Life, Byzantine 4th-6th century A.D. (Private Collection, Max Berger, Vienna).
According to Genesis 2:8–9, Man was put before the Tree of Life, indicating that he was privileged to partake of it. After the fall, Man was barred from the Tree of Life (Genesis 3:24). The New Testament concludes with the regained access to the Tree of Life, to the followers of Christ. These have the right to enjoy the Tree of Life in the holy city for eternity.

417

MAPS

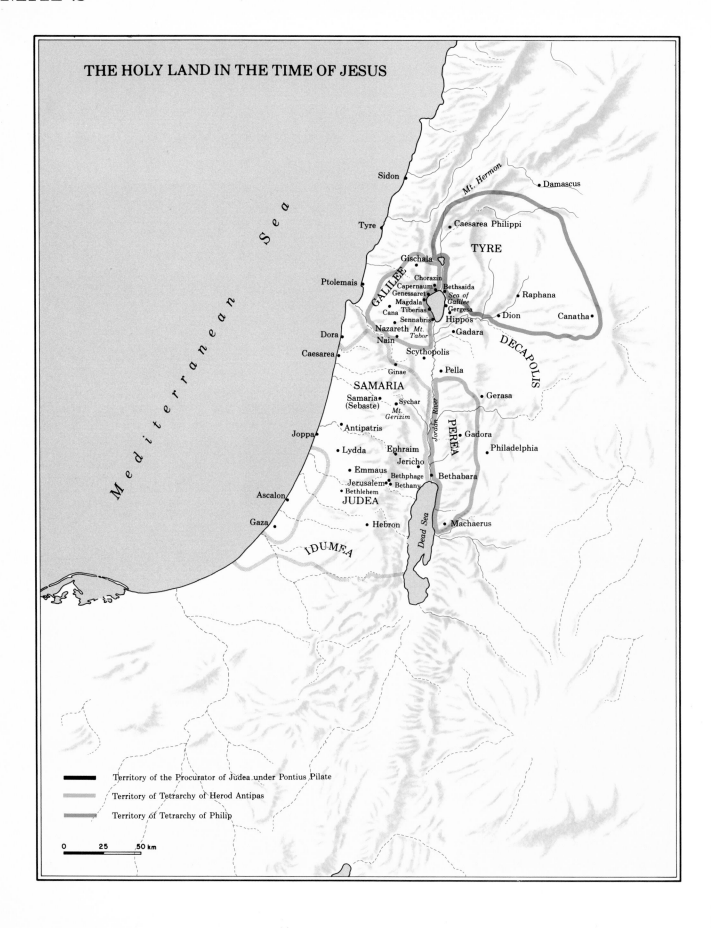

THE HOLY LAND IN THE TIME OF JESUS

Mediterranean Sea

Sidon

Tyre

Ptolemais

Dora

Caesarea

GALILEE

Gischala

Chorazin

Capernaum

Genessaret

Magdala

Cana

Tiberias

Sennabris

Nazareth *Mt. Tabor*

Nain

Scythopolis

Ginae

SAMARIA

Samaria (Sebaste)

Sychar

Mt. Gerizim

Antipatris

Joppa

Lydda

Ephraim

Emmaus

Bethphage

Jerusalem

Bethany

Bethlehem

JUDEA

Ascalon

Gaza

Hebron

IDUMEA

Jericho

Mt. Hermon

Damascus

Caesarea Philippi

TYRE

Bethsaida

Sea of Galilee

Raphana

Gergesa

Hippos

Dion

Canatha

Gadara

DECAPOLIS

Pella

Gerasa

Jordan River

PEREA

Gadora

Philadelphia

Bethabara

Dead Sea

Machaerus

Territory of the Procurator of Judea under Pontius Pilate

Territory of Tetrarchy of Herod Antipas

Territory of Tetrarchy of Philip

0   25   50 km

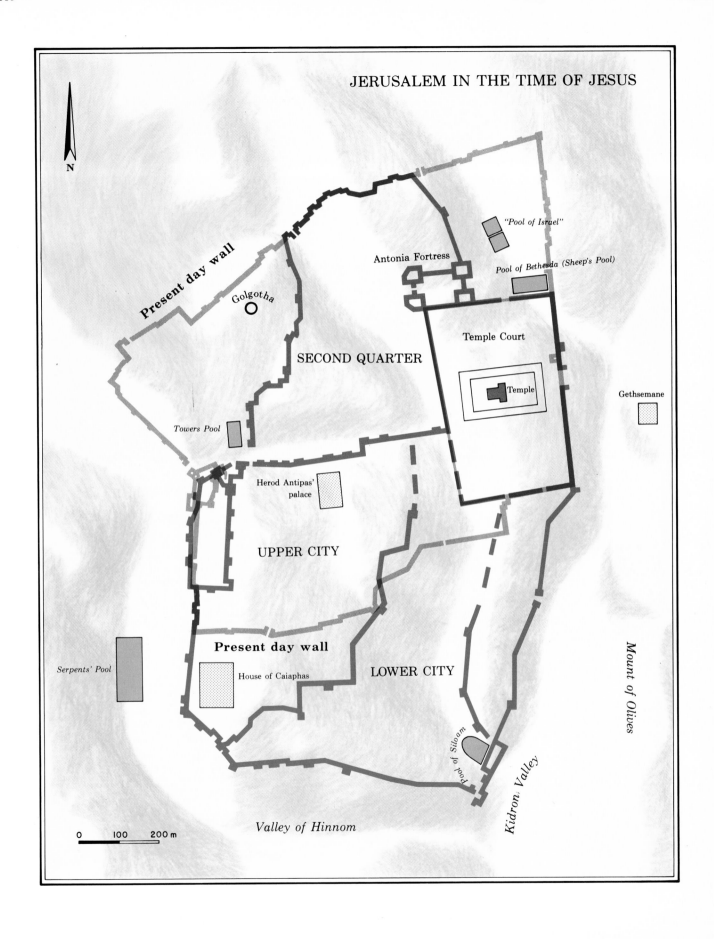

JERUSALEM IN THE TIME OF JESUS

N

Present day wall

Golgotha

"Pool of Israel"

Antonia Fortress

Pool of Bethesda (Sheep's Pool)

SECOND QUARTER

Temple Court

Temple

Gethsemane

Towers Pool

Herod Antipas'
palace

Mount of Olives

UPPER CITY

Present day wall

Serpents' Pool

House of Caiaphas

LOWER CITY

Pool of Siloam

Kidron Valley

Valley of Hinnom

0   100   200 m

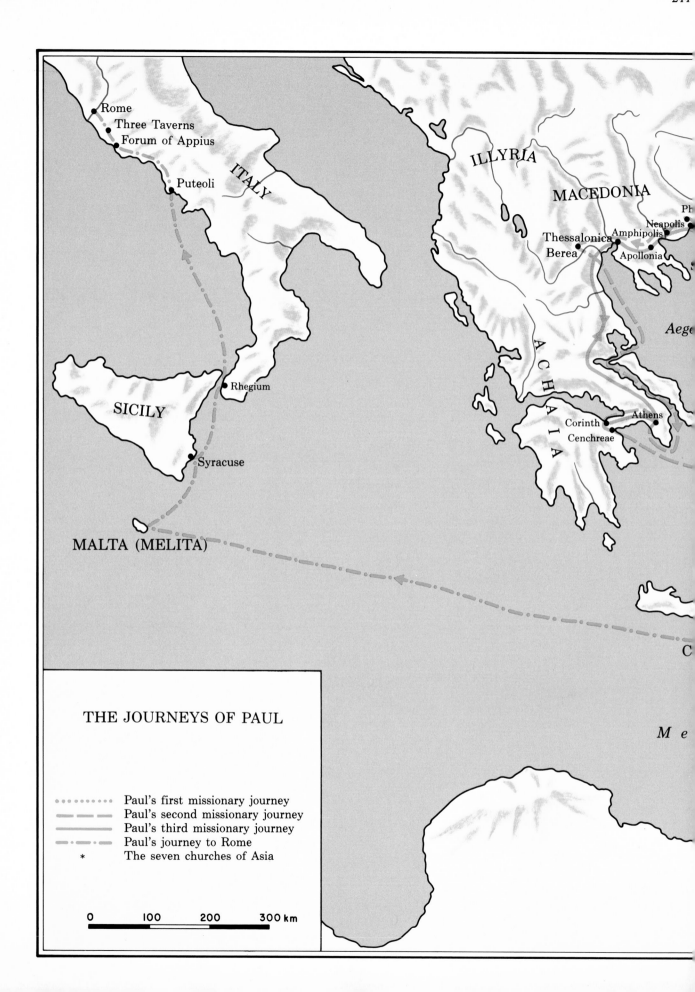

THE JOURNEYS OF PAUL

.... Paul's first missionary journey
– – – – – Paul's second missionary journey
————— Paul's third missionary journey
–·–·–·– Paul's journey to Rome
*   The seven churches of Asia

0   100   200   300 km

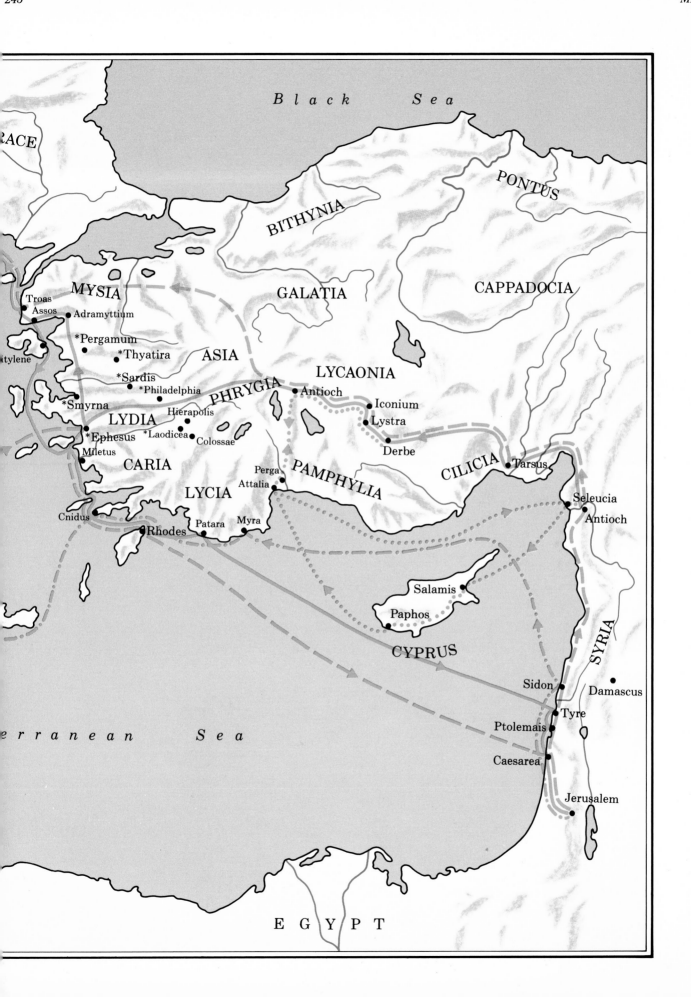

The numbers refer to pages in which the entries in this Index are mentioned in the Bible text or in the captions of the illustrations.

ACKNOWLEDGEMENTS

MATTHEW
1. The Patriarchs; sculpture at Chartres Cathedral.
2. Judea – Photo A. van der Heyden
3. Herod – Photo Alinari Fratelli, Firenze
4. Augustus; statue – Photo J.P.H.
5. Relief on column at Nativity – Photo A. van der Heyden
6. Landscape in Sinai – Photo A. van der Heyden
7. Cave of the Innocents – Photo A. van der Heyden
8. View of Galilee – Photo David Harris
9. Judean Desert – Photo A. van der Heyden
10. Thanksgiving Scroll – The Shrine of the Book, Israel Museum, Jerusalem
11. Qumran caves – Photo A. Van der Heyden
12. Jordan River – Photo A. van der Heyden
13. Jericho – Photo A. van der Heyden
14. The Baptism of Christ; painting at Armenian Monastery, Bethlehem
15. Convent of St. John the Baptist – Photo A. van der Heyden
16. Quarantal mountain – Photo A. van der Heyden
17. Quarantal Monastery – Photo A. van der Heyden
18. Quarantal, stairs to monastery – Photo A. van der Heyden
19. Caves at Quarantal – Photo A. van der Heyden
20. Chapel in grotto at Quarantal – Photo A. van der Heyden
21. Greek Orthodox monastery, Capernaum – Photo A. van der Heyden
22. Sea of Galilee – Photo Azaria Alon
23. Landscape in Galilee – Photo A. van der Heyden
24. Fishermen's nets – Photo A. van der Heyden
25. Fishermen's boat – Photo A. van der Heyden
26. Mount of Beatitudes – Photo A. van der Heyden
27. Sea of Galilee seen from Beatitudes – Photo A. van der Heyden
28. Habakkuk commentary – The Shrine of the Book, Israel Museum, Jerusalem
29. Two wolves and a ram – Musée du Louvre, Paris. Photo Erich Lessing
30. Fragment of cloth – The Shrine of the Book, Israel Museum, Jerusalem. Photo Zev Radovan
31. Chorazin, remains – Photo A. van der Heyden
32. Ruins at Chorazin synagogue – Photo A. van der Heyden
33. Wheat harvest in Galilee – Photo David Harris
34. Sign at the entrance of the "synagogue" – Photo A. van der Heyden
35. Entrance to "synagogue" at Nazareth – Photo A. van der Heyden
36. Baker's stall – Museo Nazionale, Naples – Photo Erich Lessing
37. Banias – Photo A. van der Heyden
38. Remains of Roman temple at Banias – Photo A. van der Heyden
39–40. Coin from Paneas – Dr. Grosswirt Collection
41. Mount Hermon – Photo David Harris
42. Basilica on Mount Tabor – Photo A. van der Heyden
43. Church of Transfiguration – Photo Palphot
44. Mount Tabor – Photo Azaria Alon
45. Bethphage – Photo David Harris
46. Mount of Olives seen from Bethphage – Photo A. van der Heyden
47. Palm Sunday procession – Photo David Harris
48. Tiberius – Archaeological Museum, Istanbul. Photo Erich Lessing
49. Phylacteries – The Shrine of the Book, Israel Museum, Jerusalem
50. "Seat of Moses" – Israel Department of Antiquities. Photo Erich Lessing
51. Façade of the Temple from reconstructed model – Photo David Harris
52. Judea Capta coin – Photo Zev Radovan
53. Grain mill – Photo Zev Radovan
54. Oil lamps – Photo Zev Radovan
55. Gold coins, Roman period – Photo Zev Radovan
56. Mixed flock – Photo A. van der Heyden
57. Alabastron – Israel Department of Antiquities. Photo Erich Lessing
58. Bethany – Photo A. van der Heyden
59–62. Streets in Old City of Jerusalem – Photos A. van der Heyden
63. Model of private dwellings in Jerusalem – Photo David Harris
64. The Cenacle – Photo David Harris
65. Chalice of Antioch – Metropolitan Museum of Art, New York
66. Church of All Nations – Photo A. van der Heyden
67. Olive tree in Gethsemane – Photo A. van der Heyden
68. Oil press – Photo A. van der Heyden
69. Church of St. Peter in Gallicantu – Photo David Harris
70. Steps on Mount Zion – Photo A. van der Heyden
71. Inscription Pontius Pilate – Israel Department of Antiquities. Photo A. van der Heyden
72. Detail of Lithostratos – Photo A. van der Heyden
73. Roman pitcher and bowl – Museo Nazionale, Naples. Photo Scala, Firenze
74. "The Disrobing of Christ" by El Greco – Toledo Cathedral. Photo J.P.H.
75. Fifth Station of the Cross – Photo A. van der Heyden
76. Golgotha – Photo David Harris
77. Garden Tomb – Photo A. van der Heyden
78. Carving on Lithostratos – Photo A. van der Heyden
79. Roman legionaries – Trajan's Column, Rome
80. Tomb of Joseph of Arimathea – Photo Erich Lessing
81. Women and angel; from relief at Aachen Cathedral – Photo Erich Lessing
MARK
82. The Wilderness of Judea – Photo A. van der Heyden
83. View of Judea with Herodium – Photo A. van der Heyden
84. Jordan River – Photo A. van der Heyden
85. Baptismal site – Photo A. van der Heyden
86. Capernaum; remains of synagogue – Photo A. van der Heyden
87. The cure of the paralytic; from wall painting at Dura-Europos – Photo Moshe Caine
88. Interior of Capernaum synagogue – Photo A. van der Heyden
89. Remains at synagogue of Capernaum – Photo A. van der Heyden
90. Votive relief – Archaeological Museum, Athens. Photo Erich Lessing
91. Detail from the arch of Titus – Photo Scala, Firenze

92. Mustard plant – Photo David Darom
93. Fisherman on the Sea of Galilee – Photo David Harris
94. Same as above
95. Stormy weather at the Sea of Galilee – Photo David Harris
96–97. View of Kursi – Photo Zev Radovan
98. Wild pig on mosaic – Photo Zev Radovan
99–100. Details of mosaic pavement at Kursi – Photos A. van der Heyden
101. Valley of Beth-Shean – Photo Zev Radovan
102–103. Remains of Roman theater at Beth-Shean – Photos David Harris
104. Susita – Photo Zev Radovan
105. Susita, view from Roman fortress. Photo A. van der Heyden
106. Gerasa – Photo Garo N./Erich Lessing
107. Gadara – Photo Garo N./Erich Lessing
108. Woman touching Jesus; from a relief on a sarcophagus – Photo Erich Lessing
109. Sandal found at Masada – Masada excavations. Photo Zev Radovan
110. Salome dancing – Bibliothèque Nationale, Paris. Photo Erich Lessing
111. Tomb of St. John the Baptist – Photo A. van der Heyden
112. Washing of the hands; from Barcelona Haggadah – British Museum, London
113. "Korban" inscription – Israel Department of Antiquities and Museums, Jerusalem. Photo Erich
Lessing
114. Terracotta dog – Musée du Louvre, Paris. Photo Erich Lessing
115. Hippodrome at Tyre – Photo Zev Radovan
116. Remains of Roman columns at Tyre – Photo Zev Radovan
117. Mosaic from Church of Multiplication – Photo Zev Radovan
118. Mount Hermon – Photo Azaria Alon
119. Dabburya – Photo David Harris
120. Elijah; from Verdun altar – Photo Erich Lessing
121. Bethany – Photo A. van der Heyden
122. Page from Queen Melisande's Psalter – British Museum, London
123. Near Bethany – Photo A. van der Heyden
124. "Banker" – Belgrad Museo Nazionale. Photo Scala, Firenze.
125–126. Tyrian coin – Department of Antiquities and Museums, Jerusalem
127–128. Coins of procurators – Photos Zev Radovan
129. Synagogue at Masada – Photo A. van der Heyden
130. Stones of Western Wall – Photo A. van der Heyden
131. Spikenard – Photo David Darom
132. Garden of Gethsemane – Photo Garo
133. Olive trees at Gethsemane Garden – Photo Garo
134. Reconstruction of Antonia fortress – Photo David Harris
135. The Praetorium – Photo Palphot
136. Pillar of Flagellation – Photo A. van der Heyden
137. Monastery of the Cross – Photo David Harris
138. Herod's family tomb – Photo A. van der Heyden
LUKE
139. Ein Karem – Photo David Harris
140. Incense shovel – Israel Department of Antiquities and Museums
141. Nazareth – Photo A. van der Heyden
142. Church of the Annunciation – Photo David Harris
143. The Annunciation by S. Martini – Uffizi, Firenze. Photo Scala, Firenze.
144. Madonna lily – Photo David Darom
145. Church of the Visitation – Photo David Harris
146. Grotto of St. John the Baptist – Photo David Harris
147. Courtyard of Church of Visitation – Photo David Harris
148. Emperor Augustus – Photo Zev Radovan
149. Bethlehem – Photo Werner Braun
150. Khan – Photo David Harris
151. Well of Kathisma – Photo A. van der Heyden
152. Kathisma Monastery – Photo A. van der Heyden
153. Shepherd's Field – Photo A. van der Heyden
154. Grotto of the Shepherds – Photo A. van der Heyden
155. Grotto of the Nativity – Photo Garo
156. The Star in the Grotto of the Nativity – Photo A. van der Heyden
157. Church of Nativity – Photo David Harris
158. Entrance to the Church of the Nativity – Photo A. van der Heyden
159. Interior of the Church of the Nativity – Photo David Harris
160. Reconstruction of the Second Temple – Photo David Harris
161. Cradle of Jesus – Photo A. van der Heyden
162. Presentation of Christ at the Temple; from a stone relief, church of Moissac, France
163. Emperor Tiberius, bust portrait – Photo Zev Radovan
164. The Tetrarchs; sculpture – Photo Scala
165. Jesus and his ancestry; mosaic Kariye church, Istanbul. Photo Erich Lessing
166. Corner of Temple Mount – Photo A. van der Heyden
167. Stones in the Negev – Photo Azaria Alon
168–169. Views of Galilee – Photos David Harris
170. Detail of Isaiah Scroll from Qumran – The Shrine of the Book, Israel Museum, Jerusalem. Photo
Erich Lessing
171–172. Meron – Photos A. van der Heyden
173. Mount of the Leap – Photo David Harris
174. Our Lady of the Fright – Photo David Harris
175. St. Peter's Fish – Photo David Harris
176. Zealot dwelling at Masada – Photo A. van der Heyden
177. Centurion – from Antoninus Pius Column
178. Na'im – Photo Palphot
179. Flute player – National Museum Athens. Photo Erich Lessing
180. Church of Maria Magdalane – Photo David Harris
181. View of region of Caesarea Philippi – Photo A. van der Heyden
182. On the way to Jericho – Photo A. van der Heyden
183. Inn of the Good Samaritan – Photo A. van der Heyden
184. Pater Noster Church – Photo David Harris

185. Pater Noster Church (courtyard) – Photo Zev Radovan
186. Demon – Hessisches Landsmuseum, Darmstadt. Photo Erich Lessing
187. Jonah – Archaeological Museum, Istanbul. Photo Erich Lessing
188. Flowers – Photo A. van der Heyden
189. The Good Shepherd – Archaeological Museum, Istanbul. Photo Erich Lessing
190–191. Carob – Photos David Darom
192. The Flood – Illuminated MS., Library of Gerona Cathedral. Photo Erich Lessing
193. Murex – Photo David Darom
194. Pharisee and publican – Photo Erich Lessing
195. Purse – Museo Nazionale, Naples. Photo Erich Lessing
196. View from Bethphage – Photo A. van der Heyden
197. View from Mt. of Olives – Photo David Harris
198. Fig tree – Photo David Darom
199. Chapel of the Agony – Photo David Harris
200. Garden of Gethsemane – Photo A. van der Heyden
201. Coin of Pontius Pilate – Photo Zev Radovan
202. Women mourning – Kariye Church, Istanbul. Photo Erich Lessing
203. Le Toron des Chevaliers – Photo N. Drukker
204. Emmaus – Photo David Harris
205. Emmaus – Photo A. van der Heyden
206. Dome of the Ascension (interior) – Photo A. van der Heyden
207. View of Jerusalem – Photo David Harris
208. Tower of Church of Ascension – Photo A. van der Heyden
JOHN
209. John the Baptist – Museo dell'Arcivescovado, Ravenna. Photo Erich Lessing
210. Bethsaida – Photo David Harris
211. Cana – Photo David Harris
212. Churches at Cana – Photo David Harris
213. Samaria – Photo A. van der Heyden
214. Shechem – Photo Zev Radovan
215. Mount Gerizim – Photo A. van der Heyden
216. Samaritan priest – Photo A. van der Heyden
217. Jacob's Well – Photo A. van der Heyden
218. Jacob's Well (interior) – Photo A. van der Heyden
219. St. Ann Church – Photo Zev Radovan
220. Pool of Bethesda – Photo A. van der Heyden
221. Woman reading, figurine – Musée du Louvre, Paris. Photo Erich Lessing
222. Pool of Siloam – Photo Zev Radovan
223. *Hannuka* lamp – Einhorn Collection – Photo David Harris
224. Lazarus' tomb – Photo A. van der Heyden
225. Bethany – Photo A. van der Heyden
226. Church of Lazarus – Photo A. van der Heyden
227. Resurrection of Lazarus; relief – Photo Zev Radovan
228. Model of Caiaphas' house – Photo Zev Radovan
229. Ceramic basin – Department of Antiquities and Museums, Jerusalem. Photo Erich Lessing
230. The Last Supper – Photo Zev Radovan
231. Vine and basket of fruit; mosaic – Photo Zev Radovan
232. Grotto of Betrayal – Photo David Harris
233. Prison at the high-priest's house – Photo Erich Lessing
234. Prison of Barabas – Photo David Harris
235. Chapel of the Flagellation – Photo David Harris
236. Thorns – Photo David Darom
237. Via Dolorosa – Photo A. van der Heyden
238. Holy Sepulcher – Photo A. van der Heyden
239. Aloes – Photo David Darom
240. Golgotha chapel – Photo A. van der Heyden
241. Calvary – Photo David Harris
242. Chapel of the Angel – Photo David Harris
243. Holy Sepulcher – Photo David Harris
244. Jesus and Thomas, capital of column – Photo David Harris
245. Tiberias – Photo David Harris
246. The Sea of Galilee at night – Photo David Harris
247. Church of the Primacy – Photo Palphot
248. Mensa Christi – Photo A. van der Heyden
THE ACTS
249. Church of the Ascension – Photo A. van der Heyden
250. Judas tree – Photo David Darom
251. Aceldama – Photo Moshe Caine
252. Pentecost Altar – Klosterneuburg Abbey. Photo Erich Lessing
253. St. Stephen's Gate – Photo A. van der Heyden
254. The stoning of Stephen; enamel – Eglise Gimel-les-Cascades. Photo Erich Lessing
255. Sebaste – Photo David Harris
256. Paralytics; mosaic – Church of Kariye, Istanbul. Photo Erich Lessing
257. Chariot and horse; relief – Photo Erich Lessing
258. Gamla – Photo Palphot
259. Paul in Damascus; enamel – Victoria and Albert Museum, London. Photo Erich Lessing
260. Peter healing Tabitha; sculpture – Photo David Harris
261. House of Simon the tanner – Photo A. van der Heyden
262. Jaffa – Photo Zev Radovan
263. Caesarea – Photo Zev Radovan
264. Aqueduct at Caesarea – Photo Zev Radovan
265. Coin minted at Caesarea – A. Spaer Collection
266. Cornelius and Peter; relief – Musée Lapidaire Chrétien, Arles. Photo Erich Lessing
267. Seleucia – Photo Erich Lessing
268. Tyche, goddess of Antioch – Museum Vaticani
269. Grotto of St. James – Photo A. van der Heyden
270. Santiago da Compostela Cathedral – Photo Scala, Firenze
271. Paphos – Photo Erich Lessing
272. Frieze from Antioch – Photo Erich Lessing

273. Oracles; Greek painted vase – Staatliche Münzsammlung, Berlin
274. Kavalla – Photo Erich Lessing
275. Thessalonica – Photo A. van der Heyden
276. The Parthenon – Photo J.P.H.
277. Paul disputing with Jews; enamel – Victoria and Albert Museum, London. Photo Erich Lessing
278. Claudius – Photo Dalia Amotz
279. Corinth – Photo A. van der Heyden
280. Corinth, the agora – Photo Scala, Firenze
281. Cushion merchant; relief. Uffizi, Firenze – Photo Scala, Firenze
282. Diana of Ephesus – Museo Nazionale, Naples. Photo Scala, Firenze
283. Ephesus – Turkey Ministry of Tourism
284. Theatre at Ephesus – Photo A. van der Heyden
285. Ephesus, the agora – Photo A. van der Heyden
286. Artemis temple, Ephesus – Photo A. van der Heyden
287. Troas – Photo Erich Lessing
288. Samos – Photo Erich Lessing
289. Miletus – Photo Erich Lessing
290. Rhodes – Photo A. van der Heyden
291. Steps to Temple Mount – Photo David Harris
292. Tarsus – Photo Erich Lessing
293. Beth Shearim – Photo A. van der Heyden
294. Antipatris – Photo A. Hai
295. Coin of Roman procurator Felix – Photo Zev Radovan
296. Menorah on column – Photo David Harris
297. Nero – Photo Zev Radovan
298. Caesarea – Photo David Harris
299. Knossos, Crete – Photo Erich Lessing
300. Ship in a storm; relief – Photo Erich Lessing
301. Paul at Malta; fresco – Photo Erich Lessing
302. Appian Way – Photo Scala, Firenze
303. Puetoli – Photo Erich Lessing
304. The Three Taverns – Photo Erich Lessing
305. Old houses in Rome – Photo Scala, Firenze

ROMANS
306. Glass with ritual objects – Israel Museum, Jerusalem
307. Old streets in Rome – Photo Scala, Firenze
308. Circumcision implements – Israel Museum, Jerusalem. Photo Zev Radovan
309. Adam; relief – Grotto Vaticane. Photo Erich Lessing
310. Roots of a tree – Photo Erich Lessing
311. Women gambling; painting on marble – Museo Nazionale, Naples. Photo Erich Lessing

I CORINTHIANS
312. Column from temple at Corinth – Photo Scala, Firenze
313. Portrait of Chilon; wall painting – Photo Erich Lessing
314. Aristocratic ladies – Mosaic, Kariye Church, Istanbul. Photo Erich Lessing
315. Mosaic from Beth-Shean – Photo Zev Radovan
316. Youth with effeminate hairdo; relief from Herculanum. Photo Erich Lessing
317. Sacrifice to the Delphi oracle – Lateran Museum, Rome. Photo Erich Lessing
318. Sacrificial scene; relief – Magyar Nemzeti Muzeum, Budapest. Photo Erich Lessing
319. Runner; from Attic vase – Musée du Louvre, Paris. Photo Erich Lessing
320. Child playing; sculpture – Kunsthistorisches Museum, Vienna. Photo Erich Lessing
321. Moses – wall painting from Dura-Europos synagogue. Photo Moshe Caine

II CORINTHIANS
322. Moses by Michelangelo – Photo Erich Lessing
323. Roman pottery – Israel Museum, Jerusalem. Photo Erich Lessing
324. Pillar of Flagellation of Paul – Photo Erich Lessing
325. Warriors; relief – Kunsthistorisches Museum, Vienna. Photo Erich Lessing
326. Eve and the serpent; relief – Photo Erich Lessing

GALATIANS
327. Text of the Epistle to the Galatians – Photo A. van der Heyden
328. Peter and Paul; relief – Museo Archeologico Aquileia. Photo Erich Lessing
329. Valley of the Cross – Photo David Harris
330. Woman, nurse and child – Detail of vase from Eretria

EPHESIANS
331. Hadrian's temple at Ephesus – Photo A. van der Heyden
332. Inscription forbidding Gentiles to enter Temple – Photo Zev Radovan
333. Mystic scene; wall painting – Musee du Louvre, Paris. Photo Erich Lessing
334. Sleeping goddess – Musee du Louvre, Paris. Photo Erich Lessing
335. Drinking scene; relief – Monumenti E Gallerie Pontificie, Vatican
336. Portrait of a couple, from Pompeii wall painting – Muzeo Nazionale, Naples. Photo Erich Lessing
337. Two Roman soldiers; relief – Roemisch-Germanisches Zentralmuseum, Mainz. Photo Erich Lessing
338. Roman helmet and armor; relief – Museum Carnuntum, Deutsch Altenburg, Austria. Photo Erich Lessing

PHILIPPIANS
339. Arete; sculpture – Kunsthistorisches Museum, Vienna. Photo Erich Lessing
340. "Yeshua" inscription on a sarcophagus – Photo Erich Lessing
341. Head of athlete; sculpture – Department of Antiquities and Museums, Jerusalem. Photo Erich Lessing
342. Paul on the way to Damascus – Musée des Beaux Arts, Lyon. Photo Erich Lessing

COLOSSIANS
343. Roman baths near Hierapolis – Photo Turkey Ministry of Tourism
344. Omphalos from Delphi – Photo Erich Lessing
345. Paul holding a book; ivory plaque – Musee de Cluny, Paris. Photo Erich Lessing
346. Portrait of a philosopher; sculpture – Department of Antiquities, Jerusalem. Photo Erich Lessing
347. Angel; enamel – Musée Municipal de Limoges. Photo Erich Lessing
348. Mineral springs at Hierapolis – Turkish Ministry of Tourism
349. Barbarians; relief – Photo Erich Lessing
350. Scythian horseman – Hermitage, Leningrad. Photo Erich Lessing
351. Aqueduct at Laodicea – Photo Erich Lessing

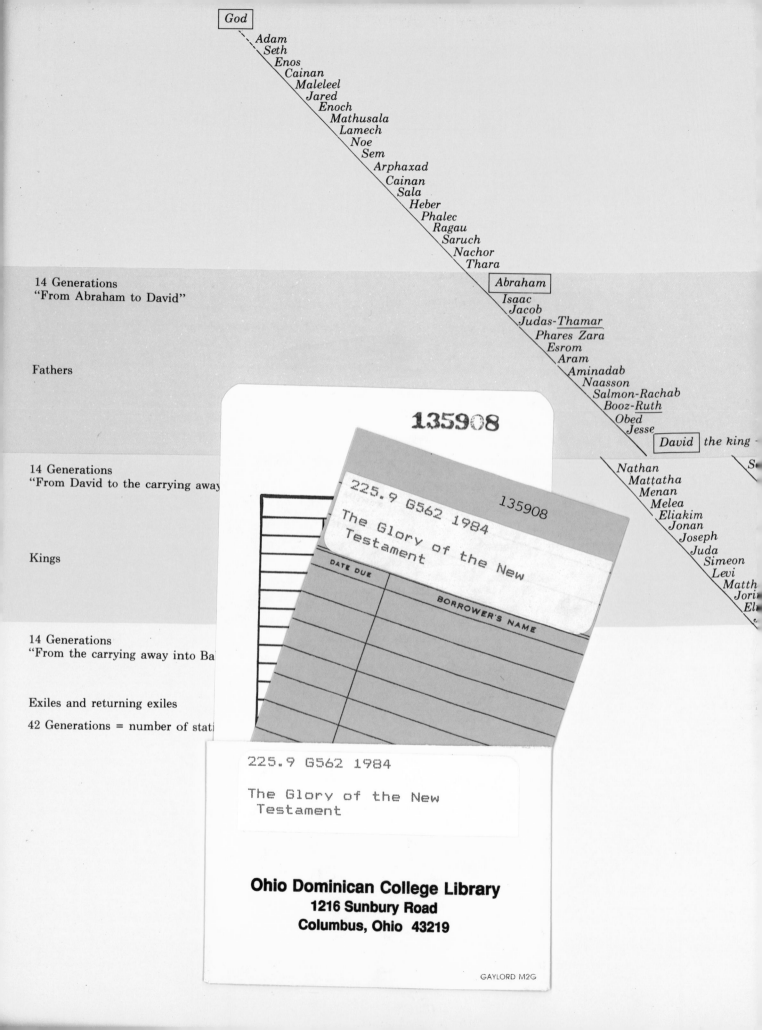

God

Adam
Seth
Enos
Cainan
Maleleel
Jared
Enoch
Mathusala
Lamech
Noe
Sem
Arphaxad
Cainan
Sala
Heber
Phalec
Ragau
Saruch
Nachor
Thara

Abraham

Isaac
Jacob
Judas-*Thamar*
Phares Zara
Esrom
Aram
Aminadab
Naasson
Salmon-*Rachab*
Booz-*Ruth*
Obed
Jesse

David | the king

14 Generations
"From Abraham to David"

Fathers

14 Generations
"From David to the carrying away

Kings

14 Generations
"From the carrying away into Ba

Exiles and returning exiles

42 Generations = number of stati

Nathan
Mattatha
Menan
Melea
Eliakim
Jonan
Joseph
Juda
Simeon
Levi
Matth
Jori
Eli

135908

225.9 G562 1984

The Glory of the New Testament

135908

DATE DUE

BORROWER'S NAME